ROUTLEDGE LIBRARY EDITIONS: COLONIALISM AND IMPERIALISM

Volume 26

THE ENGLISH AND COLONIAL BARS IN THE NINETEENTH CENTURY

THE ENGLISH AND COLONIAL BARS IN THE NINETEENTH CENTURY

DANIEL DUMAN

Routledge
Taylor & Francis Group
LONDON AND NEW YORK

First published in 1983 by Croom Helm Ltd

This edition first published in 2023
by Routledge
4 Park Square, Milton Park, Abingdon, Oxon OX14 4RN

and by Routledge
605 Third Avenue, New York, NY 10158

Routledge is an imprint of the Taylor & Francis Group, an informa business

© 1983 Daniel Duman

All rights reserved. No part of this book may be reprinted or reproduced or utilised in any form or by any electronic, mechanical, or other means, now known or hereafter invented, including photocopying and recording, or in any information storage or retrieval system, without permission in writing from the publishers.

Trademark notice: Product or corporate names may be trademarks or registered trademarks, and are used only for identification and explanation without intent to infringe.

British Library Cataloguing in Publication Data
A catalogue record for this book is available from the British Library

ISBN: 978-1-032-41054-8 (Set)
ISBN: 978-1-032-45667-6 (Volume 26) (hbk)
ISBN: 978-1-032-45673-7 (Volume 26) (pbk)
ISBN: 978-1-003-37816-7 (Volume 26) (ebk)

DOI: 10.4324/9781003378167

Publisher's Note
The publisher has gone to great lengths to ensure the quality of this reprint but points out that some imperfections in the original copies may be apparent.

Disclaimer
The publisher has made every effort to trace copyright holders and would welcome correspondence from those they have been unable to trace.

The English and Colonial Bars in the Nineteenth Century

Daniel Duman

CROOM HELM
London & Canberra

© 1983 Daniel Duman
Croom Helm Ltd, Provident House, Burrell Row,
Beckenham, Kent BR3 1AT

British Library Cataloguing in Publication Data

Duman, Daniel
    The English and Colonial bars in the nineteenth
century.
    1. Lawyers – England – History
    I. Title
    340'.23   KD460
ISBN 0-85664-468-4

Printed and bound in Great Britain by
Biddles Ltd, Guildford and King's Lynn

CONTENTS

List of Tables and Figures
List of Abbreviations
Preface
Introduction

1. THE CHARACTER OF THE PROFESSION   1

    Dimensions..   2
    Origins: Geographical, Social and Educational.....   9

2. THE GOVERNANCE OF THE BAR IN THE NINETEENTH
    CENTURY: TRADITION VERSUS REFORM   33

    Traditional Patterns of Authority and Discipline...   34
    The Customary Etiquette of the Bar.................   40
    The Forces of Change...............................   50
    Reform and Reformers...............................   55
    Reorganisation from Within.........................   66

3. CAREERS AT THE ENGLISH BAR........................   78

    Testing and Training...............................   79
    The First Steps....................................   83
    Provincial Bars....................................   86
    Connection and Patronage...........................   89
    The Ladder of Preferment...........................   94
    The Determinants of Success........................   105
    A Single-Class Profession..........................   113

4. THE COLONIAL BAR AND BENCH........................   121

    Crown Colonies and Self-Governing Colonies.........   121
    India..   130
    Professional Imperialism and the Law...............   137

5. WEALTH-HOLDERS, LANDOWNERS AND COMPANY DIRECTORS... 143

    Incomes and Fortunes................................. 143
    The Barrister as Landowner........................... 153
    Investments and Directorships in Business............ 155
    Economics and the Bar - A Summary.................... 163

6. POLITICS AND THE BAR................................. 169

    Barristers in the House of Commons................... 169
    Politics and Professional Advancement................ 176
    Barristers and the Political Elite................... 184
    The Inns of Court: Portals to Power.................. 191

7. THE BAR AND BENCH IN SOCIAL AND HISTORICAL
    PERSPECTIVE.. 199

Appendix... 210
Selected Bibliography.................................... 212
Index.. 222

TABLES AND FIGURES

Tables

1.1	Occupations of Inns of Court Men 1835 and 1885....	5
1.2	The Size of the Bar 1790-1881.....................	7
1.3	The Practising Bar in England and Wales...........	8
1.4	Geographical Origins of Barristers................	10
1.5	Geographical Origins of United Kingdom Barristers.	11
1.6	The Social and Occupational Origins of the Bar....	17
1.7	Annual Rentals of Parental Estates................	18
1.8	Public School Attendance..........................	23
1.9	University Attendance 1785-1885...................	24
1.10	Admissions to the Inns of Court 1780-1888.........	25
1.11	Inns of Court Attendance 1785-1885................	27
1.12	Ratio of Admissions and Calls to the Bar at the Middle Temple and Lincoln's Inn 1785-1884.......	28
2.1	The Benchers of the Inns of Court 1816-1877.......	36
2.2	Circuit Affiliations of the Bar 1800-1900.........	51
3.1	Provincial Barristers c. 1825-1900................	88
3.2	QCs and Serjeants Appointed to the Judiciary 1790-1901..	99
3.3	Age at Time of Becoming Queen's Counsel...........	99
3.4	Social Origins of Late Victorian Barristers and Judges..	108
4.1	The Social Quality of Colonial and English Barristers 1885.................................	124
4.2	Backgrounds and Careers of Colonial Chief Justices 1865-1901.......................................	129
4.3	The Social Origins of Indian Barristers 1885......	133
5.1	The Incomes of Barristers 1796-1913...............	145
5.2	The Wealth of Practising Barristers and Queen's Counsel...	149
5.3	The Wealth of Barristers Belonging to Various Professional, Economic and Political Elites.....	151
5.4	Social Origins and Occupations of Barrister/ Directors.......................................	157
5.5	Distribution of Directorships by Location and Type	159

6.1	Lawyers in the House of Commons 1832 to 1886	170
6.2	The Social and Occupational Origins of Barrister/MPs (1880)	173
6.3	Legal Officeholding Among Practising Barrister/MPs Elected in 1880	183
6.4	Barristers in British Cabinets 1815-1914	185
6.5	The Social Origins of Barrister/Cabinet Ministers 1815-1914	188
6.6	The Occupations of Barrister/Cabinet Ministers 1815-1914	188
6.7	Frequency of Ministerial Appointments Among Barrister and Lay MPs	190

Figures

1.1	Inns of Court Admissions 1785-1885	3
1.2	Geographical Origins of United Kingdom Barristers 1835	14
1.3	Geographical Origins of United Kingdom Barristers 1885	15

To My Parents

ABBREVIATIONS

BPP   British Parliamentary Papers
DNB   Dictionary of National Biography
Hansard Parliamentary Debates, 3rd series
LJ   Law Journal
LT   Law Times
PRO   Public Record Office

Note: All books cited in this study were published in London, unless otherwise indicated.

PREFACE

Five years ago, having nearly completed a study of the royal and ecclesiastical judges appointed in England between 1727 and 1875, I decided to broaden the perspectives of my research by embarking on an examination of the entire upper branch of the legal profession during the eighteenth and nineteenth centuries. This book incorporates the major part of that work. During the time that I have been engaged on this project I have accumulated many debts that I would now like to acknowledge.

I would like to thank those institutions and individuals who made their facilities available to me and who allowed me to consult the materials in their possession. These include: the British Library, the Public Record Office, the Principal Probate Registry in Somerset House, the Bodleian Library, the University Library Cambridge, the Institute of Historical Research, the Hertfordshire County Record Office, the director of the Sheffield City Libraries, the Masters of the Bench of the Honourable Society of the Inner Temple, the Senate of the Inns of Court and the Bar, the Wine Committees of the South-Eastern and Western Circuits, the Lambeth Palace Library, the Berkshire County Library and the Zalman Aranne Library at Ben-Gurion University of the Negev. I would like to express my appreciation to those individuals whose family papers I was privileged to consult: the Earl Cairns, the Earl of Carnarvon, the Earl of Halsbury, the Earl of Selborne, the Earl of Wharncliffe, the Baron Coleridge, the Baron Monk Bretton, Sir James Alexander Stephen Bt., and Mr John Blofeld QC.

I am also grateful to all those individuals from whose advice and help I benefited while engaged in this study: Professor W.R. Cornish of the London School of Economics, Professor Eliot Freidson of New York University, Professor Shmuel Galai of Ben-Gurion University, Professor Paul Lucas of Clarke University, Dr Christopher Brooks of Durham University, Dr Wilfrid Prest of the University of Adelaide, Mr Raymond Cock of Sussex University and Mr Thomas Telenko of the University of Michigan. This book has been much improved by the invaluable suggestions and comments made by Professor David Spring of the Johns Hopkins University, Dr W.D. Rubinstein of Deakin University and Professor Stephen E. Tabachnick and Dr Robert Liberles of Ben-Gurion University who read the early drafts of this study. Of course any remaining inaccuracies of fact or interpretation are my responsibility alone.

From the beginning of this project I received encouragement from Mr David Croom, as well as his understanding when I failed to meet more than one deadline. I want to thank Mrs Lili Lang who typed the final version of the book in preparation for publication. Travel and research grants from Ben-Gurion University of the Negev allowed me to spend several summers in England studying the gentlemen of the long robe, and aided me in transforming the raw data into a finished work. I am also grateful to the editors of the <u>Journal of Social History</u> for allowing me to use material that first appeared in that publication.

While I was engaged in this study I became seriously ill and owe an enormous debt to those doctors and nurses at Soroka and Beilinson Medical Centres who treated me during this difficult period. I want to extend my special appreciation to Drs Yona Ben-Yakar and Ferit Tovi whose concern for both my physical and emotional well-being could not have been greater, and to my dear friend Dr John Posner who was always ready with a sympathetic ear and wise counsel.

Finally I must acknowledge the help that I received from members of my family. My mother and mother-in-law allowed themselves to be recruited to type the early draft, my brother made important suggestions about the organisation of the book, my son Yoav - who was born soon after I began - permitted me to use a small corner of my study as long as I did not disturb him, and most of all my wife Marion who was more or less willing to be exploited as research assistant, editor, proof-reader, typist, nurse and companion during very trying circumstances.

INTRODUCTION

Two decades ago the professionals ranked among the most neglected of all English social groups.(1) Fortunately since then both historians and sociologists have devoted considerable energy to investigating individual professional occupations, and the process and meaning of professionalisation.(2) For the nineteenth century alone we now have monographs on the Anglican clergy, medical practitioners, army and navy officers, chartered surveyors, university dons, architects, engineers and superior court judges.(3) Yet as impressive as this list is, especially when supplemented by shorter studies of many other occupations, much remains to be done both in analysing particular professions and in placing the entire group in social and historical perspective.(4) My ultimate goal here is to contribute to the realisation of these objectives.

This book is primarily a study of the personnel and institutions of the English bar during the reign of Queen Victoria, but it is more than simply the chronicle of an ancient and respected profession. Its wider significance emanates from the fact that the bar is, in my view, the classic English profession as measured by nearly all the criteria usually associated with professionalism: autonomy from external interference, monopoly over practice, the possession of esoteric knowledge and skills, corporate unity and a position of dominance over a clientele dependent upon professional advice. Therefore an analysis of the bar will naturally shed light on the evolution of the professions as a whole. In the six substantive chapters I examine: the dimensions of the bar and the origins of its members; the governance of the profession; the careers of practising barristers in England and her colonies; the members of the bar as wealth-holders, landowners and company directors; and the place of the gentlemen of the long robe in the world of Victorian high politics. I conclude with an essay that makes use of my research on the history of the bar and the bench in the eighteenth and nineteenth centuries in order to challenge and revise the orthodox view of the character and development of the English professions.

At this point I want to comment on two vital aspects of this study, namely the scope of the subject matter and the methodology employed in analysing it. Surprisingly perhaps, the task of defining who is to be subsumed under the title of 'barrister' is considerably more difficult than might be supposed. It seems logical to assume that just as a doctor is a man who practises medicine or a clergyman is a minister of religion, so a barrister is someone whose principal vocation is advocacy in the courts of law. In fact, had I adopted this criterion, thereby limiting my research to the practising members of the English and colonial bars, I would have condemned the majority of the members of the profession to continued historical neglect. On the other hand, the inclusion of any man who had acquired the qualification of barrister-at-law regardless of his occupation creates other equally perplexing problems. For example, the call to the bar did not in itself foster the development of that corporate identity that we typically associate with members of a profession. In all likelihood barristers defined themselves according to their principal occupation rather than as inns of court men. Thus the <u>esprit de corps</u> that united practising barristers in England and Wales probably did not extend even to their colonial counterparts, much less to those country gentlemen, businessmen or civil servants who had early in their lives been called to the bar.

In order to minimise these difficulties without ignoring their existence, I have chosen to examine the bar in the most comprehensive manner possible without losing sight of the fact that our main concern here is the history of a profession. To this end I have placed the practitioners on centre stage while at the same time devoting considerable attention to the members of the bar in some of their other guises. Finally I have tried to show, especially in the chapter on politics, that while inns of court men were not all cut from the same cloth, a sojourn at the Temple, Lincoln's Inn or Gray's Inn helped a man to see the world from a lawyer's point of view even if it did not necessarily transform him into a lawyer.

Prosopography seemed the most effective means of investigating the structure and character of the bar. However, this choice created a methodological problem: what was the best way to collect the data?(5) During the nineteenth century thousands of men were called to the English bar. Not only would it have been impossible given the available resources to include them all, but such a procedure would probably have led to a situation of rapidly diminishing returns as little would have been added to the picture presented here despite the additional investment of research. Consequently I decided to make use of sampling techniques and construct random samples of the profession. This task was made considerably easier by the fact that in both 1835 and 1885 books were published that contained not only the names of all living barristers in each of

NOTES

1. Until then the most important study of the English professions was A.M. Carr-Saunders and P.A. Wilson, The Professions (Oxford, 1933).
2. For examples of the sociological literature see Geoffrey Millerson, The Qualifying Associations: A Study in Professionalisation (1964); H.M. Vollmer and D.L. Mills, Professionalisation (Englewood Cliffs, New Jersey, 1966); J.A. Jackson (ed.), Professions and Professionalization (Cambridge, 1970); Philip Elliott, Sociology of the Professions (1972); Terence J. Johnson, Professions and Power (1972); Eliot Freidson, Profession of Medicine, A Study of the Sociology of Applied Knowledge (New York, 1972); Magali Sarfatti Larson, The Rise of Professionalism, A Sociological Analysis (Berkeley, 1977).
3. Diana McClatchey, Oxfordshire Clergy 1770-1869 (Oxford, 1960); Brian Heeney, A Different Kind of Gentleman, Parish Clergy as Professional Men in Early and Mid-Victorian England (Hamden, Conn., 1976); Sir George Clark and A.M. Cooke, A History of the Royal College of Physicians of London (3 vols., Oxford, 1964-72); M. Jeanne Peterson, The Medical Profession in Mid-Victorian London (Berkeley, 1978); Gwyn Harries-Jenkins, The Army in Victorian Society (1977); Michael Lewis, The Navy in Transition (1965); F.M.L. Thompson, Chartered Surveyors: The Growth of a Profession (1968); Sheldon Rothblatt, Revolution of the Dons (Cambridge, 1968); Arthur Engel, 'From Clergy to Don, the Rise of the Academic Profession in Nineteenth Century Oxford', unpublished PhD thesis, Princeton University, 1975; Barrington Kaye, The Development of the Architecture Profession (1960); W.H.G. Armytage, A Social History of Engineering (1961); Jennifer Morgan, 'The Judiciary of the Superior Court 1820 to 1968: A Sociological Study', unpublished M. Phil. thesis, University of London, 1974; Daniel Duman, The Judicial Bench in England 1727-1875: The Reshaping of a Professional Elite (Royal Historical Society forthcoming). For a more general treatment see W.J. Reader, Professional Men (1966).
4. Examples of shorter studies are D.H.J. Morgan, 'The Social and Educational Background of Anglican Bishops, Continuities and Changes', British Journal of Sociology, 20 (1969), pp. 295-310; A.W. Coats and S.E. Coats, 'The Social Composition of the Royal Economic Society and the Beginnings of the British Economic Profession 1890-1915', British Journal of Sociology, 21 (1970), pp. 75-85; B.W.G. Holt, 'Social Aspects in the Emergence of Chemistry as an Exact Science: the British Chemical Profession', British Journal of Sociology, 21 (1970), pp. 181-99; C.J. Dewey, 'The Education of a Ruling Caste: the Indian Civil Service in the Era of Competitive Examination', English Historical Review, 88 (1973), pp. 262-85; Andrew T. Scull, 'From Madness to Mental Illness: Medical Men as Moral

the two years but short biographical entries on each man as well. Rather fortuitously these two books more or less span the Victorian era; the first was written just two years before Victoria's accession and the second, two years before her fiftieth jubilee. The former, compiled by James Whishaw and entitled A Synopsis of the English Bar, contains the names of 2477 men while the latter, Men-at-the-Bar, the work of the prolific nineteenth-century genealogist Joseph Foster, lists 7521 barristers.

Ten per cent samples of the bar in 1835 and 1885 form the centrepiece for this study. Yet while these data provide a good overview of the profession they do not tell the entire story and must be supplemented by samples of important subgroups of barristers as follows: all of the judges appointed to the superior courts between 1875 and 1901 (n=53); all of the colonial chief justices who served in the years 1865 to 1901 (n=156); a 50 per cent random sample of the County Court judges named to the bench between 1847 and 1901 (n=116); a 20 per cent sample of Queen's Counsel who took silk in the years 1800 to 1901 (n=155); all barrister/MPs elected to the House of Commons in 1880 (n=130); all barristers who sat in Cabinets between 1815 and 1914 (n=60); and all Indian (non-European) barristers living in 1885 (n=108).

In total this portrait of a profession includes data gleaned from the biographies of more than 1700 barristers. Fortunately the nineteenth century was the heyday of genealogy and so the historian has a vast wealth of printed sources and manuscripts from which to gather information about the birth, social origins, education, careers, and wealth of his subjects.(6) Nevertheless in some cases finding even the most elementary data was extremely difficult. This was especially true for the samples of the bar in 1835 and 1885, despite the works of Whishaw and Foster, since the barristers in those groups did not constitute an elite, but merely the rank and file of a profession.

The biographies compiled from this material provided both the quantitative skeleton around which the entire study is built and the details of individual careers that have been employed to exemplify the statistics. I have also endeavoured wherever possible to let the barristers speak for themselves through autobiographies, memoirs, letters, diaries, parliamentary debates and professional journals. In addition some use has been made of Victorian literature, though only with extreme care, since many fictional barristers while interesting character studies were not necessarily representative members of their profession.(7) My hope is that the combination of statistical and literary evidence will provide the reader with a balanced picture of the nineteenth-century English barrister and his universe.

Entrepreneurs', *European Journal of Sociology*, XVI (1975), pp. 218-61; Andrew T. Scull, 'Mad-Doctors and Magistrates: English Psychiatry's Struggle for Professional Autonomy in the Nineteenth Century', *European Journal of Sociology*, XVII (1976), pp. 279-305.

5. Lawrence Stone, 'Prosopography', *Daedalus, 100* (1971), pp. 46-75. In most cases the percentages given in this study have been rounded off to the nearest whole per cent.

6. The main sources for biographical information were: F. Boase, *Modern English Biography* (6 vols., 1965); *Burke's Peerage, Baronetage and Knightage*; *Burke's Landed Gentry*; W.P. Blaidon, *Records of the Honourable Society of Lincoln's Inn, Admissions* (2 vols., 1897); *Debrett's House of Commons and Judicial Bench* (1880); *Dictionary of National Biography*; *Directory of Directors* (1889); Joseph Foster, *Men-at-the-Bar* (1885); Joseph Foster, *Register of Admissions to Gray's Inn, 1521-1889* (1889); Joseph Foster, *Alumni Oxonienses 1715-1886* (4 vols., Oxford, 1888); Joseph Foster, 'Register of all Barristers called to the Inns of Court to 1887' (20 vols.), manuscript deposited in University Library Cambridge; *Law List*; *Return of the Owners of Land 1872-3*; BPP, (England, Wales and Scotland), *LXXII (1874)*; *(Ireland), LXXX* (1876); M. Stenton (ed.), *Who's Who of British Members of Parliament 1832-1885* (1976); H.A.C. Sturgess, *Register of Admissions to the Middle Temple* (3 vols., 1949); *The Times* (obituaries); J. and J.A. Venn, *Alumni Cantabrigenses 1754-1900* (10 vols., Cambridge, 1940-54); James Whishaw, *A Synopsis of the English Bar* (1835); *Who was Who*. In addition I have used the probate acts in the Public Record Office and Somerset House and a variety of school and local directories.

7. On the difficulties in using literary evidence see Peter Laslett, 'The Wrong Way Through the Telescope, a note on literary evidence in sociology and historical sociology', *British Journal of Sociology*, XXVII (1976), pp. 319-42.

Chapter One

THE CHARACTER OF THE PROFESSION

In 1888 James Bryce wrote of the bar 'Certainly no English institution is more curiously and distinctively English than this body...'.(1) He might also have added that the bar held a unique position among that relatively small group of nineteenth-century English occupations that ranked as professions. Its governing bodies - the inns of court, dating from the fourteenth century - were the oldest professional societies in England predating by more than a century both the creation of the Anglican clergy and the establishment of the Royal College of Physicians.(2) The bar was also one of the smallest of the professions, probably numbering less than a thousand members in the late eighteenth century and under 2500 by the 1830s.(3) Both socially and politically it was the most conspicuous of the professions. No other profession had so many qualified members who did not practise. The bar was the most centralised of the professions with the majority of the practising members - those men who earned their livelihood in the courts of England and Wales - spending virtually their entire careers within the two square miles that comprised legal London.(4) Finally, despite the fact that the bar had considerable claims to the title of England's premier profession it played at best a peripheral role in the professional revolution of the nineteenth century.(5) Most of these points will be elaborated upon in this study. In the first chapter I intend to set the stage for the remainder of the book by means of statistical descriptions of the admissions patterns at the inns of court, the occupations of nineteenth-century barristers and the size of the practising bar, followed by more detailed investigations of the geographical, social and educational backgrounds of the barristers in the years 1835 and 1885.

DIMENSIONS

The mid-nineteenth-century bar exemplified the overcrowded profession. The fledgling barrister was the object of both ridicule and pity as he sat 'hungry and briefless in some garret of the Inn: lived by stealthy literature; hoped and waited, and sickened, and no clients came; exhausted his own means and friends' kindness; had to remonstrate humbly with duns, and to implore the patience of poor creditors.'(6) By the 1850s the situation grew so desperate that a leading professional journal begged young men about to embark on a career to look elsewhere.

> Until the numbers of the Bar are reduced to some reasonable proportion...it will be the most unprofitable and hopeless profession for any man to adopt as a means of obtaining a livelihood; and therefore it would be wise for all who have not a fortune to maintain them, to hasten the restoration of the balance between the business to be done and the wigs to do it, by betaking themselves, as soon as possible to some more profitable and promising occupation, either at home or abroad.(7)

Before we can hope to assess to what extent, if any, the nineteenth-century bar was overcrowded, it is essential to examine the evidence concerning the membership of the inns of court, the growth of the profession and the size of the practising bar in that period.

Admissions
Figure 1.1 traces the combined admission patterns at Lincoln's Inn, Gray's Inn, the Middle Temple and the Inner Temple (after 1848 the Inner Temple cannot be included due to a lacuna in the data). Nevertheless, since the two parallel graphs have almost identical shapes, we can assume that the post-1848 pattern reflects the state of the entire profession. By and large the fluctuations in admissions were not due primarily to internal professional factors; rather they reflect the prevailing economic conditions.(8) In fact they can be related to periods of economic boom and depression, as is vividly illustrated by the graph. For explanatory purposes we can divide Figure 1.1 into five main periods and trends: a decline that began with the post-war slump in the late 1780s that followed the American Revolution. This continued through the first phase of the French Wars and ended with the signing of the Treaty of Amiens (1802); expansion during the next 35 years began with the wartime economic boom and lasted until the late 1830s, interrupted only by the crash of 1825; the decline that characterised the next 20 years commenced with

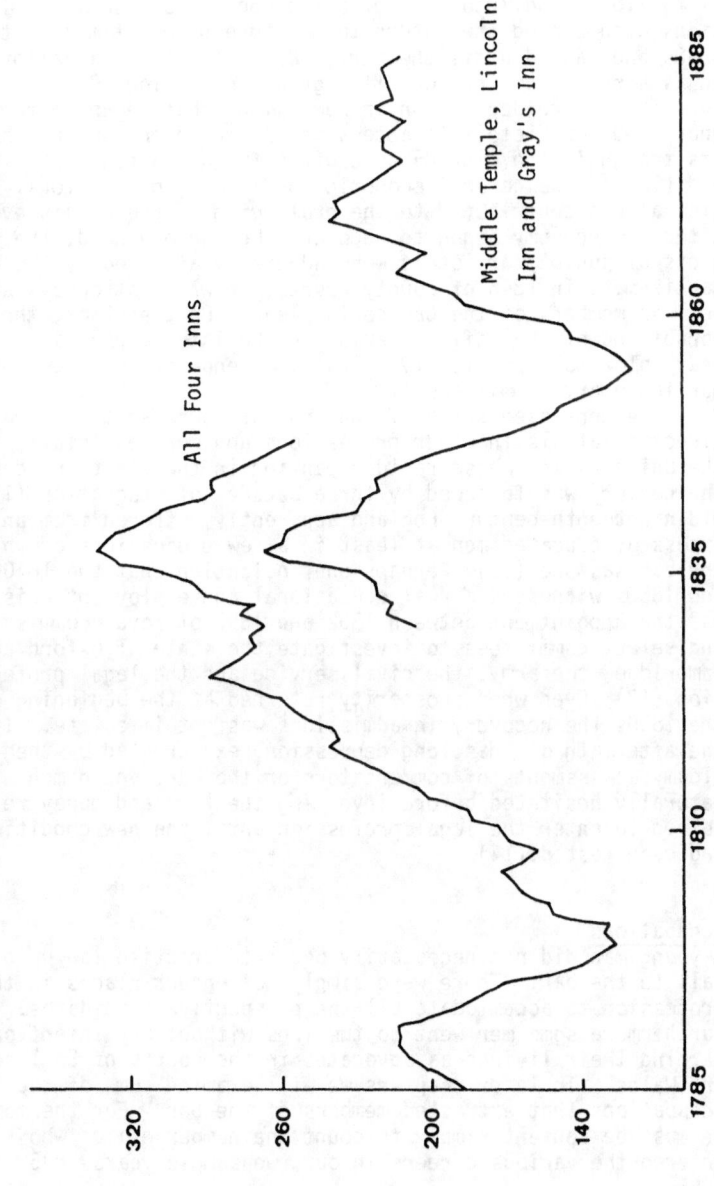

Figure 1.1: Inns of Court Admissions 1785-1885 (five-year moving averages)

the crisis of 1837 and continued through the depression years of the 1840s and into the following decade; a rise in admissions accompanied the return to more prosperous times in the 1850s and lasted until the early 1870s; finally stagnation set in as a result of the so-called great depression.(9)

The severe depression in admissions that began in the year of Queen Victoria's accession to the throne and reached its trough in the mid-1850s requires further attention. In addition to the general economic conditions, professional considerations contributed to the prolonging of the crisis even after the economy began to recover. On the one hand, the prospects of junior barristers were adversely affected by the establishment in 1846 of county courts, in which attorneys as well as members of the bar could plead. On the other, the abrupt end of the railway mania in the late 1840s was a heavy blow to a previously lucrative avenue of practice before parliamentary committees.(10)

The depressed state of the inns of court at this time had direct parallels in other professions and more especially in the universities whose rapid expansion in the first third of the century was followed by three decades of stagnation.(11) Mid-nineteenth-century England apparently suffered from an excess of educated men at least in a few professions of which the bar was one.(12) Perhaps one indication that the 1840s and 1850s witnessed a real educational and employment crisis was the appointment between 1852 and 1857 of royal commissions and select committees to investigate the state of Oxford and Cambridge, the army, the civil service and the legal profession.(13) Even when prosperity returned at the beginning of the 1850s the recovery in admissions was not immediate. In the aftermath of this long depression, exacerbated by the gloomy assessments of commentators on the bar, young men naturally hesitated before investing the time and money required to enter the legal profession until the new conditions had been tested.(14)

Occupations

A young man did not necessarily begin to practise law upon his call to the bar. There were simply not enough places in the profession to accommodate all the prospective candidates. Furthermore some men went to the inns without any intention of earning their livings as advocates in the courts of England and Wales. In later chapters we will examine some of the occupations that attracted members of the bar. For the moment we must be content simply to count the number of men who entered the various careers in our two sample years 1835 and 1885.

The practising bar is the most problematic of the categories in Table 1.1 since it is in large measure a residual

Table 1.1: Occupations of Inns of Court Men 1835 and 1885

		Practising Bar	Colonial Bar	Other Professions	Civil Service	Business	Land	Unknown	Total
1835	No.	155	9	18	4	2	17	43	248
	%	63	4	7	2	1	7	17	
1885	No.	272	79	70	52	33	73	146	725
	%	38	11	10	7	5	10	20	

one. I have included men here if according to the information in the Law List they had practised law for even a few years, on condition that they conformed to two additional criteria: that while active in the profession they had a set of chambers in London or in a provincial law centre (among the most important of these were Liverpool, Manchester, Leeds, Birmingham, Bristol, Newcastle and Cardiff), and that according to the available evidence they entered no other occupation after they left the bar. Unfortunately this method of classification inflates the number of practising barristers. In order to correct this problem I employ a variety of sources in the next section to help determine more accurately the number of advocates in England and Wales in 1835 and 1885.

Since this caveat applies equally to both samples, it should not deter us from using them to compare the occupational choices of the early and late Victorian barristers. One is immediately struck by the enormous decline in the percentage of men who entered the practising bar in England and Wales and the concurrent expansion of the colonial bar, the civil service and business. While the domestic bar supported a considerably smaller proportion of qualified barristers in 1885 than it had 50 years earlier, the emergence of alternative opportunities both at home and in the colonies prevented significant professional unemployment. In addition, while only slightly more than a third of the 1885 barristers practised in England, more than half of the men in that sample made direct use of their legal training in their subsequent careers. Included in this group are 79 colonial barristers, 15 colonial civil servants who sat as local and high court judges primarily in India, and 17 members of the home civil service and other professions who filled offices in which knowledge of the law was a prerequisite.

The Practising Bar

We can now return to the perplexing problem of the size of the practising bar in England in the nineteenth century. In fact there are no accurate data on the subject until the middle of the present century when the Bar Council issued official statistics on the subject. The extent of the difficulty that faces us is indicated by evidence given in 1850 by the Attorney-General, Sir John Jervis, before a royal commission. He told the commissioners that the number of practising barristers was between 100 and 1000, hardly a useful estimate.[15] Other members of the bar were more daring than Jervis. Joseph Napier, the future Irish Lord Chancellor, told the House of Commons in 1854 that there were '800 barristers who robed at Westminster'; he did not specify the size of the provincial bar.[16] Three years later H. Byerley Thomson told his readers that no more than 500 men earned a full-time living from practice as advocates in the courts of England and Wales.[17]

Finally in 1894 Samuel Lofthouse, who played a central role in the establishment of the Bar Council, estimated that no more than 1000 men had 'substantial work' at the bar.(18)

During most of the Victorian era the list of counsel in the Law List is of little value for our purposes here, since from 1841 there was not even a pretense that it was a register of active members of the profession, as had been the case at least in theory prior to that date. The census data is similarly unhelpful since we do not know the criteria used to classify a man as a barrister. Nevertheless the one advantage of the census over the Law List was that someone who had left the bar for another profession may have continued to include his name in the latter but would certainly have changed his occupation in the former. Despite the evident limitations of the data derived from these two sources, I have listed them in Table 1.2, since they do provide at least a starting point for our investigations of the dimensions of the practising bar.

Table 1.2: The Size of the Bar 1790-1881

1790	424	1840	1835
1800	577	1851	2816
1810	708	1861	3071
1820	840	1871	3580
1830	1129	1881	4019

Sources: Law List 1790-1840, Census of England and Wales 1851-1881.

At this juncture, it is necessary to reduce the enormous discrepancy between these data and the estimates of contemporary observers given above. To do this we must return to the samples of the bar in 1835 and 1885. In order to transform these into useful estimates of the size of the practising bar they must be refined. To this end all those men who no longer earned their livings from advocacy in those two years have been eliminated including all those men over age 65 who had presumably retired. I have divided the remainder into two groups: those men who achieved professional recognition as signified by the receipt of professional offices or honours, and those who did not. The former are the hard core of the bar, and their numbers provide a guide to the minimum size of the bar in a given year. The latter group presents an additional difficulty, namely continuity of practice. From the barristers who specialized in the common law courts (King's

Bench, Common Pleas and Exchequer, the assize courts and the county quarter sessions), the regularly updated circuit lists in the Law List indicate which men had retired. But for the chancery bar no such direct cross-check is available and we are forced to fall back upon the law reports of the Court of Chancery. The barristers who made at least one court appearance provide a rough indication of the number of active equity barristers, although a degree of under-enumeration results from the fact that some equity juniors did not appear in court, restricting themselves to chambers work as equity draftsmen and conveyancers. After making these corrections I combined the two tiers - the successful advocates and the rank and file - into a maximum to estimate the size of the bar.

Table 1.3: The Practising Bar in England and Wales

	1835		1885	
	No.	% of sample	No.	% of sample
Minimum	450	20	660	11
Maximum	1010	44	1450	24

Note: The samples used here do not include men over the age of 65.

Adding comparable data for 1785 (minimum 121 and maximum 295) provides us with a picture of the changing dimensions of the practising bar during the entire century.(19) Despite the fact that this evidence does not reveal the rate of growth, it indicates approximately the pace of professional expansion. The major spurt occurred during the first fifty years in which the size of the practising bar increased some two and a half times; by contrast in the second fifty years, the rise was just under 50 per cent. This difference is all the more significant since the rate of population growth during each of the two periods was practically identical - 80 per cent. (20) Furthermore, when we compare the practising and the total bars in 1835 and 1885, we find results that are parallel to those found in Table 1.1, namely a large decline in the percentage of barristers who earned their livings from the legal profession in England and Wales during the course of the century.

The charge of gross overcrowding levelled at the bar was

commonplace in late-eighteenth- and nineteenth-century social criticism. The evidence largely substantiates the gloomy assessments of the prospects facing fledgling barristers made by Adam Smith in the 1770s and John Campbell a quarter of a century later.(21) Nevertheless Table 1.3 indicates that despite the fierce competition, the profession was still capable of significant expansion at least until 1835. The bar at this time undoubtedly benefited from the initial phases of industrialisation that created new professional opportunities for its members, the most obvious example being legal work related to the establishment of railways. There may also have been an increased demand for legal services among the affluent middle classes, for example the purchase and sale of property, probate, and business matters.(22) Yet from mid-century onwards, circumstances were quite different: in real terms the profession was contracting. As I will show in a later chapter the fees generated by economic and demographical growth in the second half of the nineteenth century did not accrue to the rank and file of the profession but rather to an elite of successful practitioners who reaped enormous financial rewards.(23) Furthermore, changes in the distribution of work between the two branches of the profession, beginning in 1846, were almost entirely at the expense of junior barristers, and this considerably reduced the ability of new men to gain a foothold in the profession.(24)

ORIGINS: GEOGRAPHICAL, SOCIAL AND EDUCATIONAL

Having established the dimensions of the nineteenth-century bar we can now proceed to a more detailed examination of the barristers themselves by means of a collective biographical survey of their backgrounds and educational careers. Based primarily on random samples of the bar in 1835 and 1885 it will be possible to chart the evolution of the profession during the course of the century.

Geographical
In the 1830s the inns of court were almost exclusively British institutions; by Victoria's golden jubilee a significant international dimension had been added. Young men flocked to London not only from England, Wales, Scotland and Ireland but also from the British colonies and even from foreign countries in order to qualify for the bar. The colonials came in force during the latter decades of the century, though in fact their presence was not unprecedented. During the third quarter of the eighteenth century a wave of law students had arrived from North America, but as a result of the War of Independence their numbers tapered off rather quickly to a mere trickle by the 1790s.(25)

The main influx from the colonies during the first half of the nineteenth century came from the Caribbean islands, supplemented by the East Indies and Australia. The number of colonials at the inns began to increase in the mid-1860s, and by the following decade East Indians constituted the largest single group. This did not signal merely a geographical shift in recruitment patterns, but the entrance for the first time of a sizeable contingent of non-Europeans into the inns of court.(26)

Table 1.4: Geographical Origins of Barristers

	1835		1885	
	No.	%	No.	%
United Kingdom	241	97.2	631	87.0
Colonial/Foreign	4	1.6	87	12.0
Unknown	3	1.2	7	1.0

The county by county and regional analysis of the geographical origins of United Kingdom barristers (Table 1.5 columns a and b) reveals that the principal centres of recruitment throughout the nineteenth century were first and foremost London and the home counties, followed by the South and Southwest extending from Hampshire to Devon. These trends were of long standing, stretching back at least to the reigns of Elizabeth and the early Stuarts.(27) London was the focus of legal England, containing all of the major professional institutions. It is not surprising that the sons of the metropolis, who lived close to the inns of court and the law courts, were by far the largest contingent at the bar, accounting for a quarter of the total. Furthermore, the predominance of Londoners at the inns resulted from the fact that the capital was not only the wealthiest and the most populous city in the realm but also the economic and political centre of the nation. Much the same factors explain the large number of barristers who came from the Home Counties of Surrey, Hertfordshire, Essex, Sussex and Kent. Together they accounted for 14 per cent of the barristers. Thus over a third of the members of the bar in both 1835 and 1885 came from the capital or its neighbouring counties. Incidentally while the percentage of the bar from the Home Counties had declined slightly since the early seventeenth century, the percentage from London had more than doubled. The southern counties from Hampshire west-

Table 1.5: Geographical Origins of United Kingdom Barristers

	1835				1885			
	a	b	c	d	a	b	c	d
	No.	% of bar	% of pop.	b/c	No.	% of bar	% of pop.	b/c
Bedford	0	0	-	-	1	.2	.4	.5
Berkshire	5	2.1	.6	3.5	7	1.1	.6	1.8
Buckinghamshire	3	1.2	.6	2.0	2	.3	.5	.6
Cambridgeshire	3	1.2	.6	2.0	3	.5	.5	1.0
Cheshire	5	2.1	1.4	1.5	12	1.9	1.8	1.1
Cornwall	1	.4	1.2	.3	5	.8	.9	.9
Cumberland	1	.4	.7	.6	1	.2	.7	.3
Derbyshire	3	1.2	1.0	1.2	5	.8	1.3	.6
Devonshire	10	4.1	2.0	2.1	18	2.9	1.7	1.7
Dorsetshire	3	1.2	.7	1.7	7	1.1	.5	2.2
Durham	4	1.7	1.0	1.7	4	.6	2.4	.3
Essex	6	2.5	1.3	1.9	9	1.4	1.7	.8
Gloucestershire	6	2.5	1.6	1.6	16	2.5	1.6	1.6
Hampshire	10	4.1	2.0	2.1	17	2.7	1.7	1.6
Herefordshire	2	.8	.5	1.6	6	1.0	.3	3.3
Hertfordshire	3	1.2	.6	2.0	7	1.1	.6	1.8
Huntingdonshire	1	.4	.2	2.0	0	0	-	-
Kent	5	2.1	1.4	1.5	22	3.5	2.0	1.8
Lancashire	5	2.1	5.5	.4	46	7.3	9.9	.7
Leicestershire	1	.4	.8	.5	10	1.6	.9	1.8
Lincolnshire	2	.8	1.3	.6	3	.5	1.3	.4
London/Middlesex	56	23.2	4.3	5.4	162	25.7	12.0	2.1
Monmouthshire	0	0	-	-	5	.8	.6	1.3
Norfolk	2	.8	1.6	.5	9	1.4	1.3	1.1
Northamptonshire	2	.8	.7	1.1	4	.6	.8	.8
Northumberland	4	1.7	.9	1.9	6	1.0	1.2	.8
Nottinghamshire	1	.4	.9	.4	4	.6	1.1	.5
Oxfordshire	1	.4	.6	.7	7	1.1	.5	2.2
Rutland	0	0	-	-	3	.5	.1	5.0
Shropshire	5	2.1	.9	2.3	6	1.0	.7	1.4
Somerset	8	3.3	1.7	1.9	11	1.7	1.3	1.3
Staffordshire	4	1.7	1.7	1.0	6	1.0	2.8	.4
Suffolk	1	.4	1.2	.3	8	1.2	1.0	1.2
Surrey	10	4.1	.7	5.9	31	4.9	1.3	3.8
Sussex	9	3.7	1.1	3.4	19	3.0	1.4	2.1
Warwickshire	2	.8	1.4	.6	5	.8	2.1	.4
Westmoreland	0	0	-	-	0	0	-	-
Wiltshire	6	2.5	1.0	2.5	6	1.0	.7	1.4
Worcestershire	0	0	-	-	4	.6	1.1	.5

Table 1.5 (cont'd)

	1835				1885			
	a	b	c	d	a	b	c	d
	No.	% of bar	% of pop.	b/c	No.	% of bar	% of pop.	b/c
Yorkshire	16	6.6	5.6	1.2	29	4.6	8.3	.6
Wales	4	1.6	3.3	.5	18	2.9	3.9	.7
Scotland	10	4.1	9.8	.4	37	5.9	10.7	.6
Ireland	21	8.7	32.2	.3	50	7.9	14.8	.5
Total	241				631			

Source: Data on county and regional populations comes from the 1831 census for 1835 and from the 1881 census for 1885. Mitchell and Deane, <u>British Historical Statistics</u>, pp. 6-7, 20-23.

ward to Cornwall and Somerset had also had a long association with the legal profession. In 1835, 16 per cent of the bar came from the six counties in this region, identical to their contribution two centuries earlier. Their position was probably due to the importance of this region in regard to commerce and trade as well as to local and family traditions in the bar. By the later nineteenth century the proportion of the bar from the West Country had declined by a third. This was due as we shall see below both to economic and social factors.

By contrast the regions that sent relatively small numbers to the bar were the east and far north of England. The former including Lincolnshire, Norfolk and Suffolk, had been one of the major recruiting grounds for barristers before the Civil War accounting for 12 per cent of the bar, yet by the nineteenth century it had declined to a mere 2 to 3 per cent. Similar percentages of men came from the northern counties of Cumberland, Durham, Northumberland and Westmoreland; the contribution of these counties in the early seventeenth century was less than 2 per cent. The decline in the proportion of barristers from the east can probably be attributed to the fact that the region was almost entirely agricultural by the nineteenth century. As a result it had a relatively low population growth rate and suffered from the exodus of the gentry from the bar. The north not only had a low population but it was the furthest point from the centre of legal England.

When we divide the counties and regions of the United Kingdom not simply with regard to their absolute contributions to the bar but according to the ratio of barristers to population, as in Table 1.5 column d and the accompanying maps, we find that some of our earlier conclusions have to be modified. Despite the general continuity of the underlying pattern a major redistribution occurred in the geographical origins of members of the bar between 1835 and 1885.(28) In 1835 the western counties, along the Welsh border, that in absolute terms were not extremely large contributors to the bar are shown to have had a high density of barristers. A similar though even more pronounced revision is necessary with regard to the north east. But even more significantly, when we compare the two maps we find that by the late Victorian period there was a much more even distribution of barristers in the United Kingdom than had been the case fifty years earlier. Counties with 'very high', 'high' and 'low' barrister-to-population densities became fewer in number while the number of 'average' counties increased. The old centres of concentration still exist in the 1880s though in a diluted form. Most of the Home Counties had now declined from 'very high' to 'high', Berkshire and Wiltshire from 'very high' to 'average' and Somerset, Cambridgeshire, Buckinghamshire, Essex, Cheshire and Northumberland from 'high' to 'average'. In the opposite direction Ireland, Scotland, Cornwall, Suffolk, Lancashire, Worcestershire, Nottinghamshire, Monmouthshire and Bedfordshire all increased from 'low' to 'average'.

In his study of the student body at Oxford University Professor Stone found an analogous development in the geographical origins of matriculants at approximately the same time. In both instances 'high' and 'low' density regions decreased in area while the centre of gravity drifted northwards. Stone suggests that this development reflects the proportional increase in the population and wealth of midland and northern counties and the improvement in long-distance transportation due to railways.(28) There was another factor related to the redistribution of wealth and population due to the industrial revolution that deserves mention - namely changes in the social quality of the Oxford student body as well as of the members of the bar. While the social origins of the barristers will be discussed in more detail below it is worth noting at this juncture that the 50 years between 1835 and 1885 witnessed an advance in the representation of the urban middle classes at the inns at the expense of the gentry. Although the shift was relatively modest, it may have been sufficient to explain the movement away from the agricultural south and towards the urban north and the cities of Ireland and Scotland.

Figure 1.2: Geographical Origins of United Kingdom Barristers 1835

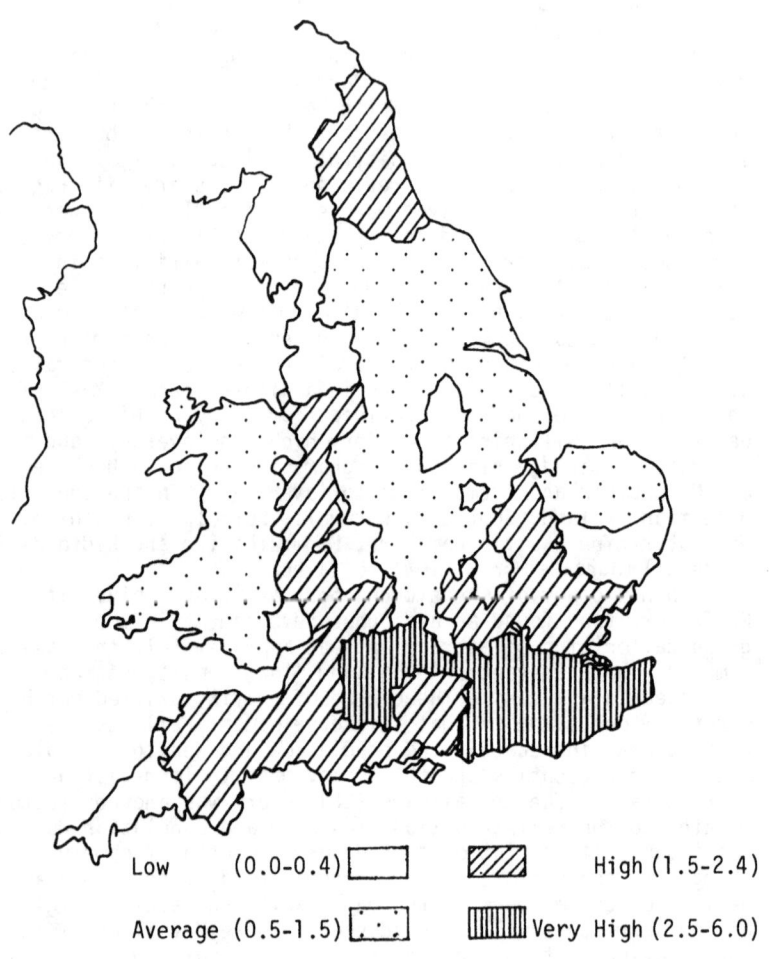

Figure 1.3: Geographical Origins of United Kingdom Barristers
             1885

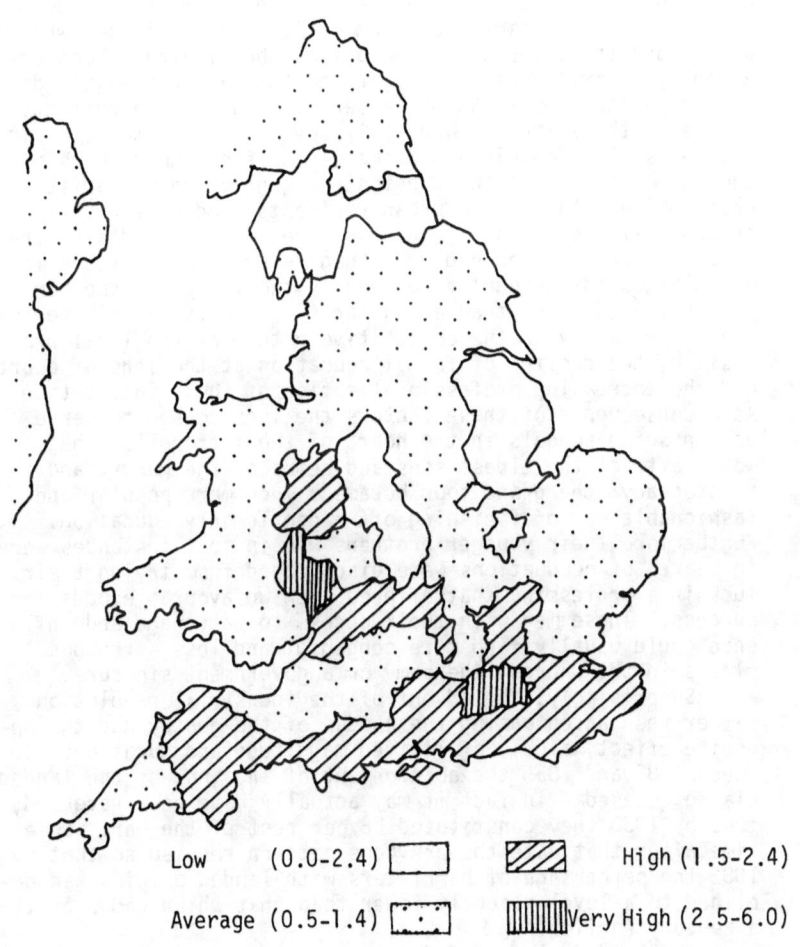

Social and Occupational

The social and occupational origins of nineteenth-century barristers are even more fundamental to our understanding of the character of the profession than are their geographical origins. Certainly by the late sixteenth century and most likely even earlier than that the inns of court had begun to witness an exodus by the sons of the gentry. In their stead came members of the professional and commercial middle classes who would form the mainstay of the bar by the eighteenth century. Recently Wilfrid Prest has suggested that a considerable dilution in the proportion of landed sons took place during the course of the sixteenth and early seventeenth centuries: in the years 1590 to 1639 approximately half of the members of the bar were sons of the substantial gentry and the aristocracy while a third were urban residents, indicating their probable middle-class origins. By the latter decades of the 1700s the proportions had more than reversed so that the middle classes now accounted for nearly two-thirds of the bar and the gentry for less than a quarter.(29) We can attribute this change primarily to the competitive nature of the legal profession, the decline of formal education at the inns of court and the increasing professionalisation of these institutions. As a consequence of these factors the inns ceased to serve as finishing schools in the heart of the metropolis, that would attract the eldest sons and heirs of the gentry and the aristocracy; the grand tour became a much more popular and fashionable way of finishing off a gentlemanly education. Furthermore their younger brothers who in most instances were in search of occupations were discouraged from trying their luck in a profession that offered such unfavourable odds for success. These men with their access to patronage and influence could usually find more congenial and less strenuous places in the Church, the army or a government sinecure.

Surprisingly, the advent of the industrial revolution rather than accentuating the exodus of the gentry had the opposite effect, albeit of limited magnitude and duration. Between 1785 and 1835 the abandonment of the inns by the landed classes ceased - in fact it may actually have been reversed; thus by 1835 they constituted 28 per cent of the bar. Some time after that date the previous pattern resumed so that by 1885 the percentage of barristers with landed origins had declined to a level slightly lower than that which had prevailed a century earlier.

The landed classes did not constitute a homogeneous socio-economic category. Thanks to the data on rental contained in the 'new domesday book' of 1874-6 we can delve in some detail into the contribution to the bar of the various strata of landed society. In Table 1.6 we see that in both 1835 and 1885 the majority of barristers from gentry origins belonged to either the greater gentry (with estates worth between £3,000 and £10,000 per annum) or the squirearchy (with estates worth

Table 1.6: The Social and Occupational Origins of the Bar

Father's Occupation		Bar	Soli-citor	Clergy	Medi-cine	Other Profes-sions	Civil Ser-vice	Busi-ness	Urban Gentry	Land	Rural Gentry	Other	Unknown	Total
1835	No.	19	14	19	7	7	7	35	43	47	23	4	23	248
	%	8	6	8	3	3	3	14	17	19	9	2	9	100
1885	No.	82	53	85	34	49	36	110	78	117	37	7	37	725
	%	11	7	12	5	7	5	15	11	16	5	1	5	100

Note: For the 1835 sample towns with populations of 3000 inhabitants or more based on the 1831 census are taken to be urban, while for the 1885 sample the minimum urban population is 5000 based on the 1841 census. In fact the figure for 1885 may well over-estimate the proportion of rural gentry.

between £1,000 and £3,000 per annum).(30) The latter was in fact the largest group in both sample years. The two extremes of landed society were poorly represented. At the top, less than 10 per cent of the barristers from landed origins were the sons of great landowners and only slightly more than a tenth came from titled (peerage or baronetage) families. At the bottom, men with land worth less than £300 annually, most of whom were undoubtedly yeoman farmers, were even less conspicuous than were the landed elite. A closer look at the middle ranks of the gentry reveals that not only did the quantity of landed recruits to the bar fall between the years 1835 and 1885 but so did their wealth. Proportionally the size of the greater gentry declined by a third and that of the squirearchy by a quarter. At the same time the percentage of lesser landowners, those with land whose annual value was less than £1,000, doubled. This pattern only emphasizes the point made earlier that the bar become less attractive over time to the more prosperous sections of landed society.

Table 1.7: Annual Rentals of Parental Estates

	1835		1885	
	No.	%	No.	%
over £10,000	3	8	10	9
£3,000 - £10,000	14	37	28	26
£1,000 - £3,000	16	42	34	32
£300 - £1,000	5	13	29	27
£100 - £300	0	0	5	5
Total	38	100	106	100

Source: Return of the Owners of Land, BPP LXXII (1874), LXXX (1876).

Note: This is based on 38 of 47 cases in 1835 and 106 of 117 cases in 1885 for which exact data on rentals have been found.

The vacuum left by the gentry was filled by the sons of professionals, businessmen and civil servants. Between 1835 and 1885 the representation of the middle classes at the bar rose from 61 per cent to 73 per cent. For these groups unlike their social betters the bar was a desirable profession despite the evident risks. Simply having been called to the bar was a mark of social standing and provided an entry card into a wide variety of occupations. Furthermore, for those who eventually made their mark in the law, no profession had greater potential for bestowing wealth and influence on its members than did the bar.

The consolidation by the middle classes of their dominant position at the bar between 1835 and 1885 was due principally to the increased representation of the sons of professional men, that grew from 27 to 42 per cent. This resulted primarily from an influx by the sons of members of gentlemanly professions - the Church of England clergy, the bar, and the military; their overall proportion rose from 17 per cent in 1835 to 26 per cent in 1885. This almost exactly compensated for the decline in the size of the landed component. During the identical 50 year period recruitment from the civil service rose from 3 to 5 per cent while the proportion of businessmen's sons remained virtually unchanged.

The opposite end of the social scale, the working classes, to all intents and purposes was non-existent as far as the bar was concerned. There were a few artisans' sons who succeeded in entering the profession, though they were far from typical members of their class. Generally they were the sons of more prosperous craftsmen - jewellers for example. Not one son of an unskilled worker has been identified although it is possible that some may be hidden within the unknown category. Additionally some of the businessmen were more than likely small shopkeepers who in terms of social status should be ranked along with the artisans. But even taking all of these possibilities into account, it seems clear that the bar was not an attractive profession for those born into the working classes.

By the late eighteenth century the bar recruited most of its members from a narrow spectrum of English society and this trend was if anything accentuated during the reign of Queen Victoria. The near to absolute monopoly by the urban professional and business classes supplemented by the greater and lesser gentry meant that the bar rarely served as an avenue along which great leaps of social mobility could be accomplished. Opportunities for upward mobility were limited in reality to the sons of small businessmen, members of the traditional lower professions such as solicitors, doctors, teachers and lower civil servants, and of the new technological and business-oriented ones such as architects, engineers and accountants. For some commentators, most notably William Blackstone, these men threatened to undermine the gentlemanly character of the profession. We must assume that Blackstone did not direct his attack on the 'obscure or illiterate men' at the few isolated instances of artisans' or shopkeepers' sons. Rather the threat he saw was posed by the influx of men from the non-gentlemanly middle and lower-middle classes who learned their law and manners at the desks of attorneys and brought with them mean careerism that undermined the traditional character of the bar.(31)

The means to solve the social problem, according to Blackstone, and at the same time enhance the legal knowledge of barristers, was to make a university education a prerequisite for admission to an inn of court. The result of this proposal, as Professor Lucas has demonstrated, was the adoption of a common rule at all four inns in 1762 which among other things allowed men with master of arts or bachelor of laws degrees from Oxford or Cambridge to be called to the bar after three years instead of the usual five. Somewhat later the inns granted the same privilege to graduates of Dublin University and in the 1840s the Middle Temple extended its provisions to include the new Universities of London and Durham. In fact these regulations had little if any effect on the social quality of the English bar.(32)

In another attempt to use education to favour gentlemanly recruits the benchers of the Inner Temple in 1829 instituted a regulation that required all new members to pass an examination 'in classical attainments and the general subjects of a liberal education', including a knowledge of Greek and Latin.(33) Writing in 1845 Samuel Warren applauded the actions of the Inner Temple:

> The right hand of fellowship is, ever has been, and ever will be, cordially extended by the Bar to the newcomer, if he be but a gentleman in his feelings, and in his conduct;....we are, at the same time, aware that desperate distress, in the presence of strong temptation, prompts its victims, when unchecked by virtuous principles, to practices which are a scandal to the Bar, to degrade it from the highest position in estimation which it has occupied from time immemorial....The root of this evil is to be sought for in the excessive facility of access to the Bar, which has existed of late years. It is impossible to guard the portals of such an edifice with too great vigilance....we feel proud in being able to bear testimony to the anxious vigilance evidenced by the Benchers of the Inner Temple to admit only properly qualified persons as students - one means being the bona fide examination....The effect has long been visible in the class of persons who have of late years become members of that ancient, wealthy, and distinguished Inn of Court.(34)

A year later Edward Creasy, Professor of History at the University of London and future Chief Justice of Ceylon told the Select Committee on Legal Education, 'I think the preliminary examination would be a guarantee against men not of a high tone of gentlemanly feeling of becoming members of the profession at all....'(35) At the same time however there were Inner Templars who felt that admissions at their inn were suffering in comparison to those of their neighbour in the Temple due to its stricter policy.(36) In fact by 1854, perhaps under the pressure of falling enrolments, the Inner Temple had abandoned the use of an entrance examination for law students.(37)

Both Warren and Creasy recognised the social implications of all those proposals that attempted to establish an educational requirement as a preliminary to admission to the bar. The demand that a classical education precede entry into the legal profession was based on the assumption that gentlemen by birth or at the very least public or grammar school old boys were much more likely to be men of 'gentlemanly and honourable feelings' than were men who came from less advantaged backgrounds.(38) Proponents of this view wanted to establish social homogeneity at the inns of court and thereby in the profession at large.(39)

Education was not the only weapon at the disposal of the inns to help ensure the gentlemanly character of the bar. A few examples should suffice. In addition to the advantages that it bestowed on graduates, the 1762 regulations stipulated that attorneys, solicitors and certain other legal functionaries had to abandon practice for two years prior to being called to the bar.(40) In 1807 Lincoln's Inn passed a controversial and short-lived regulation that prohibited the call of any man who had earned a living from journalism.(41) In 1825 the Middle Temple introduced rules barring the admission of any man 'engaged in any profession other than law, or in any trade, business, or occupation.'(42) At the same time the two Temples and Lincoln's Inn began to require that prospective members supply character references signed by two barristers.(43)

As with the educational requirements, the class dimensions of these enactments are clear. Their intention was to inhibit the entrance into the bar of men without independent means. By prohibiting alternate sources of employment while one was a student, these statutes favoured those individuals who could afford to wait in idleness prior to their call and then survive the briefless early years in the profession. Furthermore, from the 1820s the young man whose social circle did not include several barristers who could vouch for his character was at a distinct disadvantage.

Did these measures achieve their aim of limiting the admissions to the bar to gentlemen? While it is impossible to give a completely definitive answer, our samples of the bar do provide some clues concerning the efficacy of these regulations. Men who sprang from the lower middle and working classes were a rarity at the bar at least since the eighteenth century, and it seems unlikely that these rules had any effect on this tiny minority. Members of these social strata were sufficiently deterred from entering the upper branch of the legal profession by the cost and the uncertainty of success - luxuries that they could not afford. The real target would seem to be Blackstone's 'obscure or illiterate men'. In 1785 the lower professions, business and urban gentry accounted for 37 per cent of the bar. By 1835 this had risen to 43 per cent and in 1885 to 47 per cent. At the same time the proportion of gentlemen by birth, including rural gentry, as we have seen remained steady at 46 to 47 per cent.(44) Despite the assumptions of those who formulated the various requirements, the non-gentlemen were not precluded from acquiring a classical education nor were they less able than were the sons of clergymen with small livings or the less prosperous elements of gentry to find the financial resources to tide them over during the most unproductive years in the profession. In fact law students and fledgling barristers found various avenues of employment that provided them with supplementary incomes including university fellowships, special pleading and equity draftsmanship below the bar, the training of newly admitted students, law reporting and even journalism.(45) Furthermore, as we shall see below, some of the non-gentlemen, particularly the sons of solicitors, were well placed to attract clients as soon as they were called to the bar. In the light of this evidence the attempts of conservative reformers to use educational and class-biased regulations as a means of controlling the social composition of the bar must be judged a failure.

Educational
The natural complement to the preceding discussion of the social quality of the bar and attempts to control it, is an examination of the educational background of late eighteenth- and nineteenth-century barristers in school, university and inns of court. Unfortunately the data on school attendance I have collected are less than useful due to the high percentage of unknowns. Only in the case of the public schools is there sufficient evidence for us to draw meaningful conclusions. Since printed registers exist for many of these institutions, the problem of missing data is much less significant here.

The proportion of early- and late-Victorian barristers who were educated at public schools was virtually identical, though the percentage that attended elite schools declined slightly. This change was mirrored in the reduced concentration of future barristers at a few select schools. In 1835 of the public school contingent 66 per cent were pupils at only three schools - Eton (25), Westminster (13) and Harrow (12). Fifty years later four schools - Eton (50), Harrow (29), Rugby (23) and Winchester (17) accounted for 52 per cent of all the public school old boys at the bar. Of the new public schools only Cheltenham (14) accounted for as much as five per cent of public school barristers in 1885.

While the social quality of the nineteenth-century bar would certainly not have impressed Blackstone he may have

Table 1.8: Public School Attendance

	1835		1885	
	No.	%	No.	%
Elite Public Schools	68	27	175	24
Other Public Schools	8	3	54	7
Total Public Schools	76	31	229	32

Note: I have used different criteria to identify the elite institutions in the two sample years due to the increase in the number of public schools and changes in the reputation of individual institutions during the intervening period. See T.W. Bamford, The Rise of the Public Schools (1967); J.R. de S. Honey, Tom Brown's Universe (1977). The 'elite public schools' for 1835 are the nine so-called Clarendon Schools investigated by the Public School Commission of 1864: Charterhouse, Eton, Harrow, Merchant Taylors', Rugby, St Paul's, Shrewsbury, Westminster and Winchester. 'Elite public schools' for 1885 are the 22 that appear in Table 4, group I in Honey, Tom Brown's Universe, p. 264. 'Other public schools' for 1835 are, after the omission of the Clarendon Schools, all those included in Tables 4 and 5 in the preceding work. 'Other public schools' for 1885 are those in Table 4, groups II to IV, and Table 5 in that work, pp. 264 and 268.

drawn consolation from the trend towards university education. In 1758 his central proposal had been to make 'an academical education a previous step to the profession of the common law'.(46) While this goal was not realised during the nineteenth century, there was an enormous increase in university attendance by members of the bar between 1785 and 1885.(47) In fact, the timing of the increase seems to negate the possibility that the inns of court regulation influenced that process. A more likely if less dramatic cause was the general expansion of university education during the nineteenth century. Not only did the percentage of Oxford and Cambridge men continue to rise during the century, but by 1885 the university contingent had been further augmented by graduates of other universities, including four in England, three each in Scotland and Ireland, two in Germany and one each in Australia, France, India, Mauritius and the United States. Two universities dominated this group, accounting for two-thirds of the non-Oxbridge total - University of London with 36 men (38 per cent) and Trinity College, Dublin with 26 men (28 per cent).

Table 1.9: University Attendance 1785-1885

	1785		1835		1885	
	No.	%	No.	%	No.	%
Cambridge	19	18	78	31	201	28
Oxford	18	17	52	21	214	30
Other Universities	6	6	14	6	94	13
Total Universities	43	41	144	58	509	70

Just as in the case of the public schools, Oxbridge men at the bar were concentrated in a few favoured colleges. The most frequent choices in 1785 and 1835 were in order of preference: Trinity, Cambridge, Christ Church and St John's, Cambridge. By 1885 the popularity of St John's had declined and its place had been usurped by Balliol. Together these four colleges accounted for 35 per cent of the Oxbridge-educated barristers in 1785, 49 per cent in 1835 and 45 per cent in 1885, while more than a quarter of the Oxbridge men in the two nineteenth-century samples had studied at Trinity College alone.

In both their secondary and higher education the barristers gravitated towards the most exclusive schools and colleges. This was even true in the late Victorian period when they attended a larger number of educational institutions than previously. The leading position of Eton, Harrow and Rugby and of Trinity, Christ Church and Balliol was not due merely to the educational choices of the gentry sons. They were equally popular with upper-middle-class sons especially those who would eventually rise to the summit of the practising bar.

The final stage of every barrister's pre-professional career was spent at the inns of court. Until 1852 the call to the bar was a mere formality after a man had waited the prescribed length of time - three to five years - and had eaten the prescribed number of meals in the commons of his inn - three meals per term for twelve terms.(48) With the establishment of the Council of Legal Education in 1852 a student also had to attend law lectures sponsored by the Council or pass an examination. Finally, in 1872 the qualifying examination was made a precondition for admission to the bar.(49) Between the mid-seventeenth century when the previous system of legal training fell into disuse, and the implementation of these modest reforms more than two centuries

Table 1.10: Admissions to the Inns of Court 1780-1888

	Lincoln's Inn		Inner Temple		Middle Temple		Gray's Inn		Total
	No.	%	No.	%	No.	%	No.	%	
1780-1789	769	41.7	332	18.0	596	32.3	147	8.0	1844
1790-1799	638	37.6	347	20.4	395	23.2	319	18.8	1699
1800-1809	649	41.3	291	18.5	364	23.2	267	17.0	1571
1810-1819	857	41.3	365	17.6	512	24.7	343	16.5	2077
1820-1829	904	33.9	661	24.8	548	20.5	555	20.8	2668
1830-1839	1029	33.1	637	20.5	787	25.3	652	21.0	3105
1840-1849	906	33.1	694	25.3	855	31.2	284	10.4	2739
1850-1859	828	61.4	-	-	410	30.4	110	8.2	1348
1860-1869	869	43.3	-	-	1018	50.7	122	6.1	2009
1870-1879	937	42.1	-	-	1141	51.2	149	6.7	2227
1880-1888	614	31.8	-	-	1151	59.6	166	8.6	1931

Sources: W.P. Baildon (ed.), The Records of the Honourable Society of Lincoln's Inn, (2 vols., 1896); R.L. Lloyd, 'Inner Temple Admissions', (3 vols., 1960), vol. 3 (unpublished typescript); H.A.C. Sturgess (ed.), Register of Admissions to the Honourable Society of the Middle Temple, (3 vols., 1949), vols. 2, 3; Joseph Foster (ed.), The Register of Admissions to Gray's Inn, 1521-1889, (1889).

later, the aspiring barrister received little beyond a social introduction to the profession inside the inns. Legal knowledge was acquired from reading legal classics and from a period of apprenticeship, known as pupilage, in the chambers of a barrister, special pleader or equity draftsman and conveyancer.(50)

Admissions at individual inns were subject to considerable fluctuations as is clear from Table 1.10. We find between 1780 and 1888 that there was a relative decline in the popularity of Lincoln's Inn, home of the equity bar; notable expansion at the Middle Temple; relative stability at the Inner Temple at least until 1850 when the data for that inn end; and at Gray's Inn a temporary revival followed by a rather severe contraction.

While precise explanations of these fluctuations cannot be given it may be useful to mention a few possible causes. Professional prospects in the equity courts may well have influenced the fortunes of Lincoln's Inn. At the other end of the scale, Gray's Inn naturally suffered from its less than ideal location, farther away from the centre of legal London than the other three inns. Its recovery in the first third of the nineteenth century resulted from two factors. The influx of students may have meant that empty chambers were at a premium and therefore Gray's Inn may simply have benefited from the law of supply and demand. Furthermore, in this era when the final assault to exclude attorneys from the inns of court was underway, Gray's Inn alone was prepared to admit members of the lower branch 'for the purpose only of holding chambers within the Inn.'(51) Finally the Inner Temple's enrolment may have been lower than the Middle Temple's in the 1830s and 1840s as a result of the former's entrance examination for non-graduates and its more rigid residence requirements.(52)

When we examine the inns from a somewhat different perspective, in terms of attendance by sample groups of barristers in 1785, 1835 and 1885, we discover that there were in fact three major societies - the two Temples and Lincoln's Inn and one minor house - Gray's Inn. In addition we find that some of the fluctuations discussed above are reflected in the data in Table 1.11 as well. Thus the percentage at the Middle Temple is virtually unchanged throughout the century. Attendance at the Inner Temple apparently reached its nadir in the 1830s but by the 1880s it had become the largest of all. The experience at Lincoln's Inn was just the reverse having been the most popular inn by 1835 with nearly half the bar, and then falling off to a comparatively modest 29 per cent by 1885.

There was no certainty that a man who entered an inn of court would ever qualify for the bar, much less practise as an advocate. Despite the ease of becoming a barrister it was not until the 1840s that even a majority of students took this step, according to the data for the Middle Temple and Lincoln's Inn (Table 1.12). The most striking characteristic of the

Table 1.11: Inns of Court Attendance 1785-1885

	1785		1835		1885	
	No.	%	No.	%	No.	%
Inner Temple	31	30	55	22	292	40
Middle Temple	31	30	69	28	201	28
Lincoln's Inn	35	34	111	45	213	29
Gray's Inn	5	5	13	5	19	3
Unknown	2	2	0	0	0	0

table is the steadily rising percentage of members who were eventually called to the bar. The spectacular nature of the increase becomes all the more apparent when it is placed in historical perspective. During the forty years, 1590-1630, when admission levels were comparable to those in the nineteenth century, only 18 per cent of the entrants ever became barristers.(53) Just over a century and half later the proportion had risen only slightly to no more than 25 per cent.(54) By contrast in the second decade of the nineteenth century it surpassed 33 per cent; thirty years later it reached 50 per cent, and peaked at almost 70 per cent in the 1860s before beginning a modest decline. There can be little doubt that the rise in the call ratio was one aspect of the professionalisation of the inns of court.

This process had begun in the eighteenth century but it reached its climax only in the nineteenth. More and more students were intent on qualifying for practice at the bar, at least pro forma. Conversely the number of men who were content merely to live in chambers, eat dinners in the commons and mix in society for a few years diminished considerably. By the 1830s the inns had become more than ever professional societies in that more than half of the new members were eventually called.

This rise of a new professional consciousness coincided with a period of overcrowding that made the prospects of establishing a reasonable practice bleak indeed. By 1885 less than two-fifths of the bar was earning its livelihood from advocacy in England and Wales. Thus once qualified, the majority of nineteenth-century barristers - at least those who were not of independent means - had to adapt their career goals to the realities of the job market. As we shall see in detail below, those who chose to enter alternate occupations were not inevitable failures. Many men never intended to practise in the courts of Westminster or in the English

Table 1.12: Ratio of Admissions and Calls to the Bar at the Middle Temple and Lincoln's Inn 1785-1884

Decade of Admission	Middle Temple			Lincoln's Inn			Total		
	Admissions	Calls	%	Admissions	Calls	%	Admissions	Calls	%
1784-1794	525	100	19.0	836	181	21.7	1361	281	20.6
1795-1804	307	78	25.4	591	207	35.0	898	285	31.7
1805-1814	441	133	30.2	703	263	37.4	1144	396	34.6
1815-1824	552	237	42.9	936	407	43.5	1488	644	43.3
1825-1834	615	273	44.4	923	432	46.8	1538	705	45.8
1835-1844	997	606	60.8	998	434	43.5	1995	1040	52.1
1845-1854	571	353	61.8	854	478	56.0	1425	831	58.3
1855-1864	645	405	62.8	863	623	72.2	1508	1028	68.2
1865-1874	1141	664	58.2	956	710	74.3	2097	1374	65.5
1875-1884	1220	697	57.1	756	530	70.1	1976	1227	62.1

Sources: W.P. Baildon and R.F. Roxburgh (eds.), The Records of the Honourable Society of Lincoln's Inn. The Black Books (5 vols., 1897-1968), vols. 4 and 5; Sturgess, Middle Temple Admissions, vol. 2.

Note: For the Middle Temple call data are derived from men admitted in a given decade who were later called to the bar. For Lincoln's Inn it is assumed that admissions roughly correspond to calls five years later, so that admissions between 1785 and 1794 are juxtaposed to calls between 1790 and 1799.

provinces. Many colonials came to England to train and then returned home immediately. Other men went directly into the world of business or the civil service or returned to their paternal estates upon their call to the bar. Still others tried their hand at the bar for a few years, but soon found other professions which were more congenial to their characters and talents.

Increased professionalisation also meant a dramatic increase in the size of the bar in these years. In 1885 there were nearly three times as many living barristers as there had been half a century earlier. Expansion brought with it new patterns of social and geographical recruitment. Perhaps even more significant were the changes wrought in the relationships between the barristers and the central institutions of their profession. The conflicts that emerged as a result in the last four decades of the nineteenth century threatened to undermine the most basic traditions of the legal profession. But as we shall see in the next chapter the voices of conservatism prevailed and the original edifice remained with only minor alterations.

NOTES

1. James Bryce, The American Commonwealth (2nd edn., 2 vols., 1889), vol. II, p. 495.
2. Sir George Clarke, A History of the Royal College of Physicians (2 vols., Oxford, 1964-6).
3. On the size of professions in the nineteenth century see W.J. Reader, Professional Men (1966), pp. 208, 211.
4. See Duman, The Judicial Bench in England, p. 7.
5. On the evolution of the professions in the nineteenth century see Reader, Professional Men, passim.
6. William Thackeray, The History of Pendennis (Harmondsworth ed., 1972), p. 317. First published 1848-50.
7. LT, 19 (May 29, 1852), p. 66.
8. See W.W. Rostow, British Economy of the Nineteenth Century (Oxford, 1948), chapter II.
9. On the last two stages see R.A. Church, The Great Victorian Boom 1850-1873 (1975), passim; and S.B. Saul, The Myth of the Great Depression (1969), passim.
10. Barristers specializing in parliamentary work represented the initiators of new railway lines before Parliament. The function of these counsel was to secure the passage of private acts that would authorise the construction of lines and the compulsory purchase of land. Michael Robbins, The Railway Age (Harmondsworth, 1965), pp. 31-7, 89-96. This type of practice could be very lucrative. In 1847 Charles Austin, a specialist in railway matters, is reported to have earned in excess of £40,000. DNB, vol. I, p. 734. On the decline in this speciality see H. Byerley Thomson, The Choice of a Profession (1857), p. 30.

11. Lawrence Stone, 'The Size and Composition of the Oxford Student Body 1580-1910', in Lawrence Stone (ed.), The University in Society (2 vols., Princeton, 1974), vol. I, Appendix IV, Tables 1A and 1B.

12. Lenore O'Boyle, 'The Problem of the Excess of Educated Men in Western Europe, 1800-1850', Journal of Modern History, 42 (1970), pp. 78-80; see also Harold Perkin, The Origins of Modern English Society (1969), p. 424.

13. Oxford University Commission, BPP XXII (1852); Cambridge University Commission, BPP XLIV (1852-3); Report on the Organisation of the Permanent Civil Service, BPP XXVII (1854); Inns of Court Commission, BPP XVIII (1854-5); Somerset Commission on the Purchase and Sale of Commissions, BPP XVIII (1857).

14. For some representative comments on the state of the bar see Thomson, The Choice of a Profession, p. 30; LJ, 6 (March 24, 1871), p. 189; LJ, 31 (January 4, 1896), p. 3.

15. Select Committee on Official Salaries, BPP X (1850), p. 180.

16. Hansard, 3rd series, House of Commons, 131 (1854), col. 148.

17. Thomson, The Choice of a Profession, pp. 96-7.

18. LT, 95 (May 20, 1894), p. 54.

19. Daniel Duman, 'The English Bar in the Georgian Era' in Wilfrid Prest (ed.), Lawyers in Early Modern Europe and America (1981), p. 88.

20. B.R. Mitchell and Phyllis Deane, Abstract of British Historical Statistics (Cambridge, 1971), pp. 5-6.

21. Duman, 'Bar in the Georgian Era', p. 89.

22. Perkin, Origins of Modern English Society, pp. 254-5. There is much work that remains to be done in regard to the social backgrounds of nineteenth-century litigants. For an examination of this in the seventeenth century see C.W. Brooks, 'Litigants and Attorneys in the Kings Bench and Common Pleas, 1560-1640' in J.H. Baker (ed.), Legal Records and the Historian (1978), pp. 41-59.

23. See below Chapter 5.

24. Select Committee on Official Salaries, p. 178; Brian Abel-Smith and Robert Stevens, Lawyers and the Courts (1970), pp. 211-4.

25. C.E.A. Bedwell, 'American Middle Templars', American Historical Review, 25 (1920), pp. 680-9. The first Americans entered the inns in the 1680s.

26. See below pp. 131-4.

27. On geographical recruitment of barristers in the seventeenth century see Wilfrid R. Prest, The Inns of Court under Elizabeth I and the Early Stuarts 1590-1640 (1972), pp. 32-40.

28. Stone, 'Oxford Student Body', 77-8. On the regional distribution of wealth in Victorian England see W.D. Rubinstein, 'The Victorian Middle Classes: Wealth, Occupation and

Geography', Economic History Review, XXX (1977), pp. 602-623.

29. Wilfrid Prest, 'The English Bar, 1550-1700' in Prest, Lawyers in Early Modern Europe, pp. 70-1; Duman, 'Bar in the Georgian Era', pp. 90-95.

30. The nomenclature and income divisions used here are taken from F.M.L. Thompson, English Landed Society in the Nineteenth Century (1963), pp. 32 and 114-7.

31. Duman, 'Bar in the Georgian Era', pp. 91-3.

32. Paul Lucas, 'Blackstone and the Reform of the Legal Profession', English Historical Review, 77 (1962), pp. 456-96. Select Committee on Legal Education, BPP X (1846), pp. 1-8.

33. Select Committee on Legal Education, p. 4.

34. Samuel Warren, Introduction to Law Studies (2 vols., 1845), vol. 1, pp. 76-7, 79.

35. Select Committee on Legal Education, p. 36.

36. Testimony given by Thomas Starkie and Andrew Amos before the Select Committee on Legal Education, pp. 8-9, 107.

37. Inns of Court Commission, p. 53.

38. Inns of Court Commission, p. 55. J.G. Phillimore on the other hand rejected the notion that a classical education should be a mandatory prerequisite for admission to an inn of court. He told the Inns of Court Commission, p. 125, that 'I would not exclude any person in consequence of the want of possessing it [knowledge of Latin and Greek] from the opportunity of becoming a barrister'.

39. Jerold Auerbach, Unequal Justice, Lawyers and Social Change in America (New York, 1976), pp. 19-29.

40. Select Committee on Legal Education, p. 1.

41. Elie Halevy, England in 1815 (1961), p. 23, note 2.

42. At the same time the other three inns barred attorneys, solicitors or articled clerks either from admission to the society or from keeping commons. Select Committee on Legal Education, pp. 2-3, 5-7.

43. Ibid., p. 2-4.

44. Duman, 'Bar in the Georgian Era', p. 94.

45. Duman, The Judicial Bench, pp. 59-60. The special pleader and equity draftsman drafted common-law and equity pleadings respectively. Members of the inns of court who had not yet been called to the bar could take out a certificate to practise in these capacities 'under the bar'; junior barristers were also permitted to draft pleadings and conveyances.

46. William Blackstone, Commentaries on the Laws of England (4 vols., 1765-9), vol. 1, p. 33.

47. For two views of the importance of a university education for members of the bar see Edward Wynne, Eunomus, or Dialogues Concerning the Law and Constitution of England (4 vols., 1785), vol. 2, p. 20; LT, 42 (December 1, 1866), p. 83.

48. For a copy of the regulations on admissions to the inns and calls to the bar in 1846 see Select Committee on Legal Education, pp. 1-8.

49. Abel-Smith and Stevens, Lawyers and the Courts, pp. 62-73; Sir William Holdsworth, A History of English Law (17 vols., 1922-72), vol. XV, pp. 237-8.

50. For a fuller discussion of pupilage see Chapter 3 below.

51. Select Committee on Legal Education, p. 8. On the exclusion of the attorneys see H.H.L. Bellot, 'The Exclusion of Attorneys from the Inns of Court', Law Quarterly Review, 26 (1910), passim; Duman, 'Bar in the Georgian Era', p. 103.

52. See note 37 above.

53. Derived from Tables 1 and 8 in Prest, The Inns of Court, pp. 11 and 52. Calls from one decade are assumed to correspond to admissions from the previous decade because of the residence requirement of seven years in the seventeenth century.

54. Derived from Tables A2 and A7 in Paul Lucas, 'A Collective Biography of the Students and Barristers of Lincoln's Inn, 1680-1804: A Study in the "Aristocratic Resurgence" of the Eighteenth Century', Journal of Modern History, 46 (1974), pp. 247, 252. Calls from one decade are assumed to correspond to admissions from the decade beginning five years earlier since the residence requirement after 1762 was five years.

Chapter Two

THE GOVERNANCE OF THE BAR IN THE NINETEENTH CENTURY:
TRADITION VERSUS REFORM

In the scholarly debate concerning the nature and development of modern professionalism, one characteristic that has been seen by most contributors, whether historians or sociologists, as basic to the process is the creation of professional qualifying or registering associations.(1) Nevertheless, there remain several English occupations that despite unimpeachable credentials as professions have not developed associations that conform to the established models. These exceptions include the armed services, the Anglican clergy and most significantly for our purposes, the bar.(2)

While the inns of court fulfilled several of the functions that typified the professional association, they remained four independent societies collectively endowed with the exclusive privilege of conferring the degree of barrister-at-law in England and Wales. Since the late sixteenth century the call to the bar has been the only recognised qualification for advocacy in the superior courts of England and Wales; as a result, the inns became the central institutions of the bar.(3) Yet despite their pre-eminent position the inns did not enjoy an absolute monopoly over the governance of the profession in the nineteenth century. In the first place the authority of each inn only extended to its own members. In the second they shared responsibility for the discipline of the bar with the Attorney-General, the circuit messes, the judges of the royal courts and from 1884 onwards with the Bar Committee and its successor, the Bar Council.

My primary concern here is to describe the evolution of the central institutions of the bar and the means by which standards of professional etiquette were imposed on its members. After having examined the traditional system I will trace the forces that conspired to undermine its authority and the attempts both in Parliament and within the bar itself to reorganise the profession. As we shall see the results of this reform process were, to say the least, paradoxical. This was a period when the demands of men infused with utilitarian principles transformed the face of professional England. Yet the bar, with one of the most archaic of all governing organisations - the inns of court - was the only major profession to emerge virtually unaltered by the prevailing social forces.

TRADITIONAL PATTERNS OF AUTHORITY AND DISCIPLINE

In some measure the combination in each of the four inns of court of the status of a private college or club with the powers and privileges of a qualifying association is contradictory. On the one hand the inns are delegated complete control over a profession whose activities are of direct concern to the public, and on the other are not responsible to any public body or authority.(4) The most explicit description of their unique position can be found in a judgement delivered by Lord Mansfield in 1780. After consulting with the other judges he concluded:

> ...the Inns...are not corporations, and have no constitutions by charters from the Crown. They are voluntary societies, which, for ages, have submitted to government analogous to that of other seminaries of learning. But all the power they have concerning admission to the Bar, is delegated to them from the Judges, and, in every instance, their conduct is subject to their control as visitors...From the first traces of their existence to this day, no example can be found of an interposition by the Courts of Westminster Hall proceeding according to the general law of the land; but the Judges have acted as in a domestic forum. (5)

In fact the nearly absolute autonomy that Mansfield conferred upon the inns was in sharp contrast to the periodic intervention in their affairs that had been practised by both the Privy Council and the judges in the Tudor and early Stuart periods.(6)

Although as originally constituted the barristers participated in the governance of their societies, during the sixteenth century power passed from the members of the inns to self-perpetuating oligarchies known as the masters of the bench or more simply as the benchers.(7) As a result, from then on the vast majority of barristers had no influence whatsoever on the central governing bodies of their profession. During the course of the seventeenth century, the benches underwent a transformation as election to that body became a sign of professional success rather than of learning.(8) The direct result of this change was that the inns abdicated their educational functions during the second half of that century, a state of affairs which as we have seen lasted for some two hundred years.(9)

During the nineteenth century the gap between the governors

of the inns and the governed widened as a consequence of changes in the structure of the bar. Since the sixteenth century the bar has been divided into a junior order, the barristers-at-law, who along with law students were members of the inns of court, and a senior order, the serjeants-at-law who upon their creation left their inn of court and joined the Serjeants' Inn.(10) These serjeants included not only those barristers who achieved that rank in the normal course of their careers but also all common law judges who if not already members of the order were created serjeants pro-forma prior to their appointment to the bench. Thus the serjeants and common law judges did not occupy the benches of the inns of court until the mid-1870s when the order of serjeants dissolved as a result of the provisions of the Judicature Act of 1875.

In the first half of the seventeenth century the early Stuart kings added a new rung to the hierarchy of the bar with the permanent establishment of the rank of queen's counsel.(11) The QCs, unlike the serjeants, remained members of the inns of court after their appointment and they were natural candidates for co-option by the benchers. Until the 1830s the number of QCs was small and therefore they were not able to dominate the benches. However, with Lord Eldon's retirement from the Lord Chancellorship in 1827 the rank began to lose much of its previous political character and it became the standard means of denoting that a barrister was a senior member of the profession. In consequence the number of QCs multiplied during the nineteenth century and they began to monopolize the benches to the near exclusion of junior barristers. Both QCs and juniors were eligible to be benchers. Yet while election of the former almost invariably occurred soon after they took silk in their forties or fifties, life-time juniors, if ever selected, usually had to wait until they were nearly seventy.(12) In fact, newly appointed QCs were not automatically admitted to the bench of their inn; the sitting benchers ballotted for them although in the vast majority of cases the election was perfunctory.(13)

In 1877 the Law Times registered its disapproval of the overwhelming predominance of QCs, and to emphasize its point provided a breakdown (Table 2.1) of the benches of the four inns that dramatically demonstrated the erosion in the representation of the junior bar during the nineteenth century.

The benches of the inns of court stood at the centre of the system of professional discipline in the nineteenth century. C.H. Whitehurst, Treasurer of the Middle Temple, told the 1854 Inns of Court Commission that the benches fulfilled 'a very valuable function with regard to the Bar, that is a controlling power...a better power than that of any Court, is that equitable power that you have tested in the Benchers of the Inns.'(14) Another witness, J.G. Phillimore QC MP elaborated upon this when he described the character and obligations of the benchers.

Table 2.1: The Benchers of the Inns of Court 1816-1877

	Lincoln's Inn		Inner Temple		Middle Temple		Gray's Inn	
	1816	1874	1816	1877	1816	1877	1816	1876
QCs	10	66	2	49	9	45	10	12
Juniors	12	3	21	12	24	7	10	9

Source: Law Times, 62 (March 24, 1877), p. 363; Law List, 1874.

Note: The article did not give details for Lincoln's Inn for 1877 so I have taken the liberty of adding the relevant data for 1874.

> There is a high feeling of honour and a strong desire to
> do right in the men who are chosen from the leading mem-
> bers of the Bar to be Benchers of the respective Inns, to
> act in a sort of censurial capacity. They constitute an
> excellent aristocracy...(15)

As we shall see later these views did not go unchallenged either from within the bar or from without.

The power of the benchers over professional discipline rested on their control of the ultimate sanction, the power to 'disbar a man, and so turn him out of his profession altogether.' In reality however, 'This jurisdiction is hardly ever exercised at all' and only in the most extreme circumstances.(16) Together the 'general sentiment of the profession' and the circuit messes regulated the day-to-day discipline of the bar.(17) They operated mainly through the force of social pressure, and their ability to control the behaviour of members of the bar almost invariably without recourse to coercive sanctions must be attributed to the high degree of consensus which existed within the profession. The structure of the bar, at least until the middle decades of the nineteenth century, suited this informal system of discipline. As we noted already it was both the most centralised of the learned professions, with the vast majority of practitioners living and working in London, and one of the smallest.(18)

General conformity to the rules of the bar depended upon the '<u>esprit de corps</u> by which every barrister was the watchful guardian of the honour and integrity of his learned brethren.'(19) According to A.V. Dicey the socialisation process ensured that

> The power...of professional feeling is far greater than
> any one would believe who had not observed its force.
> Every barrister becomes by degrees imbued with a reverence
> for the rules of his profession, and he must be a speci-
> ally clear-headed man if he does not come to regard what
> are at best convenient rules as having in themselves,...a
> certain kind of sacredness.(20)

Yet compliance with professional etiquette did not rest solely upon voluntary submission by every member of the bar. The judges of the superior courts exercised 'a superintendance and a discipline abundantly sufficient to keep up all wise and salutary rules regarding the profession without any legal enactment.'(21) According to Fitzjames Stephen, supervision by the judges was so effective because they were full-fledged members of the professional family:

> The judges are simply barristers who have succeeded in
> the profession of which they are still members, and they
> carry to the Bench the professional habits and ways of
> thought acquired in the course of a professional lifetime

...This gives them an influence in the administration of justice which those who have neither felt nor exercised it can hardly appreciate. The judges can hardly fail to understand the unwritten rules and sentiments which determine the duties of counsel, and when they so understand them and apply them fairly, they have the sentiment of the profession on their side.(22)

The bar messes of the six English circuits exercised a more parochial though related authority over professional discipline. These clubs, about which very little was known until recently when some of the circuits permitted scholars to study their records, brought together the barristers who practised in each of the six regional groupings of assize courts.(23) While on circuit for four to six weeks bi-annually the members of the mess travelled, lodged and dined together. Not every barrister went to all the assize towns; many men restricted themselves to those counties in which they had connections and therefore the greatest chance of attracting business.(24) Membership of the mess was open to anyone who practised on the circuit, although formal admission was by way of ballot and a candidature could be rejected. A barrister could only join one circuit and the rules of etiquette often placed time limitations on his freedom to change to another one.(25)

The origins of the messes are obscure, but by the early nineteenth century they combined both social and professional functions. In addition to serving as dining clubs they were also responsible for the conduct of members while on circuit. The members of the mess governed it according to democratic principles, unlike the inns, and disputes were put to an open vote. They established their own rules of etiquette and in circuit courts tried men who were accused of breaches of professional conduct. Much of the time the trials contained an element of humour but they could be in earnest as well. The sanctions available to these courts were limited to social pressure, token fines (usually in bottles of wine) and in extreme cases expulsion from the mess.

The significance of the circuit messes was that they were the only professional institution that took formal charge of supervising the day-to-day professional conduct of barristers. Nevertheless the effectiveness of the messes in fulfilling this function cannot be taken for granted. In the first place their combined authority only extended to common-law practitioners during meetings of the assizes.(26) They had no control over equity specialists, who did not go the circuit, nor even over their own members during the major part of the professional year. Secondly, contemporary observers disagreed on the power of the messes and their ability to control the behaviour of their members. A defender could describe the mess as a 'beautiful system for keeping men in order by word of mouth - not the cannon's mouth...the system of trusting one another, and looking to one another.'(27) But to a detractor it was 'purely a social institution' whose members once during the circuit 'hold a sort of high jinks, more or less puerile, called the circuit court, at which men are fined for the benefit of the cellar, half in joke, half in earnest, for a variety of trivial conventional offences.'(28)

On balance professional opinion seems to have supported the view that the circuit messes were in the final analysis effective watchdogs over professional etiquette.(29) This opinion was most cogently argued by A.V. Dicey in an article which appeared in the Fortnightly Review. He wrote:

> All the strength of professional feeling supports the authority of the mess. This authority may not be often put forth, but the very fact that it is not often exerted arises in part from its being generally obeyed...it is clear enough that the social powers of the Bar practically exercise considerable control over the freedom of its individual members.(30)

Furthermore, Dicey rejected the assertion that expulsion from the mess was a mere gesture which could not affect a barrister's professional prospects, since it did not prevent him from practising in the assize courts. He explained:

> a person who sets the authority of the circuit at defiance places himself in a position of hostility to the members of his profession...and would probably soon find that any advantage gained by defying the social code of the circuit was dearly purchased by incurring the disapprobation and tacit opposition of the members of his profession.(31)

None of the elements of professional discipline that existed in the nineteenth century could be totally effective in their own right. Yet together they seem to have been reasonably able to supervise and control the behaviour of the members of the bar. When a case of extreme misconduct galvanised the opinion of the entire profession, all of the disciplinary mechanisms could be engaged to punish the offender. Undoubtedly the most dramatic instance of this process was the case of Dr Edward Kenealy, counsel for Arthur Orton, the Tichborne claimant, in his trial for perjury in 1873. Kenealy's handling of the case violated the canons of professional ethics and as a result the jury which found his client guilty also censured him in their verdict. Kenealy continued his intemperate conduct after the trial ended and he publicly attacked both the Lord Chief Justice and the Solicitor-General in an attempt to defend his client. As a result of these unorthodox tactics, which may have been due to mental illness brought on by diabetes, the mess of the Oxford circuit expelled him, he had his patent as a QC invalidated and the benchers of Gray's

Inn debenched and disbarred him.(32)

There was one evident weakness in the system, namely its informality. In the later decades of the nineteenth century as we shall see, this characteristic put severe strains on the administration of professional discipline and etiquette. Before proceeding to examine the impact of social change on the traditional methods of governance and discipline, it is necessary to look in some detail at the nature and evolution of professional etiquette.

THE CUSTOMARY ETIQUETTE OF THE BAR

Little is known about the early history of the etiquette of the bar. Until at least the mid-nineteenth century, the rules were unwritten and there was no uniformity from court to court or from circuit to circuit. In this respect, customary etiquette differed significantly from the strict codes of professional regulations that many professions formulated in the late nineteenth and twentieth centuries. As Lord Brougham told the House of Lords in 1852: 'Professional etiquette was a flexible rule, it went to circumstances, it admitted of exceptions in cases of necessity.'(33)

Inherent in the informality of legal etiquette was an uncertainty about the exact limits of acceptable professional behaviour. The problem facing members of the bar in the nineteenth century and for that matter historians of the profession today was described by a barrister in a letter to the Pall Mall Gazette in 1867. 'It would be a very difficult matter to say what the rules of the bar are, or what is their sanction, and probably no two members of the profession would give the same account of them.'(34) A few months later the Law Journal supported this view: 'The truth is that the rules of the Bar...are admitted to be of a very fluctuating and uncertain character...'.(35)

There are evident difficulties in moving beyond these rather unsatisfactory generalisations about legal etiquette due to the informal nature of those rules. Fortunately the records of the circuit messes that scholars have examined, most especially those of the Norfolk circuit that run from 1818 to 1876, provide valuable clues about the evolution of professional etiquette in the nineteenth century.(36) That process has recently become a subject of debate involving not only historians, lawyers and sociologists, but policy-makers as well.(37) At issue here are the historical origins and the development of legal etiquette, both of which must have a direct bearing on our understanding of the structure of the bar in the nineteenth century. In order to shed some light on these controversial subjects I propose in the following pages to trace the development of legal etiquette and to re-examine the views expressed both by contemporary and modern writers concerning the impact of these rules on the barrister and his client.

Legal etiquette, as it existed in the nineteenth century, can be divided into four categories: 1. rules defining the parameters of professional practice and the relationship between barrister and lay client; 2. restrictive practices relating to the employment of barristers; 3. regulations concerning the conduct of barristers on circuit; 4. rules of circuit membership. Most of these had general applicability serving to delimit areas of professional authority and responsibility, to control competition between barristers and to define the division of labour and maintain honourable relations between the upper and lower branches of the legal profession. These to a greater or lesser degree became the basis of the modern code of conduct for the bar. A few others, especially in categories three and four, were more narrowly concerned with the social rules of the circuit and the mess.

The aim of the categories described above is to help us divide the rules which constituted the etiquette of the bar according to their functions, and to explain the evolution of that code in its formative stages. Naturally there are dangers inherent in this type of explanation since it tends to oversimplify the phenomena that it pretends to describe. The various categories are not discrete and the borders between them are much more fluid than our framework would seem to suggest. In addition, while the quadripartite division of professional etiquette will accommodate all of the most important rules and customs of the bar, we cannot fit every one into the suggested categories with ease. No attempt will be made to discuss all or even most of the rules that together constitute the etiquette of the bar. Specific examples have been chosen for this survey because they are found in the records of the circuit messes, because they exemplified the privileged status of the bar that became an issue after mid-century or because they helped to ensure the independence of the barrister from his client.

Parameters of Professional Practice

The rules that defined the scope of the barrister's practice, as well as his rights and duties, were unquestionably the most fundamental ones of all. They included a complex variety of regulations but we can reduce them to the following premises: The barrister is an independent practitioner; his fee is an honorarium and not a wage; and he does not advise or act on behalf of a client without the intervention of a solicitor. Each rule, despite the fact that it consists of several distinct professional customs, will be treated as a unit since it defines or regulates a specific aspect of professional behaviour.

The barrister is the epitome of the independent professional practitioner and has been so for centuries.(38) He cannot engage in a partnership with either another barrister or a solicitor nor can he become a permanent employee and continue to practise as an advocate.(39) He is also forbidden to enter into an agreement with a client or solicitor by means of which he would be retained for a fixed annual salary or for a standard fee for every piece of work, although this has not always been the case. As Dr Baker has shown, advocates in the late Middle Ages, for example Chaucer's Serjeant-at-Law, probably had patrons and certainly accepted permanent formal retainers.(40)

If, as has been argued recently by historians and sociologists alike, (correctly, I believe) the two distinguishing characteristics of the professions are independence and autonomy, then the extinction of the formal retainer was one important step in the professionalisation of the bar.(41) It helped to destroy the dependence of the advocate upon a patron or a group of patrons. The process had begun by which the flow of dependency was reversed. Together the customs of the bar whose object was to guarantee that barristers remained solo practitioners, also helped to transform the patron into a client. In this way the rules of legal etiquette promoted the autonomy of the profession, although at the expense of the fledgling barrister who was, as it were, confined to his chambers without the means of acting in his own interest.

Of equal importance in the process by which the patron became a client was the concept of the honorarium. The earliest precedent thus far is from 1607,(42) while the most famous statement of the rule was written by William Blackstone in his Commentaries. His formulation makes clear the effects of the honorarium on the locus of power in the relationship between counsel and litigant. Professional custom, as understood by Blackstone, dictated that,

> all the serjeants and barristers indiscriminately (except in the Court of Common-Pleas where only serjeants are admitted) may take upon them the protection and defence of any suitors, whether plaintiff or defendant; who are therefore called his clients, like dependants upon the ancient Roman orators. These indeed practised for gratis ...so likewise it is established with us, that a counsel can maintain no action for his fees; which are given, not as locatio vel conductio, but as quiddam honorarium, not as a salary or as hire, but as a mere gratuity, which a counsellor cannot demand without doing wrong to his reputation.(43)

In fact the honorarium was not a free gift from the litigant. By the seventeenth century a barrister, it seems, expected to be paid a certain fee based on his professional reputation and status and the type of work to be undertaken.(44) He also had the possibility of refusing to accept a brief if the fee was not sufficient.

As Blackstone makes clear, the honorarium is inextricably connected to two other rules: that a barrister is not permitted to sue for the recovery of his fees, and that a barrister cannot be sued for non-attendance in court or for negligence in the conduct of a case.(45) Interestingly enough these are among those few rules of professional etiquette which have not merely become part of the tradition of the bar, but which the courts have recognised as binding on both barrister and client.

According to a court decision in 1863 (Kennedy v. Broun) there can be no legally binding contract between barrister and client with regard to the services of counsel as advocate or his remuneration for these services.(46) In theory there is no financial relationship between counsel and client. The client pays the solicitor for the supply of legal services and the solicitor remunerates the barrister according to the fee marked on the brief. In the case of non-payment the barrister could not recover his fees from the solicitor in court. This state of affairs gave rise to a question posed by William Graham to the Norfolk Circuit mess in 1867 concerning 'whether the Bar have the right to combine to refuse to hold briefs for an attorney who has not paid his fees to one of their number.' In the debate that followed it was suggested 'that the interests of the Bar were subservient to those of the Public & that no Barrister was justified in refusing a brief on those grounds'. The proposal was abandoned without a vote when the circuit was reminded of a decision by the Attorney-General at a meeting of the entire bar in Lincoln's Inn that 'no combination of the Bar to collect past fees was legal.'(47)

Barristers were able to protect their interests by other means, namely by demanding the pre-payment of fees. This was in fact a common practice. As a result an unscrupulous member of the profession could have his cake and eat it too, since he was under no _legal_ obligation to return a fee even if he was unable to represent his client in court. This possibility led in part to the parliamentary attack on the honorarium and its related immunities during the 1870s.

The last and most complicated of the rules in this category required that a barrister accept a brief only through the agency of an attorney. With respect to this custom Lord Brougham told the House of Lords in 1852

> that counsel was not in the habit of taking briefs from clients themselves but from attorneys...With respect to the Superior Courts, there was no inflexible statute law or common law which prohibited counsel from taking briefs from clients themselves; but they had always been prevented from doing so by usage or custom, the etiquette of the Bar.(48)

Despite the strength of custom, it is clear that still in the middle of the nineteenth century, the prohibition against direct access by clients to barristers was not absolute. Lord Campbell recognised this state of affairs when in a high court decision of 1850 he expressed the opinion that while the rule 'that a barrister ought not to accept a brief in a civil suit, except from an attorney' had no basis in law, 'the almost uniform usage which had prevailed upon the subject for more than a century' should be preserved. The most important exception to this rule, as suggested by Campbell, was in criminal cases where a counsel had the right or more correctly the obligation to accept a dock brief from a prisoner without intervention by an attorney.(49) Evidence from the Norfolk Circuit indicates that the rule also prevailed in the assize courts. In 1868 the Norfolk Circuit Club 'decided unanimously to adhere to the "old custom" so that "no barrister can take instructions from any but an attorney except from a prisoner in the dock".'(50) Thus despite its extra-legal character, direct access was respected by the profession at large.

Restrictive Practices
The most important and historically the most controversial of the bar's restrictive practices were the two-counsel rule and the special retainer. According to the former a client who wanted to be represented in court by a QC or serjeant also had to brief a junior barrister who usually received a fee equal to two-thirds of the leader. The special retainer related to the appearance by a barrister on a circuit of which he was not a member. In order to protect the monopoly of the circuit bars, a non-member had to charge an additional fee - £100 for QCs after 1876 - thereby discouraging solicitors from retaining barristers from outside the circuit. The pre-nineteenth-century histories of these customs are unknown and our knowledge of them rests solely upon evidence contained in the circuit mess records. Recently the dating of these rules has become the subject of controversy with one side contending that they originated at the beginning of the last quarter of the nineteenth century while the other side pointed to precedents for both rules in the Norfolk Circuit records prior to 1850.(51) While it is not necessary to review all of the arguments represented by each side, we must consider the central points at issue since they bear directly upon the evolution of the etiquette of the bar in the nineteenth century.

There can be little doubt that the formal codification of these rules only occurred during the last quarter of the century. In order to understand the earlier development of these customs, it would probably be wise to analyse them separately. The two-counsel rule is found in the records of the Norfolk Circuit in various forms beginning in 1818.(52) In 1828 the mess applied the rule to counsel representing the plaintiff in both civil and criminal cases,(53) while just over a quarter of a century later the membership by a show of hands rejected a resolution to repeal the rule in its entirety.(54) In 1869 P.F. O'Malley QC asked the circuit to extend the two-counsel requirement to defence counsel as well since 'he [O'Malley] had lost many briefs in the criminal court because he invariably demanded a junior.' Apparently O'Malley's argument was persuasive since the mess reacted by giving unanimous approval to his proposal. (55) Against this evidence, Sir Alexander Johnston has reported an instance in 1851 in which the Attorney-General of the day overturned an attempt by the Chester Circuit mess to impose the two-counsel rule on barristers representing plaintiffs.(56) The evidence presented here is not unequivocal. With regard to the Norfolk Circuit mess we can safely conclude that that body recognised the two-counsel rule, with certain limitations, as a binding and integral part of professional etiquette. Yet with regard to the bar as a whole, the situation at mid-century is unclear and it may have been that the rule only existed on some circuits; it seems that there was no general professional consensus on the issue.

We possess even less evidence on the early history of the special circuit retainer than on the two-counsel rule, though from the 1860s we are on much firmer ground here. The special retainer may have been part of professional practice on the Norfolk Circuit as early as 1818.(57) After that date there is an absence of references to the rule until 1862 when the English circuits attempted to formulate a common policy with regard to special retainers. In the event, the absence of representatives from the Home and Midland Circuits frustrated this object. Nevertheless, the delegates who were present agreed unanimously that they would recommend to their circuits that they adopt a standard schedule of special retainer fees for the winter [sic spring] assizes in both criminal and civil cases.(58) The issue of special retainers again came to the forefront of professional concern in 1876, when members of the Home Circuit proposed to abolish the rule.(59) Raymond Cock is entirely correct in taking issue with the description of the events of 1876 with respect to special retainers which was presented by Professors Abel-Smith and Stevens. Collective action on special retainers did not date from 1876, as we noted above. On the contrary, the circuit messes at that time merely confirmed the system that had been established in 1862, while lightening the financial burden on clients and facilitating the retention of barristers from outside each circuit by sharply reducing the level of fees. The available evidence indicated that the special retainer had become an integral part of the custom of the bar considerably before the last quarter of the nineteenth century.

If we take formal and nationwide codification as the criterion for the existence of a system of professional etiquette, then those who claim that restrictive practices became binding rules only in the last quarter of the nineteenth century carry the day. However, if we assume that legal etiquette, like other oral laws, may have existed and influenced behaviour despite the fact that it was only 'of a fluctuating and uncertain character', then we must inevitably conclude that restrictive practices were part of the etiquette of the bar and that the barristers adhered to them long before the passage of the Judicature Acts of 1873 and 1875 or the formation of the Bar Committee.

Conduct on Circuit

The primary object of these regulations was to prevent members of the bar from using unfair means to procure briefs. Dicey suggested that their combined purpose was to 'promote honourable conduct...and may be summed up under the one law - thou shalt not hug attorneys.'(61) By trying to assure the segregation of barristers on circuit from members of the lower branch and from lay clients, the customs included in this category sought to impose limitations on the use of connections in the quest for briefs. The bar recognised and accepted respectable connections based on 'family interest, which naturally enough goes a very long way, and possesses the advantages to the young aspirant for fame, of being brought under the notice of the public much sooner than otherwise would be the case.'(62) But the unrespectable variety, that obtained through touting for business or by fraternising with attorneys, was prohibited by the messes and the profession. Thus a barrister on the Norfolk Circuit was forbidden to travel directly to a circuit town in a private conveyance accompanied by an attorney or in a public coach, to enter a circuit town before the opening of the assizes there, and until the 1850s to lodge in public hotels in most of the circuit towns.(63)

One interesting problem relating to influence and practice in the assize courts was the position of justices of the peace who were members of the circuit that included their home counties or boroughs. Certainly a possible case of conflict of interests existed here since JPs committed accused criminals for trial before the courts of assize. In the first discussion of this issue by the Norfolk Circuit bar mess in 1866 it was 'the unanimous opinion...that a Barrister acting as a County Magistrate should not hold criminal briefs at the Assizes in that County.'(64) In 1888 the South-Eastern Circuit mess considered a motion by Mr W.N.M. Geary, JP for Kent, that all restrictions on JPs practising in their home counties be removed with the single exception of cases in which they had acted in their official capacities. Geary rejected the charge that a barrister/magistrate exercised undue influence in his home county by reminding the mess that 'recorders & MPs practised in their own boros and they had more influence than a simple JP. Moreover barristers joined a session or circuit on which they thought they had influence.'(65) In deciding this delicate issue the mess felt it prudent to consult with the other circuits before making a final decision. These consultations revealed that three messes, the Midland, Oxford and North Wales and Chester had no rules whatsoever; on the North-Eastern Circuit the rule conformed to Geary's proposal; while on the South Wales and Western Circuits the regulations were identical to that on the South-Eastern. In the event, the mess decided by a large majority to retain the standing rule that prohibited barrister/JPs from doing criminal work in their home counties or boroughs, with the exception of recorders.(66)

Rules of Circuit Membership
These rules have a more limited significance than those already discussed. The single exception to this generalisation was the rule limiting the number of years during which a barrister could change his circuit. In fact while this was a membership rule, it also was directly related to the issue of restrictive practices - most especially with the question of special retainers. In 1856 the Norfolk Circuit Club allowed a barrister who had been a member of another circuit for up to ten years to join the mess.(67) But the days of the ten-year rule were numbered, and in 1858 the Norfolk Circuit adopted the policy used since 1856 by the neighbouring Home Circuit of setting the time limit for membership at three years.(68) By contrast, the Western Circuit mess permitted barristers of more than three years' standing to join, though the procedures for admissions were slightly more stringent than for those who were recently called and had never been members of another circuit.(69) The remainder of the rules on membership were concerned with details of election, which are not of particular interest for our study, though they were vital to the members of the mess. In fact the majority of the club's codified rules were concerned with the election of members.

The Bar - 'A Learned Trades Union'?
Before concluding our survey of the traditional patterns of discipline and etiquette of the bar, we must look at that system from a somewhat different perspective, namely within the context of the mid-Victorian debate about whether the bar constituted in fact a 'learned trades union'. The controversy revolved around two inter-related questions: Was the system of etiquette and discipline of the bar identical or similar to the rules of trades unions? And should the existing regulations remain unaltered, be reformed or even abolished? Our present concern is with the first question only: consideration of the second must be deferred until a later section.

The debate was initiated by a letter to the Pall Mall Gazette in May, 1867 by a correspondent signing himself 'a journeyman engineer'. He suggested that professional associations and trades unions were virtually identical. He wrote:

> Try to prevent a working mechanic from working for less than the average wages of his trade, or call him a 'nobstick' or a 'black sheep' if he goes against the general regulations, and you strike at the root of free trade and are guilty of intimidation. But rule that a barrister must remain briefless for life rather than work for less than the regulation fee...and you simply show a just regard for the interests and dignity of your calling. The union of the legal profession certainly contains some of the worst features of the unions of the mechanical trades...(70)

These contentions elicited a variety of responses from members of the bar. Within a few days the Pall Mall Gazette published a second letter from 'a barrister', who unequivocally rejected the arguments contained in the first. He claimed: 'There is not a single bar rule which either does prevent, or is meant to prevent, the most unrestricted competition between man and man for business.'(71) A third letter followed quickly on the heels of the second. The author, also a barrister, countered most of the assertions of his colleague concerning the nature of the system of etiquette and discipline which governed the bar, although he stopped short of saying that the bar functioned as a trade union.(72) The letters page of the Law Times also became a forum for the debate. A correspondent found fault with the comparison between the bar and a trade union. He contended that while the object of the latter was to raise wages, lower hours of work and at the same time preserve the equality between workers, the former 'prescribes nothing more than the minimum fee that shall be accepted, and certain restraints in the manner in which business is to be sought.'(73) By far the longest and most thorough analysis of the problem came from the pen of A.V. Dicey. In the Fortnightly Review he marked out the middle ground between 'a journeyman engineer' and his critics by noting both points of similarity and dissimilarity between the bar and a trade union. He concludes: 'the Bar is a protected profession, governed by certain rules enforced upon its members chiefly by the strength of professional feeling, which is represented partly by the Benchers and partly by the Circuit Courts.'(74)

Although differences of opinion abound in this debate, there is one point of consensus: the professions, including the bar, had a higher social and legal standing than other occupations. They possessed officially sanctioned monopolies over particular types of work, and in return were responsible, at least in theory, to the public for the protection of these trusts.(75) In fact, all professions were not equal, and there were great differences in the extent of their monopolies and in their autonomy. If one were to construct a hierarchy of nineteenth-century English professions based on their authority over their members, their independence from external supervision and their ability to define the content of their work and their relationship with clients, then the bar would undoubtedly rank at the top. The unique position of the bar in this regard was due partly to its code of etiquette and partly to historical accident.

Legal etiquette, despite its informal character, was instrumental in shaping the identity and corporate unity of the bar. This process occurred during a period extending at least from the Reformation to the industrial revolution and we must be careful not to foreshorten its evolution. By the 1830s the system was practically complete.(76) Distinct boundaries separated the functions of the barrister from those of the attorney. The position of the barrister was now established as a consultant. He was a member of a small high-status profession which had bequeathed the legal drudgery to a larger but inferior class of lawyers. The attorney served as a middleman; it was his responsibility to choose the barrister who would represent his client in court. Thus the client usually played no role in selecting his own counsel, and he was effectively deprived of the possibility of consulting with a barrister except through the intervention of an attorney. The lack of direct contact between the lay client and the barrister helped to shield the latter from the accusations of pettifoggery often directed at the attorney. Finally, the rules of legal etiquette concerning the employment and remuneration of barristers established their dominance in the client/professional relationship. These rules prevented the barrister in his capacity as advocate from becoming either a permanent employee or retainer of an aristocratic or wealthy patron.

The effectiveness of this informal system of legal etiquette is testimony to the unity of the bar. Alone social pressures were sufficient to guarantee compliance by the vast majority of barristers to the customs of their profession. Furthermore, the fact that barristers possessed esoteric knowledge of the law and were members of a privileged fraternity with its own rules and trappings both separated them from the lay public and fostered their esprit de corps. On the circuit they dined, travelled and lodged exclusively with their fellows; in court their wigs and gowns marked them off from other men. In London the cloistered precincts of the inns served not only as a refuge from the hustle and bustle of the metropolis but as a training ground for future generations. Here in chambers, commons and in the nearby courts, barristers inculcated novices with the traditions and wisdom of the profession.

The bar had succeeded in fashioning a corporate identity for its members, yet this did not exempt it from the forces

that were transforming the face of professional England in the
middle decades of the nineteenth century. On the one hand
demographic, technological and administrative changes
were undermining the powers of the circuit messes, and on the other
the winds of reform were threatening to strip the inns of
court of their privileges. In the remainder of this chapter
I will be examining the dual challenge that this posed to the
profession's traditional institutions.

THE FORCES OF CHANGE

Together the enormous increase in the number of barristers,
the advent of railway travel and the reorganisation of the
assizes had a deleterious effect on the informal system of
etiquette and discipline; this was exemplified most clearly
by the declining status of the circuit messes during the last
three or four decades of the century.

Increase in Numbers

The number of counsel whose names appeared in the Law List
increased fivefold in a matter of fifty years between 1785
and 1835 from 379 men to 1,835 men. Between 1835 and 1885,
total membership of the bar nearly trebled - from just under
2,500 to 7,250.(77) Thus during these one hundred years the
bar grew from a small profession with hundreds of members to
a relatively large one numbering in the thousands. This
growth had a harmful effect on certain professional institutions, most especially the circuit messes that were ideally
suited to governing a small rather than a mass profession.

Of course it can be objected that the statistics presented above are inflated and do not accurately represent the
increase in the size of the practising bar. An examination
of the membership lists of the six English circuits printed
in the Law List should help to dispel these doubts. Unlike
the main list of counsel, there was an attempt on the part of
the compilers of the Law List to revise and update the circuit
registers annually by removing the names of men who had
ceased to attend the assizes. Consequently these sources are
invaluable for us in our study of the growth of the practising
bar. The number of barristers going each of the circuits are
displayed in twenty-year intervals in Table 2.2. During the
100 year period covered, the total circuit membership increased by 800 per cent while for individual circuits it ranged from 300 per cent on the Oxford Circuit to nearly 1100
per cent on the old Northern Circuit, that in 1876 was divided
into the Northern and North-Eastern Circuits.

The inflation in numbers led to a revolution in the social
and disciplinary institutions of the bar. The enormous influx
of men into the profession undermined the face-to-face

Table 2.2: Circuit Affiliations of the Bar 1800-1900

	Home	Norfolk	Midland	Oxford	Western	Northern	Total
1800	65	19	26	62	44	63	279
1820	69	21	24	62	58	82	316
1840	142	42	54	100	109	179	626
1860	285	51	63	120	120	267	906

	South-Eastern	North-Eastern	Midland	Oxford	Western	Northern	Total
1880	607	206	190	167	201	247	1618
1900	697	275	221	239	227	335	1994

Source: Law List.

relationships upon which the enforcement of the unwritten rules of etiquette had depended. Undoubtedly spurred on by two examples of less than honourable conduct at the bar by Digby Seymour and Edwin James in the early 1860s, commentators lamented the decline in professional morality.(78) In 1866 the Law Journal felt the need to warn the bar that unless it put its house in order, it would jeopardize its privileged status:

> it is above all things necessary to assume and protest that our profession is pure and honest, for otherwise the standards would be lowered, and impurity and dishonesty will cease to be looked upon as disgraceful...It is, moreover, only on this assumption that the freedom from responsibility - and the enormous authority with which the law has clothed counsel could for a moment be justified. If the time should come when we can no longer boast ourselves as we now do, our Courts will have to consider the question, how far it is well that counsel should enjoy their privilege of control over matters, which concern the deepest interests of social life, and the innermost feelings of the human soul.(79)

Circuit Messes
The effects of expansion on the circuit messes were striking. In place of the small, intimate clubs of the late eighteenth and early nineteenth centuries with their active social lives, we find large cumbersome organisations that had lost much of their internal cohesion. The railway accentuated this process by enabling barristers to travel to many assizes from London for the day only to return in the evening. In the 1860s a commentator on the bar wrote nostalgically, 'The railway has done much to destroy the ancient sociability of the circuit... pleasure and pomp, the leisurely progress and social friendliness of the old circuit life are no more.'(80) Similarly 40 years later a former barrister wrote:

> Social life on the Circuit, I am told, is not what it used to be. Men no longer travel the Circuit. They only visit it, and their visits are marked with impatience. Their hearts are with their return tickets, and I suspect there are more "Bradshaw's" [railway timetable] than briefs in their blue or red bags.(81)

The messes suffered further attrition when concurrent sittings of the assizes and Westminster courts were established in 1876. The result was as we shall see later that barristers had to choose between going on circuit or concentrating on a London practice. Sir Edward Clarke, the Solicitor-General who had been called to the bar in 1864, told guests at a dinner given in his honour in 1886 by the South-Eastern circuit, 'I remember when the S.E.C. had a more corporate existence than it has now I am sorry to say.'(82) By 1889 a mere 20 barristers dined regularly in the circuit mess, and men harked back to the days when there had been 60 or 70 in attendance.(83) Recalling the state of the Western Circuit mess in the 1870s one member wrote:

> In those days a considerable number of barristers of all ages regularly went to circuit, not only without any business to do but without the slightest desire of obtaining any. Forty or fifty men would in those days sit down at dinner on the first business night at a small assize town, where a quarter of that number is now regarded as more than average attendance. As a natural consequence, the social side of circuit life was much more developed than it is at present. (84)

Or on the Oxford Circuit at the same time:

> Men no longer travel the Circuit. They only visit it... The old repose has gone, and the Mess is in danger of becoming a memory. This is to be regretted, for the Circuit Bar Mess was, if it is not now, a thoroughly wholesome institution. It served to allay animosities, to take the edge off forensic strife, to encourage the amenities of a social life. It promoted feelings of esprit de corps, and was useful in preserving a high standard of professional honour.(85)

According to the author of these sentiments, Alfred Plowden, 'There is no longer the same cohesion, or the old esprit de corps. It has become a thing of shreds and patches, loose and disconnected...'.(86)

While the reader may be tempted to dismiss these recollections as merely the nostalgic ramblings of old men, the unanimity of the case they presented supported by other evidence suggests that they reflected real changes in the profession. Revisions of the traditional etiquette of the messes were indicative of the new environment. Plowden for one welcomed the abandonment of regulations that attempted to prevent contact between the bar on the one hand and the public and attorneys on the other. He applauded the abolition of rules preventing barristers from lodging in hotels or travelling in other than first-class carriages on circuit, since these rules 'under changed conditions and with the growth of broader views gradually became unworkable by reason of the sheer inability to enforce them.'(87) Here the issue was not the survival of a particular rule of etiquette, but the breakdown in the previously existing consensus upon which the mess was founded.

The debates in the South-Eastern Circuit mess in the

1880s and 1890s that were primarily devoted to the future role of the bar mess reflected the lack of agreement. Traditionalists defended the social and disciplinary functions of the mess and rejected attempts to limit its sovereignty. The issue came to a head in 1891 over the question of whether or not to expel J.W.W. Livett, who earned his living as a surveyor and land agent.(88) Some members suggested that the issue be referred to the benches of Livett's inn, the Inner Temple. To Thomas Blofeld, the Solicitor-General of the circuit, this step was superfluous. His objection went to the heart of the matter:

> What was the mess? Was it coextensive with the bar? If so, what was the use of the ballot, or of the rules? The mess was <u>imperium in imperio</u> they chose to dine together. It would be absurd to refer the matter to the benchers - the question was not whether Livett should remain a member of the bar but whether he should remain a member of the mess.(89)

Others felt that the mess could not continue in its present form and preferred reform. This was the position taken by Samuel Bristowe QC MP when he added his support to a proposal to abolish special retainers already in 1876. He told his colleagues 'that the Circuit System was necessary to maintain discipline. He therefore wished the old System to be retained, but was glad to see a great modification.'(90) Still others saw little point to the mess, except perhaps as a social club. In 1886 the <u>Law Times</u> proposed changes in the rules concerning the right of QCs to take briefs on any circuit without the need for a special retainer. This step, it acknowledged, would inevitably lead to 'the total abolition of the Circuit Bar system', and added: '...its abolition we intended to advocate in the plainest terms.'(91) Similarly Frederick Crump QC, one of the original sponsors of the movement that brought about the creation of the Bar Council, told fellow South-Eastern circuiteers in 1894 that:

> what the meeting had to face was the moribund condition of the Circuit. What affected the South Eastern Circuit also affected the others. On the Northern Circuit many men did not belong to the Mess, because of the heavy entrance fee and subscriptions. The old Northern Circuit could not be said to exist. Was the South Eastern Circuit to be kept alive by the institution of dinners in London? He thought not. He would not object to the members of the Circuit dining together; but if the dinners were meant to keep the Circuit system, & maintain the payment of fees the change was not worth making.(92)

The breakdown of the earlier consensus about the function and importance of the circuit mess bore witness to a general malaise and concern about the future, prevalent in the profession towards the end of the nineteenth century. Traditional institutions and patterns of organisation were in decline, yet so far no system had been created to fill the void.

REFORM AND REFORMERS

Three times between 1834 and 1854 parliamentary commissions had conducted inquiries into the state of the legal profession. Little in the way of substantive reforms had resulted, and so in the 1860s and 1870s a number of parliamentary assaults were made on the privileges of the bar.(93) In the ensuing struggle it is possible to distinguish three contending factions: The first consisted of traditionalists committed to preserving the status quo, namely the absolute autonomy and authority of the bar, from lay interference including that of Parliament. The second was composed of radical reformers who were equally determined to strip the bar of its unique legal status and privileges and to make it accountable to Parliament by the imposition of statutory controls. The third included moderate reformers, several of whom were leading lights of the bar. They felt that the profession had to become more responsive to the needs of the public and of its own rank and file, and were willing to ensure this by legislative means if need be.

The moderates, unlike the radicals, were willing to see if pressure from within Parliament supported by public opinion could yield voluntary reforms by the benchers of the inns of court. The most significant gain registered in this way was the introduction of a compulsory qualifying bar examination in 1872 after decades of procrastination. The moderate reformers led by Roundell Palmer (Lord Selborne) were not content to wait for voluntary concessions from the inns of court, rather they pinned their hopes on parliamentary intervention. But this course was far from simple, and success was most certainly not inevitable. As early as 1846 Lord Brougham told a House of Commons select committee:

> The Commission could only recommend to the Inns of Court, for the Inns of Court are in such a position that they cannot be touched, and it is hardly possible to suppose that Parliament would interfere with the undoubted rights and present possession of the Inns of Court...(94)

Two years later a similar view was expressed by the Attorney-General, Sir John Jervis, in reply to a question about the implementation of the educational recommendations of the 1846 committee. He told the Commons that 'the government had no authority to interfere in the matter. It rested in a great degree with the inns of court.'(95) These conclusions may be surprising when applied to an age in which Parliament imposed reforms on other leading occupations namely the Anglican Clergy, the officer corps of the Army, the medical profession and the Indian and Home civil services. However, in the end, the predictions of Brougham and Jervis proved to be correct.

The 1860s
The first attempt to alter the constitution of the bar by means of parliamentary intervention occurred in May 1862. The principal sponsors of this initiative - Sir George Bowyer, William Ewart and John Pope Hennessy - were all members of the bar, although only Bowyer practised. He was the eldest son of a Berkshire landowner and baronet. Called to the bar at the Middle Temple in 1839 he practised as an equity draftsman and conveyancer and was appointed a reader of his inn in 1850. In 1860 he succeeded to his father's title and estates. It is not clear from the available evidence whether he retired from the bar at this time. Bowyer's primary concern was to curb what he saw as the arbitrary and oligarchic powers of the benchers of the four inns of court by means of the democratisation of the benches. In the opening debate on the second reading of his bill, Bowyer told the Commons that in disciplinary proceedings against a member of the bar, the benchers of his inn act as both prosecutors and judges. This went against the very principles of English justice, he argued.(96) In order to correct these abuses he proposed the establishment of a joint court for all four inns whose function would be to try all barristers and law students accused of unprofessional conduct. The court would be empowered to administer oaths and compel the attendance of witnesses, and in most cases hearings would be open to the public. The second part of his proposal was even more revolutionary from the point of view of the profession. It envisioned the enfranchisement of the rank and file of the bar for the first time in centuries. They would be responsible for electing slightly more than half of the benchers; the sitting benchers would choose the remainder in the traditional manner.(97)

The opponents to the bill, while conceding that some reform might be useful, rejected the attacks levelled against the inns and their supposedly unrepresentative character. The main case for the opposition was put to the Commons by Richard P. Collier, who later served as Solicitor- and Attorney-General and as a Superior Court judge. In summing up the debate, the Law Times wrote:

> Mr. Collier...argued that the proposed interference was altogether needless; that the Benchers enjoyed the full confidence of the Bar, who by an overwhelming majority are opposed to any changes in the government of the profession, and that in fact they do maintain the honour and dignity of the Bar, and that they send forth as many

good men, and as few bad ones as could be hoped for from
any substitution by popular election. Some improvements
might be made in the procedure in case of complaints
against individual members of the Bar; but these could be
better accomplished by voluntary action of the Benchers
than by the compulsory interference of the Legislature.(98)

Collier, supported by both the Attorney-General, Sir William
Atherton and Montague Smith QC MP, maintained that the democratisation of the inns 'would be so distasteful to them that
the great majority of the profession would not exercise it'.(99)
His contention that most barristers supported the status quo
was rejected by Edward Crawfurd, a barrister of the Middle
Temple and member of the Home Circuit. He noted that no one
could speak on behalf of the bar concerning its attitude towards the popular election of benchers and concluded that 'It
was...very difficult to elicit a general expression of the
opinion on the part of the Bar, since they had very little
opportunity or inducement to consider questions of this
nature.'(100) In fact no one asked the rank and file of the
bar for their opinion on this subject until the closing decades of the nineteenth century. The opponents of reform were
victorious and Bowyer was forced to withdraw his bill as a
result of lack of support in the Commons.

The issue was not allowed to rest there. During each of
the following four years, the reformers led by Bowyer brought
in bills designed to restructure the judicial proceedings of
the inns. Despite the fact that the sponsors omitted any reference to the popular election of benchers, these initiatives
fared no better than the original one. The general drift of
opinion expressed in the debates was that the system worked
tolerably well and thus legislative intervention was not justified. The simple fact was that no one was much interested
in the proposed reform, and the bills of 1863 and 1865 expired
for lack of a quorum.

Bowyer, determined to try yet again, introduced a revised
proposal in 1866. Not only had he gained the qualified support
of the Attorney-General, Sir Roundell Palmer, the previous
year, but the inns of court after securing amendments apparently gave their assent to the bill.(101) The willingness of
the benchers to compromise may have resulted from the public
chiding that they had received from the chief law officer of
the Crown in 1865, though in fact the bill was consistent with
a resolution adopted in March 1863 by the benchers of Lincoln's
Inn supporting the establishment of a profession-wide court
of discipline.(102) Despite Bowyer's sponsorship the 1866
proposal was far from radical. George Denman QC told the
House of Commons that 'There was no innovation of principle
involved, the only object of the Bill being to establish a
better tribunal for the investigation of complaints against
barristers'.(103) Not surprisingly in these circumstances,

barristers John Locke and John Roebuck, co-sponsors of one
of Bowyer's previous reform initiatives, now opposed him since
they contended that the bill would not curb the powers of the
inns of court but strengthen them.(104) The second reading of
the bill was then deferred and that was the last that was
heard of it.

The Early 1870s
During the next five years the movement for reform of the legal
profession was quiescent, but it became reinvigorated in the
first years of the 1870s. Not only were the issues involved
debated within Parliament, but also in the pages of the day -
the Law Journal and the Law Times. At first they took opposing
stands on the issue of reform. The Law Journal rejected a
proposal put forward by W.T. Charley MP in the spring of 1871
resurrecting the question of democratisation of the benches of
the inns of court.(105) A few months later Roundell Palmer
began his campaign for the creation of a general school of
law in London that would take over the responsibility for
legal education that had been exercised, though in the most
cursory fashion possible, by the inns of court. Though his
proposals were not particularly radical, they contained elements that threatened the traditional organisation of the bar.
In the first place barristers and solicitors would be educated
side by side, a step that could have led eventually to the de-
struction of the divided profession. Furthermore, such a law
school could render the inns of court redundant since once
stripped of their educational aspects they lost much of their
raison d'être as professional governing bodies. This was the
tack taken by the Law Times in lending its support to Palmer's
bill.

> For our part we have no tenderness for the Inns of Court.
> We regard them as traitors to their trust. For genera-
> tions past the Benchers have sanctioned a state of things
> which is a scandal and a reproach to an educated commu-
> nity....We should rejoice to see the breath of public
> opinion scattering not only pretentious nothings of the
> existing system, but the very walls of the old Inns
> themselves....There are difficulties in denuding the Inns
> of their property, but surely a Government which has
> swept away the Irish Church can root up the rotten gover-
> ning system of a great profession,...there is really no
> reason why the Inns of Court should retain any jurisdic-
> tion when the education of the Profession is taken out of
> their hands.(106)

Palmer made no attempt to hide his feelings about the
character of the benches of the inns. He told the Commons in
1871 that the inns 'have no corporate character, no legal

organisation, no acknowledged public trust or public responsibility.'(107) He was hardly more conciliatory the following year when he re-introduced his resolution. While stating his belief that the inns would cooperate with Parliament in the founding of a school of law he issued a threat: 'If...the heads of the Inns of Court should be found unwilling to co-operate in supporting such an institution, it would be in the power, and within the right, of the State to take them in hand and reform them.'(108) Here was the nub of the issue. Would the state as a final recourse intervene in the affairs of the bar, as it had in the case of other professions, thereby reducing its autonomy? For Sir Richard Baggallay, a former Solicitor-General and future Lord Justice of Appeal, this was the ultimate threat posed by Palmer's proposal and the reason that it had to be opposed.(109) In the event this bill met the same fate as those submitted in the 1860s, although more interest was shown now and the profession itself was more evenly divided. On the 16th of March 1872 the proposal was defeated by a vote of 116 to 113.

Six months later Palmer succeeded Lord Hatherley as Lord Chancellor taking the title of Baron Selborne. Upon entering office he received advice from Lord Cairns, Disraeli's Chancellor in 1868, concerning the objects of professional reform.

> The first [priority] is legal Education. If you touch this, I hope you may feel yourself able to deal with the Inns of Court - to make their governing bodies really representative,...The public rights and sole privileges they enjoy, are amply sufficient to justify public interference and control.(110)

Together Selborne and Cairns monopolised the woolsack for thirteen years (1872-85) yet despite their reformist inclinations they failed to accomplish even the most minor revisions of the constitution of the bar, as we shall see. Both men found that upon assuming ministerial office, their power to initiate or even to support reform projects was severely proscribed and even neutralised.(111) There is no apparent explanation of the behaviour of successive Liberal and Conservative governments which effectively gagged their Lord Chancellors on the issue of professional reform. The best we can do is to suggest some possible reasons for this phenomenon, without however being able to prove any of them. The interpenetration of legal and political elites may have been one reason for the immunity of the bar from the general reformist mood of the times. Furthermore ministers may have felt that it was not in their power to impose reform on the inns of court with their centuries-old tradition of absolute control over the certification of barristers. The unwillingness to impose reform on ancient corporations is also evident in the Medical Act of 1858 that left the Royal Colleges untouched and in possession of all their

privileges.(112) Finally the politicians may have felt that
to press for reform of the bar, an issue about which there was
public apathy and professional hostility, could have jeopardized other more urgent proposals.

The Conservative election victory in 1874 freed Selborne
from the restrictions of office. He then returned to the offensive on the issue of professional reform. In July he introduced a bill making the governing bodies of the inns more
representative of the bar. This proposal was reminiscent of
the one first made by Sir George Bowyer 12 years earlier.
Selborne began by commending the inns on their voluntary improvement of legal education, but went on to suggest that members of the practising bar be given a say in electing the benchers of their inns. In addition the inns were to be incorporated and a combined judicial tribunal that would have authority
over disciplinary matters would be established.(113) Cairns,
now in office, speaking on behalf of the government, publicly
contradicted the stand he had taken in private two years earlier
probably in response to government constraints.(114) He told
the Lords that 'He could not...concur in his noble and learned
Friend's proposal that Parliament should interfere to incorporate the Inns of Court and regulate their internal government and management.'(115) As with all the previous attempts
to reform the bar in Parliament, this also failed.

The Honorarium Under Attack
A new challenge faced the English bar in the years 1875 and
1876, the implications of which were more threatening to the
profession's autonomy and authority than was the democratisation of the inns. Late in the 1875 session, Charles Norwood,
a Hull merchant and shipowner, introduced an amendment to the
Judicature Acts that would allow a barrister to sue for his
fees and also make him responsible for fulfilling his professional obligations to his clients. He told the House that
this measure was meant to halt the phenomenon of barristers
taking on more work than they could properly handle, with the
result that they failed to appear in court without returning
the fee they had been paid. In return for surrendering his
immunity from prosecution for non-appearance in court and
negligence in the conduct of a case, the barrister would be
permitted to sue in court for the non-payment of fees. Thus
the barrister and client would henceforth be parties to a contract with the consequent obligations and remedies that this
entailed for both parties.(116)

Proponents of this measure appealed for support on the
basis that they were merely rationalising the relationship between barrister and client in accordance with the other individually practised professions. Charles Lewis, a London solicitor who supported Norwood's motion, told the House of Commons
that:

> He could not understand why, when engineers, surveyors, and surgeons were liable to the extent of their whole fortunes for unskillfulness, barristers should be exempt from the rule that a man undertaking a duty for fee or reward should be liable not only to perform it to the best of his ability, but should also be responsible for gross negligence. This peculiar state of things arose from the old notion of patron and client; but the system of <u>honorarium</u> had been long since exploded.(117)

After having presented the case for the abolition of the honorarium, the supporters of the measure bowed to the request not to pursue the issue at that time since the session was almost over. The amendment was withdrawn.(118)

The following February, Norwood and Lewis along with George Leeman, a solicitor from York, Sampson Lloyd, a banker in Birmingham and George Anderson, a Glasgow merchant, introduced the Barristers and Advocates Fees Bill essentially identical to the amendment which had been abandoned the previous session. The proponents adjusted their appeal this time to emphasize that the measure was not meant as an attack on the bar as such. In fact its object was to protect the interests of both the public and of the members of the junior bar who suffered because of the rapacity of their seniors.

The opponents of the bill painted a black picture of the likely results if the honorarium was abolished. Serjeant John Simon suggested that the change did not merely concern the members of the bar, rather 'It was a question affecting the rights and liberties of Her Majesty's subjects.'(119) While according to Sir Henry Jackson the proposal was injurious to both the bar and the public: 'The interests of the Profession and the public are identical in this matter.'(120) Yet even when the air is cleared of the rhetoric on both sides, the remaining issues are evidently of fundamental importance. Not only would the passage of this measure have been the first example of direct parliamentary intervention in the relationship between barrister and client, but it would have gone a long way in destroying the special status of the bar. Jackson came close to summarizing the crux of the matter:

> If this Bill were to become law, every barrister would become liable to his client for the conduct of the case, and for the opinion he gave upon it. Sir, if this were to be law it would put an end at once to all that was worthy and noble in the <u>status</u> of the Bar....The position of a barrister in relation to his client is well understood, though it is difficult to define....It is the position of the advocate as distinct from that of agent or servant and this distinction depends upon the absence of that very right to recover the promised honorarium which it is the object of the Bill to confer. Once

61

establish the right to recover the fee, the relation of
advocate ceases, and that of principal and agent takes its
place.(121)

By the beginning of the nineteenth century the bar had
achieved the status of a totally autonomous profession, with
complete authority over the relationship between its members
and prospective clients. This was coupled with the profession's
absolute monopoly over advocacy in the superior courts. No
other English profession ever achieved this degree of unrestricted power. Norwood's bill would have reduced the power of the
bar greatly. Norwood may well have been correct when he said
that he 'could not conceive how the independence of the Bar,
and their power to advocate efficiently the cause of clients,
should be bound up with immunity from the ordinary obligations
of law and morality that affect every other class of the
community.'(122) Nevertheless, abolition of the honorarium and
its corollary reforms would necessarily have restricted the
previously unlimited autonomy and authority of the bar. The
traditionalists won the day and the proposal was decisively
defeated 237 votes to 130.

The Failure of Reform 1875 to 1878

While the Commons discussed the merits of Norwood's proposal,
Lord Selborne continued to lobby for his reform proposals in
the upper chamber. In 1875 he introduced two bills: one
dealing with the disciplinary aspect of the inns of court and
the other with the establishment of a general school of law
in London. He thus divided his 1874 initiative into two for
technical reasons. The Inns of Court Bill received a more
favorable reception than did the General School of Law Bill.
Lord Chancellor Cairns accepted the former in principle, though
he differed with Selborne on details. His objection to the
latter, however, was much more fundamental for he believed
'that it was not the business of Parliament or of the State,
to create or constitute a school for the teaching of Law.'(123)
The Inns of Court Bill was passed through the House of Lords in
1875 and again in 1876, but it was not introduced into the
Commons in either year.

Despite Selborne's lack of legislative success, his initiatives may have catalysed the government and the inns of court
to consider seriously the need for some kind of reform. As we
saw earlier the inns had been virtually silent about the various proposals, and with the exception of the still-born bill
of 1866, they ignored demands for change. As late as May 1875
Lord Cairns could say that the inns had failed to take any
position on the legislative proposals that affected them.(124)
A year later the situation had changed completely; Cairns reported that he was in consultation with the inns about Selborne's proposals, and that he hoped to be able shortly to

introduce a reform measure that was supported by both the government and the inns of court.(125) Cairns fulfilled his promise in 1877 when he introduced the Bar Education and Discipline Bill in the Lords on behalf of the government and with the concurrence of the inns.(126)

The core of the proposal was the creation of a thirty-member Council of the Four Inns of Court, six to be appointed by the benchers of each of the inns and six by the Crown. Eligibility was restricted to privy counsellors, judges of the Supreme Court of Judicature and barristers of ten years' standing. The Council was to absorb the jurisdictions previously exercised by the benchers over matters of discipline including the right to censure, suspend or disbar barristers, and by the Council of Legal Education over the training and examination of candidates for the bar. In disciplinary matters the Council would be invested with the power to summon witnesses and its decisions could be appealed to the Supreme Court of Judicature. The bill preserved the monopoly of the four inns of court over calls to the bar, although students first had to satisfy the educational requirements set down by the Council. The inns were to provide the funds for the Council with the maximum yearly contribution set at £4,600.(127) In some respects the Council resembled the General Medical Council established in 1858, but there were basic differences as well. The powers of the Medical Council were limited to registration and disciplining of practitioners, while education remained the preserve of the medical corporations and the universities.(128)

The bill guaranteed the continued authority of the benchers since they were responsible for the selection of four-fifths of the Council members. Furthermore it made no concessions to those reformers who hoped to see a democratisation of the bar. Consequently the reformers rejected the bill as merely a legislative confirmation of the status quo. In fact the bill introduced two innovations that in theory reduced the absolute autonomy of the bar. The provision for six Crown appointees meant that it was possible that laymen could have a share in determining professional policy. Additionally, the bill conceded the right of appeal to the Supreme Court. As noted earlier there was already a right of appeal to the judges, but as Lord Mansfield's decision of 1780 made clear the judges sat as 'in a domestic forum'.(129) Thus an appeal was made to the judges as senior members of the profession. By contrast according to Cairns' bill the judges derived their authority not from their professional status but from their official position. Instead of the judges presiding as internal referees they would now be acting as disinterested outsiders. Had Parliament enacted this measure it would have placed the bar on an equal footing with the other professions with respect to autonomy and self-discipline.

The bill faced little trouble in the House of Lords. Selborne was, not surprisingly, disappointed with the

compromise worked out by Cairns and he still hoped to create
his general school of law. The bill received a second reading
on June 7, a third on June 19, and was sent on to the Commons
for approval. The opponents of the bill mounted their attack
in the lower house. They succeeded in having it withdrawn after a second reading on the grounds that it was too late in the
session to give the proposal the careful consideration that it
deserved.

In February 1878 the Bar Discipline and Education Bill
was reintroduced into the House of Commons. The radical reformers once again tried to delay the bill and while the manoeuvre failed, they succeeded in making their grounds for opposing the measure abundantly clear. According to James Barclay, an Aberdeen merchant, the object of the bill was not to
control the irresponsible and oligarchic power of the inns and
their benchers; but on the contrary 'to perpetuate and extend
a trades' union of an objectionable character...the reason why
the additional powers were asked for was that the trades'
union found itself in the present day unable to exercise proper
control and supervision over its members.'(130) He charged
that the proposal was tailored to promote the interests of
the profession alone; he suggested that the interests of the
public might 'be better served if the Legal Profession were
entirely thrown open, and the close corporations called
Inns entirely abolished.'(131) Even more moderate spokesmen
did not feel that the provisions of the bill went far enough
in correcting the real problems of the profession. The Law
Journal, that had in the meantime been won over to the need
for reform, commented that the benches had to become elective
bodies, representative of all the members of the inns.(132)

In February 1878 the bill in its original form received
its second reading and its ultimate adoption seemed assured.
The Law Journal confidently predicted: 'it is a Government
measure, prepared and brought in by the law officers of the
Crown; and it may, therefore, be assumed that it will, with
some modifications more or less, pass into law'.(133) This
was not to be. The government formally withdrew the bill
without explanation on July 25. Five days later, in reply to
a question about its possible future reintroduction, the
Chancellor of the Exchequer told the House that no decision
had been made, but he cast doubt on the prospects of the measure, which had failed to win approval in two successive sessions.(134) Thus a decade and a half of activity in Parliament on behalf of reform of the legal profession came to an
end. We shall probably never know the real reason why the
government decided to abandon the Bar Discipline and Education
Bill. It had the support of the cabinet and the inns, and
the opposition was not powerful enough to prevent its passage.
Perhaps its ultimate failure can be attributed to the fact
that it was a compromise that no one really wanted. It did
not satisfy the radicals and even the moderates saw it as only

a half-measure. The consent of the inns may have been only a tactic to prevent massive reform. If the inns had been serious about change they could have introduced some of the provisions unilaterally without the need for parliamentary approval, but they did nothing.

Alone among the English professions the bar entered the last two decades of the nineteenth century with its ancient constitution and privileges completely intact. Clearly Parliament was unwilling or unable to reform the governing bodies of the bar; we are now in a position to evaluate the factors that led to legislative impotence on this issue. The suggestion that the large number of barrister/MPs blocked the restructuring of the profession by act of Parliament is not supported by the evidence.(135) Only 20 per cent of all MPs were barristers, and the majority of these men did not practise. Not only did the nominal members of the bar have no interest in protecting the special status of the profession, but some of them became leaders of the radical reformers. Furthermore even the practising barristers did not present a united front in favour of the inns. As we have seen, leading moderates were drawn from within the profession.

Certainly respect for the long tradition of professional independence and autonomy helped to ward off the onslaughts of reform, but it seems doubtful that this alone was sufficient to preserve the status quo. Its perpetuation depended on the tacit sanction of both branches of the legal profession and of educated public opinion. If these bodies, or even major elements within them, had made a concerted effort they may have succeeded in imposing parliamentary reform on the reluctant inns of court. But this did not transpire. The practising members of the bar were naturally most immediately concerned with the government of the profession. Of these the senior barristers - the QCs - had no desire to institute changes. As for the struggling and even moderately established juniors, they probably had neither the time nor the inclination to challenge the professional establishment, though they may have supported a reform movement from within as they were to do in the 1880s and 1890s. The more successful juniors, who had their sights set on silk gowns, were content to leave things as they were. As for the solicitors, their social standing and share of the available legal business had been steadily increasing. This was one of the main grievances of the junior bar. Furthermore, the County Courts Act of 1846 granted members of the lower branch the right to plead as advocates, and the etiquette of the bar protected their professional monopoly by prohibiting barristers from having direct access to clients. Thus the solicitors had as large a stake in preserving the existing modus vivendi between the two branches as had the barristers. Finally the public and politicians were unwilling to take the lead in professional reform. Clearly if any fundamental changes were made in the governance of the bar they would have to come from within. The crucial question facing the bar as it entered the 1880s was whether its traditional institutions could survive the demands of a mass profession.

REORGANISATION FROM WITHIN

By the middle of the nineteenth century members of the bar were beginning to recognise that the traditional governing apparatus of the profession was in need of reorganisation due to the unprecedented expansion in the size of the bar. The decline in the status and authority of the circuit messes that had been the principal agencies overseeing the day-to-day etiquette and discipline of the bar, meant that there was an urgent need for the centralisation and formalisation of both activities. There was also a growing feeling that the division of the central authority of the profession between four independent and autonomous bodies - the benches of the inns of court - weakened the bar. William Whately QC, Treasurer of the Inner Temple, told the 1854 Inns of Court Commission, 'I believe it [combined action among the inns] would be very beneficial. I think it would give a greater control over the members of the Profession, and more unity of action.'(136) The only unifying force at that time came from the Attorney-General who as the leading member of the bar had the authority to decide questions of professional etiquette.(137) But his authority was not absolute and this prompted Whately to tell the Commission:

> I should like to have some person in a similar situation to the Dean of the Faculty in Scotland, someone who would be at the head of the profession....The office of Attorney-General is not, I think, equal to the situation which a person in [sic] as Dean of Faculty would hold. The Attorney-General has not the same influence...(138)

Another witness, George Woodyatt Hastings, a junior barrister and secretary of the Law Amendment Society, was asked whether he thought that the discipline of the bar was sufficiently strict. He replied, 'it is not; and the Rules of the Bar are not sufficiently defined.'(139)

The Inns of Court were aware of the need for some kind of united action on their part. In 1861 the Inner Temple appointed a committee to 'consider the expediency of establishing some authority to which all questions connected with the practice of the Bar might be referred...'.(140) The report of that committee, which was read to a special council of Lincoln's Inn benchers declared 'that a body of Members of the Profession might advantageously be constituted in England, to which questions affecting the interests and character of the Bar of England might be referred.'(141) Unfortunately, there are no details of the reaction that this resolution, which apparently favoured the creation of a democratised bar association, elicited from the rulers of Lincoln's Inn. In fact the plan never came to fruition and the status quo prevailed. Ten years later the Law Times resurrected the idea of a bar association in its proposal for the establishment of a barristers' guild. The main responsibility of this organisation was to have been the supervision of the day-to-day discipline of the profession, a function that according to the journal neither the circuit messes nor the inns of court were capable of filling.(142) It told its readers: 'We believe we are proposing nothing Utopian. A society formed as we suggest would be the best security which could be provided for the preservation of the honour and reputation of the Bar.'(143) In late 1873 a group of barristers attempted to found the Legal Practitioners' Society outside the aegis of the inns. The society was to have as its major goals: 1. the codification of legal etiquette; 2. the explicit definition of the obligations and privileges of the two branches of the profession; 3. democratisation of the government of the profession; 4. protection of qualified practitioners against incursion by unqualified men. But this proposal failed to attract support or attention.(144)

The etiquette of the bar also came under periodic attacks during the middle decades of the century. In 1851 the Law Times prodded members of the bar to consider seriously the rules of etiquette as they affected the ability of junior barristers to earn a living. It proposed that a committee be established that would revise the rules of the bar in accordance with the temper of the times, and then submit its recommendations to the entire profession for approval.(145) A similar stand was taken by A.V. Dicey in 1867. He questioned the efficacy of many of the rules of etiquette, although he stopped short of calling for their total abolition. At the very least, he wrote, 'it is greatly to be desired that rules which are out of date should be distinctly and by common consent abolished.'(146) By 1872 the Law Times felt compelled to call for more drastic action. 'The honourable, hardworking, meritorious members of the Bar must for their own protection scatter existing etiquette to the winds.'(147) According to that journal the influx of uneducated and socially inferior men had destroyed the consensus upon which the unwritten rules of professional conduct were based. As a result it was essential 'that the rules of etiquette should no longer be recognised, every member of the profession acting as becomes a gentleman'.(148)

Attempts at internal reform during the 1860s and 1870s were no more successful than were those in Parliament. As a result the bar drifted into the 1880s devoid of real leadership and desperately trying to shore up archaic governing institutions that were incapable of fulfilling the demands placed on them. The etiquette of the bar predicated on the informal customs of six circuit messes and on unrecorded ad hoc decisions by the most senior members of the profession was, to say the least, inappropriate for a profession with thousands of practising members scattered through England and Wales. A feeling that paralysis had overtaken the profession was fostered by its inability to take a firm stand on new rules of court procedure introduced in the early 1880s. These rules simplified the system of pleading and conveyancing and transferred much of the work to solicitors; in addition members of the lower branch also took over a large share of the responsibility for interlocutory proceedings which dealt with the issuing of summons and orders by Masters of the Supreme Court and the judges in chambers. In both instances the losers were the junior barristers.(149) The introduction of these rules was the catalyst which finally stimulated the members of the bar to demand the establishment of a united bar association. According to the Pall Mall Gazette 'The bar...is beginning to be conscious of the disadvantages it suffers by observing the extreme care bestowed nowadays on the interests of solicitors, who are a fully organised body represented by a powerful society.'(150) Likewise the Law Times declared, 'matters have come to a crisis which renders thorough organisation imperative.'(151)

The barristers heeded this call and the result was the creation of the Bar Committee. The early response to its establishment was auspicious. In December, 1883 two thousand barristers, apparently the entire practising bar along with quite a few non-practising members, voted in the first elections for the Committee. Nevertheless there were many difficulties that stood in the way.(152) Its mandate was far from clear; neither the circuits nor the inns had delegated any of their authority to the new organisation. It had no financial resources and was dependent upon voluntary contributions by members of the bar. While the Committee was consulted about professional etiquette and discipline, its decisions were not binding. But with regard to rules governing court procedure and protection of the interests of the profession it registered some successes, especially after 1885 when the Committee's first chairman, Sir Stanley Hardinge Giffard, was raised to the woolsack as Lord Halsbury.(153)

Within a year of its creation, criticism of the ineffectiveness of the Bar Committee began to appear. According to the Law Times:

> ...the trades union of barristers had done little or nothing to forward the interests of those whom it professes to represent, and that the great reforming body has been at work more or less diligently for a year to no purpose. Certain it is that the time-honoured abuses of the Legal Profession hold their heads as high as ever. Leading barristers still undertake more work than they can honestly accomplish, and the struggle for existence is as hard as

ever for the junior Bar, and we are not aware that the
body which was the centre of so many hopes has remedied
a single evil or redressed a solitary grievance.(154)

The Committee also came in for criticism for its failure to act decisively on professional etiquette. It occasionally received referrals from the Attorney-General on such questions, and made rulings from time to time.(155) Yet on an issue of vital importance - direct access - the Committee lamely 'decided by a majority of the members present that it was not expedient in the interests of the Bar that the Committee take action in the matter.'(156) In this uncertain atmosphere it is not surprising that splinter movements were formed and that some Middle Temple juniors in 1885 received the support of the Law Journal in their struggle to democratise their inn.(157)

After a short time criticism of the Committee died down and the old apathy and inertia returned to the bar. By the early 1890s only 200 or so barristers were paying their annual half guinea subscription fees, and less than 750 voted in the Committee's elections.(158) Then suddenly in 1893 the profession was infused with a new life which first manifested itself in the form of attacks on the professional status quo. In March, the Law Times laid its accusations at the gates of the inns of court.

> The Bar is the most remarkable profession in existence.
> The solicitors have one great central society. The Bar
> is cut up into four Inns of Court. Each one has its sep-
> arate interests...Law reform has been in the air for
> months and years past. Not one of the Benches of the Inns
> of Court has had a word to say about it. Not only so,
> but they have allowed an Imperium in Imperio to grow into
> a flagrant ineptitude under their very noses - the Bar
> Committee....When and how grew up the notion that the
> governing bodies of the Inns of Court are a kind of emas-
> culate creation, unprogressive, uninitiating, torpid,
> useless? It is not only a notion, it is a conviction.
> More, it is a fact.(159)

Within two months the cudgels were taken up by members of the bar at their annual meeting held under the auspices of the Bar Committee. The lead was taken by Frederick Crump QC who suggested the creation of a new bar association to replace the ineffectual Committee.(160) Both of the two main professional journals supported the demands, although they preferred to see the Bar Committee become the 'nucleus of the organisation which must, admittedly be constituted.'(161) The reception given to the proposed association within the bar was not unanimously favourable. The Western Circuit mess, for one, resolved 'that the Circuit sees no reason for assisting, as a Circuit, in the formation of the Association.'(162)

By April 1894 preparations had been completed to present the new bar association to the profession. Some 800 barristers gathered in their traditional venue, the dining hall of Lincoln's Inn, for the occasion. In reporting the meeting the Law Times described it as presenting 'an appearance quite phenomenal in the history of the Bar.' It continued, 'The traditional character of the Bar is deadly apathy. The meeting was a revelation. The result arrived at was a consummation devoutly wished by many barristers.'(163) A committee containing both senior and junior members of the profession was formed to write the governing regulations for the association which had now been christened the General Council of the Bar. In June 1894 the organising committee submitted its report. This envisioned a society with wide-ranging powers and duties including the defence of professional privileges and interests, supervision of professional discipline and examination of legislation in the name of the bar. Furthermore, in order to correct the deficiencies of the Bar Committee it was proposed that the Council be granted an annual contribution of £1,000 by the inns of court. In return for their monetary support and to coordinate the policies of the leading professional bodies, the inns were invited to appoint representatives to the Council.(164) Not surprisingly the inns resisted all the attempts by the Council to absorb their traditional functions and jurisdictions. Protracted negotiations between the inns and the Bar Council continued for a year beginning in November 1894. (165) The compromise that they hammered out reserved the right to discipline barristers for the inns, but permitted the Council to speak on behalf of the profession in matters of etiquette. In addition the inns agreed to grant the Council £600 per annum, but refused to have the benchers co-opted by the Bar Council, perhaps fearing that this would lead to fusion.(166)

The creation of the Bar Council fulfilled the demand for a truly representative and officially sanctioned professional association encompassing the entire practising bar from the rawest junior barrister to the Attorney-General. There was now a single voice that could speak with authority on behalf of the bar in parliamentary committees, with government ministers, before the judges and in the press. In addition the power to establish and codify rules of professional etiquette was now centralised in the hands of the Council. The result was that under its aegis a uniform code of conduct recognised by barristers, solicitors and the public alike began to take shape.

Nevertheless the creation of the Bar Council did not usher in a professional revolution. Rather it signalled the transfer of much of the power of the circuit messes and of the Attorney-General over etiquette to the bar itself. Yet the inns of court conceded very little in 1894/5, certainly less than they were apparently prepared to give in 1877/8. They retained their customary privileges and identities. Moreover their dominance in professional affairs and the oligarchic character of their benches were left unimpaired. Lacking coercive powers the Council functioned solely as a consultative body and in no way threatened the hegemony of the inns. Without doubt the Bar Council filled the void that had developed in the bar as it was transformed from an intimate into a mass profession. It provided a focus for corporate unity that had been missing and may even have encouraged a feeling of esprit de corps. Yet in the end the establishment of the Council was a conservative victory. In the time-honoured English tradition, the inns of court gave in to mild reform before it turned into rebellion, and by that strategy assured the integrity of the essential elements of the status quo. The authority of the inns of court was confirmed and the absolute autonomy of the bar was preserved.

NOTES

1. Geoffrey Millerson, The Qualifying Associations (1964), Chapter 1 and Table 1.1.
2. G. Harries-Jenkins, 'Professionals in Organizations' in J.A. Jackson (ed.), Professions and Professionalization (Cambridge, 1970), pp. 65-6.
3. J.H. Baker, 'Solicitors and the Law of Maintenance 1590-1640', Cambridge Law Journal, 32 (1973), p. 65.
4. LJ, 9 (March 14, 1874), p. 140.
5. My italics. R.v. the Benchers of Gray's Inn (1780), 1 Dougl. 353.
6. Prest, Inns of Court, pp. 73-4, 136; Baker, 'Solicitors', pp. 58-9.
7. A.W.B. Simpson, 'The Early Constitution of the Inns of Court', Cambridge Law Journal, 28 (1970), pp. 241-256.
8. Prest, Inns of Court, pp. 59-70.
9. Ibid., Chapter VI; Holdsworth, History of English Law, vol. VI, pp. 481-90.
10. J.H. Baker, An Introduction to English Legal History, (2nd edn. 1979), pp. 135-7.
11. Ibid., pp. 142-3; Holdsworth, History of English Law, vol. VI, pp. 472-481. A barrister who became a QC was said to have taken silk. This was due to the fact that QCs wore silk gowns instead of the usual stuff ones.
12. Inns of Court Commission, pp. 50, 66.
13. There are exceptions to this rule, for example the case of William Digby Seymour MP, who was named a QC in February 1861. In the normal course of events he would have been elected a bencher of his inn, the Middle Temple, during the course of that year. But as a result of events that had transpired some years before, Seymour never became a bencher. Early in his career he had entered the world of business. By 1852 he had become the chairman of the Waller Gold Mining Company. Subsequently this venture failed and Seymour became embroiled in

financial difficulties. As a result he was brought before the benchers of his inn who censured him for business dealings which cast disrepute upon his character. It was on account of this action that Seymour was refused election to the bench. DNB, vol. XVII, pp. 1273-4.

14. Inns of Court Commission, p. 70
15. Ibid., p. 124.
16. Pall Mall Gazette, 5 (May 17, 1867), p. 4.
17. Hansard, 3rd series, House of Commons, 118 (1851), c. 785. The circuit messes have recently been described in Raymond Cock, 'The Bar at the Assizes: Barristers on Three Nineteenth Century Circuits', Kingston Law Review, VI (1976), pp. 36-52.
18. Daniel Duman, 'Pathway to Professionalism: The English Bar in the Eighteenth and Nineteenth Centuries', Journal of Social History, 13 (1980), pp. 616-8.
19. A.V. Dicey, 'Legal Etiquette', Fortnightly Review, n.s. 2 (1867), p. 175.
20. Ibid.
21. Hansard, 3rd series, House of Lords, 119 (1852), c. 490.
22. James Fitzjames Stephen, A History of Criminal Law in England (3 vols., New York, 1973), vol. 1, p. 452. First published in 1883.
23. Before 1876 the six circuits were: the Home, Midland, Norfolk, Northern, Oxford, and Western. After 1876 due to re-organisation the circuits were: Midland, North-Eastern, Northern, Oxford, South-Eastern, and Western. The initial work on these records was undertaken by Raymond Cock in 1976. See also note 36 below.
24. Western Circuit list of members and circuit fees 1814-52. By the 1850s only just over half of the members of the circuit attended the assizes in three or more towns. I would like to thank Mr. Barry Carter, Wine Treasurer of the Western circuit for permission to consult the records in his possession. Cock, 'The Bar at the Assizes', p. 36-7. For an examination of this problem in a frontier region of America in the early nineteenth century see Daniel Calhoun, Professional Lives in America (Cambridge, Mass., 1965), Chapter III.
25. See above p. 47.
26. With regard to the extent of the disciplinary powers of these courts the Law Journal contended that 'The jurisdiction of the "mess" is over its own members, not over strangers.' LJ, 8 (March 8, 1873), p. 141.
27. Hansard, 3rd series, 178 (1865), col. 1048.
28. Pall Mall Gazette, 5 (May 17, 1867), p. 4.
29. The usual distinction made between professional etiquette and professional ethics is that the former relates to the behaviour of professionals towards their colleagues while the latter concerns the conduct towards the lay public. Ivan Waddington, 'The Development of Medical Ethics - A Sociological

Analysis', Medical History, 19 (1975), p. 39; Burton J. Bledstein, The Culture of Professionalism (New York, 1976), pp. 107-8.

30. Dicey, 'Legal Etiquette', pp. 175-6.
31. Ibid., pp. 174-5.
32. DNB, vol. X, p. 1299.
33. Hansard, 3rd series, House of Lords, 119 (1852), pp. 488-9.
34. Pall Mall Gazette, 5 (May 17, 1867), p. 4.
35. LJ, 2 (August 16, 1867), p. 371.
36. The nineteenth-century circuit mess records that have been studied so far are: Norfolk Circuit 1818-76; Home Circuit 1873-76; South-Eastern Circuit beginning in 1876; Western Circuit from 1876. I would like to thank the Wine Committee of the South-Eastern Circuit and Mr. John Blofeld QC for permitting me to study the records in their possession. It should be noted that the data at our disposal are not necessarily representative. The Norfolk Circuit was the smallest of the circuits throughout the nineteenth century while the Home and South-Eastern Circuits were dominated by their proximity to London.
37. For example Abel-Smith and Stevens, Lawyers and the Courts, chapter 9; Cock, 'The Bar at the Assizes', passim; The Monopolies and Mergers Commission, Barristers' Services, a Report on the Supply by Her Majesty's Counsel Alone of Their Services (July 6, 1976), p. 9; Alexander Johnston, 'The History of the Two Counsel Rule in the Nineteenth Century', Law Quarterly Review, 93 (1977), pp. 190-1. Johnston was the deputy chairman of the Monopolies and Mergers Commission cited above.
38. The physician is usually taken to be the prime example of the independent professional man though this seems to be based on the American experience in particular. My contention is that for England the barrister is a much better model. For a discussion of the statutory limitations on the professions see Duman, 'Pathway to Professionalism', pp. 626-7 note 18.
39. W.W. Bolton, Conduct and Etiquette at the Bar, 5th edition (1971), pp. 6, 14-15, 46.
40. Ibid., p. 48; Dicey, 'Legal Etiquette', p. 172; J.H. Baker, 'Counsellors and Barristers', Cambridge Law Journal, 29 (1969), pp. 208-10.
41. For example, Eliot Freidson, The Profession of Medicine, A Study of the Sociology of Applied Knowledge (New York 1972), especially Chapters 2 and 4; Peterson, The Medical Profession, passim.
42. Baker, 'Counsellors and Barristers', p. 225.
43. Blackstone, Commentaries, vol. III, p. 28.
44. See W.R. Prest, 'Counsellor's Fees and Earnings in the Age of Sir Edward Coke' in Baker (ed.), Legal Records and the Historian, pp. 166-71.
45. Ibid., p. 29.
46. Baker, 'Counsellors and Barristers', p. 229.

47. Norfolk Circuit Club (March 5, 1867).
48. Hansard, 3rd series, House of Lords, 119 (1852), col. 488-9.
49. Doe d. Bennett v. Hales (1850) 15 Q.B. 171.
50. Norfolk Circuit Club (March 27, 1868). See also Norfolk Circuit Club (March 12, 1846).
51. Abel-Smith and Stevens, Lawyers and the Courts, pp. 211, 221, 223; Cock, 'The Bar at the Assizes', pp. 44-7.
52. Norfolk Circuit (March 9, 1818).
53. Quoted in Cock, 'The Bar at the Assizes', p. 46.
54. Norfolk Circuit Club (July 22, 1855).
55. Norfolk Circuit Club (March 20, 1869).
56. Johnston, 'History of the Two Counsel Rule', p. 190.
57. Cock, 'The Bar at the Assizes', p. 45.
58. Norfolk Circuit Book 1853, p. 3. The meeting was held in the chambers of William Whately in February 1862. The special retainers fees that were proposed to the circuits were 300 guineas for QCs and serjeants, 100 guineas for juniors who lead, and 50 guineas for other juniors.
59. Home Circuit special meeting (February 16, 1876). This position was supported by the Law Times, 61 (1876), p. 281, but opposed by the 'late Norfolk Circuit', Norfolk Circuit special meeting (February 21, 1876).
60. South-Eastern Circuit special meeting (July 19, 1876). The new fees were 100 guineas for serjeants and QCs and 50 guineas for juniors including those that lead. According to Cock, 'The Bar at the Assizes' p. 51, the general meeting was held in the Inner Temple Lecture Hall June 19, 1876.
61. Dicey, 'Legal Etiquette', p. 173.
62. Robert Walton, Random Recollections of the Midland Circuit (2nd series, 1873), p. 108.
63. Norfolk Circuit (July 27, 1827); Norfolk Circuit Club (July, 1849); Norfolk Circuit (July, 1876); Norfolk Circuit (August, 1821); Rules of the Norfolk Circuit Club (July 18, 1856) see Appendix.
64. Norfolk Circuit Club (July 16, 1866).
65. South-Eastern Circuit (February 13-4, 1888).
66. South-Eastern Circuit (July 12, 1888).
67. Rules of the Norfolk Circuit Club (1856).
68. Norfolk Circuit Club (March 18, 1858); Home Circuit (Summer, 1873).
69. Western Circuit Membership Rules (Spring 1875), p. 3; Western Circuit (February 12, 1895), pp. 42-3.
70. Pall Mall Gazette, 5 (May 15, 1867), p. 4.
71. Ibid., 5 (May 17, 1867), p. 4.
72. Ibid., 5 (May 21, 1867), p. 4.
73. LT, 43 (June 1, 1867), p. 38.
74. Fortnightly Review, n.s. 2 (1867), p. 177. More recently Millerson has commented on this point. The Qualifying Associations, pp. 14-16.
75. For a discussion of the professional association as

a guild and the implications of this for ethics see Emile Durkheim, Professional Ethics and Civic Morals (1957), pp. 6-9, 16-17, 19-20, 23-4, 28-9.
76. Duman, 'Bar in the Georgian Era', passim.
77. Whishaw, A Synopsis of the Bar; Foster, Men-at-the-Bar.
78. On the career of Edwin James see J.R. Lewis, Certain Private Incidents. The Rise and Fall of Edwin James Q.C., M.P. (Newcastle upon Tyne, 1980); DNB, vol. 10, pp. 643-4.
79. LJ, 1 (June 8, 1866), p. 309.
80. John C. Jeafferson, A Book About Lawyers (2 vols., 1867), vol. 1, pp. 144-5. See also John George Witt, Life in the Law (1906), pp. 84-5.
81. Alfred Chichele Plowden, Grain or Chaff? The Autobiography of a Police Magistrate (1903), pp. 133-4.
82. South-Eastern Circuit (December 12, 1886).
83. South-Eastern Circuit (February 19, 1889).
84. A Circuit Tramp, Pie Powder, Being Dust From the Law Courts (1911), p. 44.
85. Plowden, Grain or Chaff?, pp. 133-4.
86. Ibid., p. 121.
87. Ibid., pp. 98-9.
88. South-Eastern Circuit (Summer 1891).
89. South-Eastern Circuit (Norwich, Summer 1891).
90. South-Eastern Circuit (July 19, 1876).
91. LT, 81 (July 31, 1886), p. 242.
92. South-Eastern Circuit vol. for 1891-7, pp. 124-5.
93. Here I am indebted to Professors Abel-Smith and Stevens for their study, Lawyers and the Courts.
94. Select Committee on Legal Education, p. 287.
95. Hansard, 3rd series, House of Commons, 100 (1848), col. 109.
96. Hansard, 3rd series, House of Commons, 167 (1862), col. 1037.
97. Ibid., col. 1037-8.
98. LT, 37 (1862), p. 441.
99. Hansard, 3rd series, House of Commons, 167 (1862), col. 1041-2, 1046, 1053-4.
100. Ibid., col. 1045-6.
101. Hansard, 3rd series, House of Commons, 178 (1865), col. 1050-1; 182 (1866), col. 1092-3.
102. Baildon and Roxburgh, Lincoln's Inn Black Books, vol. 5, pp. 110-11.
103. Hansard, 3rd series, House of Commons, 182 (1866), col. 1092-3.
104. Ibid., col. 1093.
105. LJ, 6 (April 7, 1871), p. 277.
106. LT, 51 (July 15, 1871), p. 189.
107. Hansard, 3rd series, House of Commons, 207 (1871), col. 1497.
108. Hansard, 3rd series, House of Commons, 209 (1872),

col. 1237.
109. Ibid., col. 1257-8.
110. Papers of Roundell Palmer (First Earl of Selborne) MS 1865f, fo. 88.
111. The Law Journal wrote on this matter, 'the Cabinet condemned him [Selborne] to silence and inactivity in the matter.' LJ, 9 (July 18, 1874), p. 421.
112. Peterson, The Medical Profession, pp. 23-7, 34-7.
113. Hansard, 3rd series, House of Lords, 220 (1874), col. 1457-62.
114. See below note 120.
115. Hansard, 3rd series, House of Lords, 220 (1874), col. 1468-9.
116. Hansard, 3rd series, House of Commons, 226 (1875), col. 626.
117. Ibid., col. 628.
118. Hansard, 3rd series, House of Commons, 229 (1876), col. 307-10, 343.
119. Ibid., col. 332-3.
120. Ibid., col. 322-3.
121. Ibid., col. 321-2.
122. Ibid., col. 312-14.
123. Hansard, 3rd series, House of Lords, 224 (1875), col. 997-8.
124. Ibid., col. 997.
125. Hansard, 3rd series, House of Lords, 229 (1876), col. 587-8.
126. Hansard, 3rd series, House of Lords, 233 (1877), col. 1253.
127. Bar Education and Discipline Bill, 40 & 41 Vict. (1877), no. 221.
128. Carr-Saunders and Wilson, The Professions, pp. 83-5.
129. See note 5 above.
130. Hansard, 3rd series, House of Commons, 238 (1878), col. 129.
131. Ibid.
132. LJ, 13 (March 2, 1878), p. 146.
133. Ibid., p. 145.
134. Hansard, 3rd series, House of Commons, 242 (1878), col. 642-3.
135. Abel-Smith and Stevens, Lawyers and the Courts, p. 460.
136. Inns of Court Commission, p. 55.
137. Personal communication from Sir William Bolton who also said that no written records of the decisions of the Attorney-General exist to his knowledge. The Attorney-General was nevertheless subject to the disciplinary control of the members of his inn. J.Ll.J. Edwards, The Law Officers of the Crown, (1964), p. 277.
138. Inns of Court Commission, p. 55.
139. Ibid., p. 137.

140. Baildon and Roxburgh, Lincoln's Inn Black Books, vol. 5, p. 95.
141. Ibid.
142. LT, 52 (November 11, 1871), p. 22.
143. Ibid., p. 21.
144. LJ, 8 (November 29, 1873), pp. 699-700.
145. LT, 17 (July 12, 1851), p. 129.
146. Dicey, 'Legal Etiquette', pp. 177-9.
147. LT, 53 (July 20, 1872), p. 211.
148. Ibid.
149. Abel-Smith and Stevens, Lawyers and the Courts, pp. 213-14.
150. As quoted in LJ, 17 (June 10, 1882), p. 320.
151. Cited in Abel-Smith and Stevens, Lawyers and the Courts, p. 215.
152. The Times, December 25, 1883, p. 5.
153. Abel-Smith and Stevens, Lawyers and the Courts, pp. 215-16.
154. LT, 77 (June 14, 1884), p. 112.
155. For example see LJ, 19 (April 5, 1884), p. 231.
156. Bar Committee, 4th Annual Statement, 1887, pp. 1-2.
157. LJ, 20 (August 1, 1885), p. 465.
158. LT, 95 (May 13, 1893); LJ, 27 (July 2, 1892).
159. LT, 94 (March 18, 1893), p. 454.
160. LJ, 28 (May 13, 1893), pp. 339-40; LT, 95 (May 13, 1893), pp. 29-30.
161. LJ, 28 (June 3, 1893), p. 393; LT, 95 (June 24, 1893), p. 179.
162. Western Circuit Minutes (July 28, 1893), p. 39.
163. LT, 96 (April 14, 1894), p. 552.
164. LT, 97 (June 30, 1894), pp. 189-90.
165. Baildon and Roxburgh, Lincoln's Inn Black Books, vol. 5, pp. 307-10.
166. Ibid., p. 311.

Chapter Three

CAREERS AT THE ENGLISH BAR

The professional career of the practising barrister in England and Wales began with his entry into an inn of court. Here he acquired a basic knowledge of the law, of the principles of practice and of the culture of his chosen profession. Although from 1872 he had to attend lectures and pass a qualifying examination, apprenticeship remained a central feature of his education. Under the supervision of his seniors he underwent training in the practical side of business that despite its drudgery was essential for a man who hoped to make his way at the bar. As Blackstone had recognised a century earlier, this system was not designed to provide law students, many of whom had no intention of practising, with grounding in the science of jurisprudence, but to impart to the legal careerist the technical knowledge and skills that he would need in the profession.(1) But this was not all. In chambers and commons the novice assimilated the values and norms of the bar that each professional generation transmitted to the next. The period of studentship insured that all barristers underwent identical rites of passage that created as far as possible a standard professional outlook and fostered occupational solidarity.

The ideal end of a career at the bar was an appointment to the bench of the superior courts. After his call to the bar the fledgling barrister who hoped to reach that objective would probably try to follow a more or less standard career pattern. This typically included the acquisition by a successful junior of a medium-level professional office, such as a recordership. Then after the lapse of some years he would almost invariably take silk. If extremely ambitious he could then try his hand in politics by running for Parliament with the eventual aim of an appointment as Solicitor- or Attorney-General. Depending on his success in achieving these ends and his professional and political standing, he could end his career as a puisne judge, a member of the Court of Appeal, a law lord, Chief Justice or even Lord Chancellor.

My primary aim in this chapter is to describe the stages in a barrister's career beginning with his admission to an inn

of court and ending with his elevation to the bench of the
Supreme Court of Judicature. I have chosen the metaphor of a
ladder to describe the path of advancement in the profession
but in fact this image may be misleading. A more accurate description might be a tree. Some barristers followed the trunk
directly to the top while others made their way up by a longer
and more circuitous route. However, the majority who began
the ascent became stranded on the lower or intermediate limbs
without any possibility of extricating themselves.

We will begin by following the various stages of a career
at the English bar: the professional training of barristers;
the opening stages of practice; the expansion of provincial
bars; and the receipt of important professional offices and
ranks. We will then examine the various factors that contributed to a barrister's success in the law. The chapter concludes with a comparison between the bar and medicine with regard to their internal coherence and unity.

TESTING AND TRAINING

During the eighteenth century and the first half of the nineteenth the inns of court let law students fend for themselves
in acquiring the tools of their future profession. As a result young men often turned to established practitioners for
advice on the best way to prepare for a career in advocacy.
A typical reply to such an inquiry is found in a letter written
by William Plunkett (1807-44), a well-known conveyancer and
pupil master.

> I am clearly of [the] opinion that the study of the law
> should be commenced with conveyancing, a man should know
> the rights of property before he ventures on the study of
> remedies for the disturbance of those rights. For this
> reason I advise you to begin with conveyancing. If this
> argument prevails with you--It will give me much pleasure
> to receive you at the end of Oct. If however you prefer
> the remedies I shall be most happy to assist you in your
> search for a special pleader.(2)

In addition to the practical training that this afforded, students were also encouraged to establish a grounding in the
principles of English law by reading some of the classics of
the discipline, for example Coke on Littleton and Blackstone's
Commentaries, as well as the Law Reports.(3)

As we noted earlier the inns of court did not establish
a formal syllabus and a mandatory bar examination until 1872,
despite the fact that historians and sociologists of the professions have traditionally associated the rise of professionalism with the introduction of these reforms. Objections to
the introduction of a qualifying examination were ideologically

based. Sir Fitzroy Kelly, Treasurer of Lincoln's Inn and future Lord Chief Baron, told the 1854 Inns of Court Commission, 'I do not see the mischief of men being called to the Bar, who are after all incompetent, whether it is from want of means, or from idleness, or from incapacity, or anything else.'(4) Kelly justified this rather surprising assertion by claiming that 'If a man is not competent, he will never succeed at the Bar; and if he be, he ought not to be excluded.'(5) The Law Journal that took a similar stand in 1873 reminded its readers that the barrister stood in a very different relationship with his immediate clients, than did the members of the other independent practising professions:

> The clients of the barrister are not the uneducated laymen but the solicitors, and at every step in his career the barrister is sharply criticized by the most competent judges of his fitness and ability. No examination that can be demanded from candidates for a call can be so effective as the continuous examination of solicitors who give the briefs.(6)

A second objection to examinations was that they would discourage landed gentlemen from going to the inns of court. These men had no interest in practising law but merely wanted to acquire knowledge of the law that would be useful to them in managing their estates or in fulfilling their duties as justices of the peace or members of Parliament. The professionalisation of legal education and the introduction of rigorous examinations, it was argued, would result in the exodus of the remaining gentlemen amateurs from the bar. Not only would the gentry thereby be deprived of an opportunity to acquire an introduction to legal studies but the social quality and tone of the inns would inevitably deteriorate.(7)

The proper education for the bar, Kelly contended, was not lectures and a bar examination but a liberal education at a public school and Oxbridge, followed by an apprenticeship in the chambers of a special pleader, barrister or conveyancer, depending upon whether the student intended to specialise in equity or common law.(8) Another member of the bar, John George Witt, who had been called at Lincoln's Inn in 1864, went even further than Kelly in condemning examinations which he called 'pernicious'. He argued that they distracted the law student from his real task, namely 'learning his business'. He concluded,'...the paramount evil of the ordeal of examination is that it discourages what I may call the principle of "apprenticeship". The three years' preparation for the Bar ought to be spent in the chambers of counsel.'(9)

Thus those opposed to formal tests of a barrister's competence believed that on the one hand professional certification was unnecessary since quality would be regulated by the natural forces of supply and demand as overseen by the members of the lower branch. On the other hand the proper education for the bar did not, in their view, consist of academic knowledge of the law but rather the kind of vocational and technical training that students could only acquire from practical on-the-job experience.

Proponents of examinations took a diametrically opposed stance on the objectives of a legal education. Joseph Phillimore for one insisted 'that everything that prevents an education from being merely technical - savouring too strongly of the attorney's desk - is good.'(10) Lord Campbell believed that a formal preparatory course combined with examinations provided essential professional quality control, and in this respect the law was no different from medicine.(11) According to Edward Creasy, Professor of History at the University of London and future Chief Justice of Ceylon, such a course 'would tend to raise the character of the bar, not only with reference to their legal qualifications, but also with reference to that general high tone of feeling which I think so desirable for the sake of all the community that the bar should possess.'(12)

After 1872 both of these two contrasting conceptions of the proper education for the bar were united in the typical course followed by law students. Even with the introduction of compulsory examinations many and perhaps most of the students who intended to practise at the bar spent a year or more as apprentices or pupils in the chambers of practitioners to whom they paid a standard fee of 100 guineas. This phase of legal education, despite its popularity, was entirely voluntary until the mid-twentieth century.(13) The reason that examinations did not obviate the value of pupilage was twofold. In the first place the tests were far from rigorous. According to a leading article in the Law Times in 1875, 'the paper requires such a small knowledge of the law that practically the examination affords no test of legal knowledge.'(14) Consequently, as opponents of the reforms had predicted, cramming became an integral part of a future barrister's education.(15) In the second place, the practical introduction to the law that a student gained in the chambers of a good pupil master could not be acquired as easily, if at all, from any other source.

The life of a pupil and his education in chambers naturally varied from master to master, as the following two examples indicate. In the late 1820s James Stuart Wortley, a future Solicitor-General, described a typical day to his mother:

> This life in a special pleader's office, does not appear to me near so bad as I had been led to expect. We sit (6 or 7 of us) in a tolerably comfortable room variously at different desks & tables, in reading cases [and] putting them in legal form. I am writing out all the different forms required by the law; we are in no way confined but at liberty to employ as many as four hours as we like between 10 in the morning & 10 at night. I find that the 6

> hours which I have always proposed to myself will be considered good application. My companions, though not perhaps the most refined, are by no means deficient in intellect, & are very obliging and good humoured - The intervals of our labours are occupied with lively & tolerably agreeable conversation though frequently upon the merits of some case of the day.(16)

A quarter of a century later William Harcourt wrote to his sister:

> At ten I go into my tutor's chambers where I work like a horse till five at pleadings, opinions, etc. I then scramble to get a little dinner, then a leading Art. [for the Saturday Review] till ten, then my own private law studies till two, and so to bed....One has no time to do what Palmerston calls 'meditate on the immensity of the universe,' which is a most unsatisfactory occupation. I am at this moment attending a lecture of J.G. Phillimore on Constitutional Law [one of those instituted in 1852], and take the liberty of writing this letter as more improving than his inflated and ignorant declamations.(17)

In the eighteenth century attorneys had often served as pupil masters for future members of the bar. However, due in part to the condemnations of purists, most notably Sir William Blackstone, special pleaders, conveyancers and barristers came to be the preferred teachers of law students. Nevertheless the break was not complete and some prospective barristers chose to begin their professional training in the offices of attorneys at least prior to entering formal pupilage. Here they learned not only the principles of practice and the procedures of the lower branch but they were able to make contacts with potential clients. All of this was invaluable for the ambitious barrister. One man who followed such a course was Richard Webster, later Chief Justice of England.

> In the autumn of 1865, my father [himself a barrister], who had great knowledge and wisdom of all things connected with the legal profession, sent me for six months as a pupil to Messrs. Young, Maples, Teesdale and Nelson of No. 6, Frederick Place, Old Jewry, a well known firm of solicitors who had a very large commercial business. This led to my going in the summer of 1866 to work as a pupil at the Great Western office of that firm, where I made the acquaintance of Mr. R.R. Nelson, the leading solicitor of the Railway. My obligations to him will appear more than once in these pages.(18)

THE FIRST STEPS

Upon completing his pupilage, the student had two courses open to him. If he had eaten the prescribed number of meals in the dining hall of his inn and if he had passed the final examination (after 1872) he could be called to the bar. Alternatively he could delay his call and practise as a special pleader or equity draftsman under the bar for several years. The advantage of the latter course, which was especially popular in the late eighteenth and early nineteenth centuries, was that it allowed a man to gain experience and make connections before taking his chances at the bar.(19) However, despite the benefits that might accrue from delaying one's call, success was by no means assured. As John Taylor Coleridge wrote to his uncle in 1819 upon having decided to give up this intermediate status:

> I may not do more at the bar [than he had done as a not very successful special pleader] but probably the sooner I begin my course of barren years the sooner I shall end them and enter on the years of harvest. I own I am not sanguine of the kind of success which will alone satisfy my mind.(20)

Upon his call to the bar the young barrister had to find himself a set of chambers in or near the precincts of the inns and then wait for attorneys to brief him. As a result, for a man without connections the early years in the profession could be very precarious. But by the mid-nineteenth century a lucky minority of newly-qualified barristers became the beneficiaries of changes in the traditional chambers system.(21) In 1854 the Treasurer of the Inner Temple described the innovations to the Inns of Court Commission:

> ...so many men have ceased to live in Chambers, whom the railways take out of town [to residential suburbs]; and there are other changes in the business of the Profession. Gentlemen now find it convenient and more economical, for two or three to take a set of Chambers;(22)

The modern pattern existed only in its embryonic form in these early years. Barristers merely clubbed together, and 'the system of carefully graduated seniority with the theory of work passing down from hand to hand had scarcely evolved.'(23) Yet there were opportunities for able law students and young barristers to act as devils to senior members of the profession.(24) This employment provided them with an income before they began to receive briefs on their own account. In his memoirs John Gorell Barnes describes his position and advancement in the chambers of J.C. Mathew, a leading member of the commercial bar:

> Mathew was overworked, and there were great chances for a
> devil. I had more business and other experience, than
> these two [other pupils], and I saw my chance. In a
> short time I had learnt to be a fair pleader, and I gra-
> dually worked into Mathew's style and really went through
> practically all his Chamber work till, at the end of my
> first year, he asked me to stay on, and let me put my
> name on his door.(25)

Barnes remained in Mathew's chambers for a few years and then he and his mentor decided that it was time for him to establish independent premises.(26) This would suggest that in the 1870s tenancy in a set of chambers was not necessarily permanent for a barrister, as it is today, but rather a prelude to striking out on his own. Though the evidence is thin, it would seem that by the end of the century not only were senior barristers taking juniors into their chambers but in some instances two QCs were sharing a set.(27) Apparently the earlier temporary character of the system had begun to disappear.

Those young men who were fortunate enough to have bene-fited from this type of relationship were sure to take with them valuable professional experience, connections and perhaps even a few clients. For the majority of recently called bar-risters, prospects were far less happy, as we can gather from a letter written to James Bryce by Edward Augustus Freeman in 1868:

> you don't say whether anything at all has happened to lift
> you out of your state of brieflessness. The first stages
> of the law must be very dreary. I suppose in the essence
> those of any other profession are much the same, only in
> no other have you actually to sit, while the man who is
> preferred to you is doing what you would wish to be doing
> instead.(28)

With the advent of strict separation between equity and common law practitioners in the early decades of the nineteenth century, the former confined themselves almost entirely to chancery work in the London courts.(29) While waiting to es-tablish a senior courtroom practice they engaged in conveyanc-ing and equity draftsmanship. By contrast, common law barris-ters had opportunities to make their mark in the profession outside of the hectic metropolis. The assizes and in the early years the county quarter sessions served as arenas in which the fledgling advocate could display his talents.(30) Here he was not competing with the entire profession but with a relatively small group of colleagues. He therefore had a much better op-portunity of attracting the attention of provincial attorneys. In addition as we shall see, it was at the sessions and assizes that local connections could be of most use in providing a young man with the opportunity to make his mark in the profession.

Even for a man without local interests, constant attendance at the sessions could serve as a first step to professional success. In his memoirs James Scarlett, later Lord Abinger, ascribed his advance to his decision in 1792, on the advice of Samuel Romilly, to attend quarter sessions in Lancashire. Not only did he become a leader of the sessions bar but his reputation spread to the assizes as well.(31) Yet even in the provinces competition could be fierce and success was by no means assured.(32) According to one late-nineteenth-century barrister, while the

> Quarter Sessions is an admirable school for the training of a young barrister...the field is necessarily much restricted and it takes time therefore to lay even the foundations of success....To mount a long ladder step by step takes time, and there are so many steps to be climbed before the terminus is reached that few survive to the end, however much they persevere.(33)

But even for those who did survive and prosper at the sessions bar, it was only a first step. The time eventually came when a barrister who hoped to make a reputation had to leave the security of the sessions and risk his future in a more competitive and more lucrative arena. This was the choice that faced Fitzjames Stephen in 1862:

> I am pretty well persuaded now, that I shall neither learn nor earn much more at Sessions. I have got to the top of this little hill, or as near as I shall get, & I have rather a notion that it might be well to take some opportunity of giving them up. Though it is far too serious a thing to do without considering. I think that we must aim at doing without the Revisorship,& saving it up for the purpose of paying for the silk gown, to which I must begin to look forward.(34)

Prior to 1876 common law barristers did not even have to choose between attending the circuit and appearing in Westminster since the assizes met only out of term. Consequently the junior barrister could test his mettle at the assizes in front of High Court judges and in competition with leading counsel and also try his hand in the superior courts of London if briefs came his way. According to a Western circuiteer reminiscing about the 1870s, that was an era 'when the common-law barrister who did not go the circuit was a rare phenomenon ....the great majority of the profession looked to the circuit as the mainstay of their livelihood, and certainly the surest road to professional success.'(35)

There was another side to the life of a barrister travelling to the assizes. For many, if not most aspiring members of the bar, the reality was rather grim, as the following description of the Oxford circuit suggests.

> The real wonder was, that with the truth staring them in the face, a barren land without milk or honey, so many men had the patience to tramp round the Circuit for six weeks at a stretch, twice in the year, in the vain hope of picking up briefs...out of the whole two hundred or more pilgrims I do not believe that a dozen paid their expenses.(36)

Not surprisingly one barrister in the early part of the nineteenth century likened his circuit to a comet, 'our tail is large, and of changing materials, the body tough and small.'(37)

PROVINCIAL BARS

London was the centre of practice at the English bar. The vast majority of barristers had chambers there and most successful advocates left the metropolis only occasionally for a special fee, preferring to concentrate their efforts in the superior courts of Westminster. Nevertheless there was a small coterie of practitioners who practised exclusively in the provinces and only had chambers in one of the larger provincial towns or cities. Their numbers began to increase during the first third of the nineteenth century but the growth of significant concentrations of provincial barristers that justified the formation of local bars did not occur until the last quarter of the century.(38) This phenomenon was due to the establishment of concurrent sittings in London and at the assizes which discouraged ambitious men in London from going the circuit, especially the distant Northern Circuit. As John Gorell Barnes explained in his memoirs:

> time was too valuable in London, and the opening on the Northern Circuit was difficult if one did not localize, which I was very adverse to doing. I preferred the practice of a barrister in London to that of a barrister in Liverpool.(39)

Furthermore the County Courts began to attract a portion of the civil business previously heard in the assizes. Therefore it was possible for a man to make a decent living as a barrister in one of the larger provincial centres, especially Manchester, Liverpool, Birmingham, Leeds and Bristol.(40)

Changes on the Northern Circuit between 1874 and 1895 demonstrate the expansion of provincial practice.(41) In 1874 there were 213 members of the circuit for whom we have business addresses. Of these, 161 men (76 per cent) had chambers in London, 51 (24 per cent) had chambers in a provincial city and one man had chambers in both London and Liverpool. Twenty-one years later of the 303 Northern circuiteers for whom I have found addresses, 176 (58 per cent) had chambers exclusively in London, 111 (37 per cent) had provincial chambers only and 16 (5 per cent) had chambers in both locales. The rise of a few large provincial bars is further demonstrated in Table 3.1. Urban Lancashire became the great provincial law centre due to the volume of commercial business in and around Manchester and Liverpool, and to the combined effects of concurrent sittings and its distance from London as noted by Barnes above. By comparison to these giants the other provincial law centres were small indeed, though several were large enough to justify the establishment of a locally organised bar.

Members of the bar had long been opposed to the decentralisation of their profession. In 1833 Lord Lyndhurst told the House of Lords that barristers who practised permanently in the provinces 'would be inferior in learning, would be inferior in talent, would be inferior in intelligence, would be inferior in all those great and glorious qualifications which had so long distinguished the bar of England.'(42) Fifty years later the Law Times was still fighting the same battle:

> To the mediocrity, which of course is characteristic of seven tenths of the Bar, the prospect of decentralisation is doubtless attractive. What are now called local barristers would then practise continually before High Court judges instead of before the County Courts. More barristers would get work and small incomes would be made. Circuit life with all its social advantages would be a thing of the past; the Inns of Court would lose half of the little influence which they now exercise; and generally the Bar would sink down from the atmosphere, pure, bracing, and invigorating through which they now rise to eminence into a lower sphere where the struggle for existence would be greater and the competition keener for diminished business.(43)

As local bars began to develop, assuring their members of year-round professional contacts and companionship, attitudes towards them began to change.(44) In 1878 Lord Bramwell told a parliamentary select committee, 'I think I can say of my knowledge that the local bar of Liverpool is as good as the London bar.'(45) London still retained its dominant position, and once a man took silk he had to have a set of chambers in the metropolis; but barristers who began to practise in the provinces were no longer excluded from senior professional offices, as the careers of a number of superior court judges demonstrate.(46) By 1893 the Law Journal was praising the decentralisation process as beneficial to the bar and the public alike.

It is difficult to see why the legal profession any more

Table 3.1: Provincial Barristers c. 1825-1900

	c. 1825	c. 1830	c. 1840	c. 1845	c. 1850	c. 1860	c. 1870	c. 1875	c. 1880	c. 1890	c. 1900
Birmingham	-	-	-	4	-	1	5	-	13	19	22
Bristol	-	-	-	6	-	9	11	-	11	11	19
Leeds	-	-	-	2	-	0	6	-	14	23	20
Liverpool	13	-	12	-	17	26	34	-	59	69	95
Manchester	-	5	10	13	-	25	-	34	56	81	99
Newcastle	-	-	-	7	-	7	-	8	-	11	-
Sheffield	-	-	-	2	-	0	4	-	8	3	6

Source: Provincial and City directories.

Note: (-) indicates that no information was available for that year.

than the medical profession should be concentrated in the
capital, or why in these days the vast commercial communi-
ties of the North should have their justice periodically
ladled out to them from the Metropolis....The only objection suggested to the localisation of justice appears to
be that the best men would not settle in the provinces.
But there is no particular art or mystery in the law...It
is only in a small proportion of cases that the best man
is needed, and for many purposes the local man is the best
man....in no way would merit stand a better chance against
nepotism and connection than by the thorough decentralisation of the administration of justice. The best men
would find their way to London....and London would still
be the centre of the Courts of Appeal. Strong local bars
would be an advantage in every way, and might allow the
'mute inglorious', but latent powers in many a briefless
but scholarly barrister enduring the pangs of disappointment....to enjoy a fair field and reasonable opportunities
which are now denied him.(47)

In the view of the Law Journal local bars could never com-
pete with the one in London. Their value stemmed on the one
hand from the fact that they provided population centres far
from London with a resident pool of barristers and on the other
that they were arenas of practice in which advocates could
prove their ability free from the nefarious influences of 'nepotism and connection'. This latter contention naturally
raises a question essential to our understanding of the career
patterns of the English bar in the nineteenth century: What
was the relationship between influence, merit and professional
advancement? It is to this issue that we must now address ourselves.

CONNECTIONS AND PATRONAGE

Touting by members of the bar or their agents was against the
custom of the profession at least since the later eighteenth
century, although there were always a few barristers who flout-
ed 'the general opinion, that it is improper in a lawyer to so-
licit employment'.(48) While, as previously noted, the bar
was willing to countenance a friend or relative using their
influence to secure business for a young practitioner, it condemned a barrister or his clerk directly approaching a solicitor in order to obtain a brief. In 1870 a barrister wrote in
the Law Journal suggesting that this distinction was based on
an arbitrary double standard:

> I have known a young barrister, upon attending his maiden
> sessions in his native province, obtain more briefs than
> the leader of the sessions [from magistrates' clerks]...

This young gentleman belonged to one of the richest though not the oldest of the county families. Was there no touting here by the great unpaid? Even attorneys, who ought to have been independent of such influence, were not behind in the plutocratic struggle....Again, sir, I can call to mind the son of an eminent provincial physician in whose hands are the mortal destinies of the families of attorneys in two or three neighbouring counties. To say nothing of the power of life and death...the physician's fees have sometimes been set off or cancelled in consideration of a little timely patronage bestowed upon the son ...No doubt it is very unprofessional to make use of ignoble touters, but the same ban it appears does not attach to noble, wealthy, and influential aid. The vulgar word touting must not be applied to such.(49)

Without doubt these views were eccentric within the context of the opinion of the nineteenth-century legal profession. Apparently, as long as briefs were secured without the direct connivance of the practitioner all was considered above board. Nevertheless these examples of touting provide an instructive introduction to the ways in which 'primary contact networks', those based on family influence, could be employed to secure business for a fledgling barrister at the quarter sessions of the assizes.(50)

The scions of county families were often able to count upon receiving business in their home assizes and sessions, often to the total exclusion of outsiders.(51) This type of connection could be especially important in securing prosecution briefs in criminal cases that were in the gift of the magistrates' clerks. Henry Clark, a member of the Western circuit who owned an estate near Plymouth, was acquainted with most of the clerks in Devon and as a result he had 'more prosecutions to conduct at sessions and assizes than any other member of the Bar'.(52)

The sons of professional men, as in the case of the physicians quoted above, were sometimes able to secure circuit briefs through influence, as were the sons of local businessmen. Robert Gifford, a future Master of the Rolls, was the son of a 'dealer in a large way of business' in Exeter. In 1813 John Campbell attributed Gifford's success on the Western circuit to his 'very powerful patronage joined to very considerable abilities.'(53) Another example of business connections, this time with a national and religious emphasis, is found in the career of Charles Russell, the future Lord Chief Justice. Russell had benefited from a letter of introduction written by his uncle, the President of Maynooth College, to James Whitty, an influential Liverpool merchant and fellow Irish Catholic. Through Whitty he made the acquaintance of John Yates, a Catholic solicitor, who brought Russell clients both in Liverpool and in London.(54)

Members of the legal profession could also help promote the interests of a young barrister.(55) As we saw earlier, one of the most useful methods was for a barrister to give work to a former pupil. In this regard, Farrer Herschell told the House of Commons in 1876 that 'the only way almost in which a young man of ability and talent for the law, who had no influence, ever got into work, was by his merits becoming known to counsel, who in an emergency called for assistance, knowing what was in the young man on whom he called.'(56) On the other hand Charles Cripps, later Lord Parmoor, upon his call to the bar in 1877 had no need to devil for an established practitioner. He stepped directly into the parliamentary practice from which his father was retiring, and he was also helped on his way by his brother Henry, a partner in a firm of parliamentary agents.(57)

Judges in criminal cases were sometimes in a position to aid fledgling barristers by appointing them to defend prisoners at the assizes who had no counsel.(58) There was of course some fear that relatives of judges could be given unfair advantages over other counsel. Towards the end of the nineteenth century this gave rise to criticism in the House of Commons of the sons of county court judges practising before their fathers.(59) In 1892 the Bar Committee ruled that this should be discouraged, and the Attorney-General stated: 'I have always felt that in every Court, members of the family of the Judge should abstain from practising before him as much as possible.'(60)

Despite this restriction on them, the sons of judges were inordinately successful in rising to the top of the legal profession. Examining the occupational connections of the judges appointed to the benches of the superior courts between 1850 and 1901 we find that 9 per cent belonged to judicial dynasties: seven were sons of former judges; one was the nephew of a judge; two were both fathers and grandfathers of future judges. In addition five other members of the judiciary who served in the second half of the nineteenth century were the sons-in-law of superior court judges.(61)

By common agreement the most useful of all connections for the young barrister were those with members of the lower branch. However in contrast to most of the sources of influence discussed above, these were most often though not exclusively 'casual contacts' based primarily on occupational considerations. Attorneys and solicitors were said to be 'not only judges but patrons, who by employing young men early, give them not merely fees, but courage, practice, and the means of becoming known to others.'(62) Members of the bar had no doubts about the value of these connections. In 1864 James Bryce, later a cabinet minister and ambassador to the United States, gave his assessment of the requirements necessary to achieve success at the bar:

> Some powers of thought and speech are needed to make a
> man a leading Q.C., and something still more to make him
> Solicitor-General, but to get into a steady £800 a year
> practice, improveable [sic] by fair diligence to £1,200,
> the one thing needful is interest with Solicitors...(63)

In the twentieth century Sir Gervais Rentoul wrote in his memoirs:

> ...I would suggest that success lies in a knowledge of
> the rules of practice, in an instinct for sizing up quick-
> ly any situation that may arise, in a faculty for ready
> thought, a capacity for hard work, and attention to detail
> and a willingness to face drudgery, while last, but most
> important of all, is an acquaintance with as large a num-
> ber as possible of those in the so-called 'lower branch'
> of the profession who are willing to back their fancy and
> give a young barrister a chance.(64)

These views were not confined to members of the bar. Towards the end of the nineteenth century T.H.S. Escott commented:

> Success at the Bar depends on a combination of circum-
> stances and on a variety of gifts, physical quite as much
> as mental. A good presence, an agreeable manner, are as
> valuable as the powerful, but slowly moving intellect...
> In addition to this, there should be, if possible, some
> connection with a few influential solicitors, or the oppor-
> tunity of establishing such, and then, if most of these
> conditions are forthcoming, there will be a certainty of
> moderate success.(65)

A few examples should suffice to illustrate the power of attorneys to promote the career of fledgling barristers. Crabb Robinson tells us that he decided to be called to the bar and to join the Norfolk circuit due to the persuasion of a Norwich attorney, Adam Taylor, who promised him his patronage.(66) In the early years of his career at the equity bar Roundell Palmer received support from Messrs Freshfield, solicitors to the Bank of England, as a result of the intervention of his uncle, a businessman in the City. In his memoirs Palmer wrote, 'they gave me from that time steady support, and were my principal clients.'(67) Edward Clarke benefited from his friendship with W.R. Stevens, clerk to the solicitors of the South Eastern Railway, while Richard Webster, as we have seen, received business from R.R. Nelson, solicitor to the Great Western, in whose office he was a pupil in the mid-1860s.(68)

Judicial biography gives some indication of the value of connections with the lower branch for promoting a career at the bar. Ten judges who took office between 1850 and 1901 (9 per cent) were the sons of solicitors. Another 15 judges (14 per cent) benefited from close relationships with members of that profession: 10 (9 per cent) served as clerks to solicitors or attorneys in the early years of their careers; 2 (2 per cent) practised as attorneys for a time; 3 (3 per cent) received substantial patronage from members of the lower branch. Taking these as minimal figures we can say that at least a quarter of the mid- and late-Victorian judges were on intimate terms with men who belonged to a profession that controlled the flow of briefs and fees to members of the bar.

Of course useful connections for barristers were not confined to the legal professions. The sons of businessmen were exceptionally successful in reaching the benches of the superior courts (see Table 3.4) and this may be attributed in part to the business that their families could put their way. For example, Sir Henry Cotton, son of William Cotton - Governor of the Bank of England - became counsel to the Bank largely as a result of his father's influence. Sir John Bigham, later Lord Mersey, whose father was a leading Liverpool merchant and member of the city council, was able to establish himself as one of the leading commercial lawyers in his home town, in part as a result of his connections with its mercantile community.

There seems little doubt that connections and patronage could be powerful forces especially in the opening stages of a legal career, and that men with influential friends and relatives had significant advantages in the quest for professional honours. But as John Campbell wrote soon after his arrival in London in 1800, influence alone was not sufficient:

> Those who have powerful connections no doubt have a much better opportunity of displaying their talents, but if they are dull or dissipated no interest however great can push them on. They must yield to those who, joining attention to talent, have shone into notice notwithstanding the seemingly impenetrable fog in which fate has enveloped them.(69)

The career of A.G.C. Liddell provides eloquent testimony in support of Campbell's observation. Liddell was the son of a permanent under-secretary in the Home Department, who was also a QC and a former member of the Northern Circuit. In addition he was the grandson of the first Earl of Ravensworth. Liddell was well acquainted with two judges - Sir Samuel Martin and Sir G.W.W. Bramwell - and marshalled for both of them on the Western Circuit.(70) Upon his call to the bar in 1872 Liddell joined his father's old circuit. He received several early briefs from solicitors, but according to his own testimony he was uniformly unsuccessful.(71) Despite his failures Sir Henry James appointed him counsel to the Mint and Post Office at the Durham and Northumberland sessions in the early 1880s. Nevertheless he never made a mark in the profession and in 1886 he left the bar to accept the chief clerkship in the Crown Office. Upon this occasion he wrote in his diary:

> No one who has not followed the Bar and spent his time in laborious idleness, with rare intervals of hard work done in terror of failure, nor has not felt the degradation of a small attorney passing you by with contempt, and handing a guinea prosecution to the next man, or the apprehension of growing old in an unsuccessful life, can tell what a joy it is to me to quit the profession.(72)

Connections based largely though not exclusively on primary (family) contact networks played a central role in the promotion of the careers of individual barristers, especially during the early years of practice.(73) Here as in most other high-prestige occupations the rhetoric of equality is not fully borne out by social analysis. Some members of the bar were more equal than others in the quest for the great prizes of the profession especially the sons of businessmen and to a somewhat lesser degree those of barristers and solicitors. Others benefited from professional contacts made while students and/or during the early stages of their legal careers. While the prevalence of influence violated strict meritocratic principles, it did not lead to an infusion of incompetent but well-connected men into senior legal offices. This was due in large measure to the competition for briefs mediated by the lower branch. As a result in most instances personal and political influences, where they operated at all, only tipped the scales in deciding between candidates of more or less equal professional standing.

THE LADDER OF PREFERMENT

As I mentioned in the introduction to this chapter, although I have adopted the metaphor of the ladder to describe careers at the English bar, its resemblance to reality is limited to those few cases of men who took the shorter route to the top of the profession. For the vast majority of practising barristers, the alternate picture of a tree with a few intertwining branches that reached upward and many that went nowhere was much closer to the truth. A counsel's final destination depended on speed of ascent so that an office that for a man of 40 promised a bright future represented a final destination for a man of 55.

The entry point, the first rung, was identical for all barristers - namely the call to the bar at one of the inns of court. In this way the bar was unique among nineteenth-century professions, at least prior to the 1870s, since there was a single portal of entry. Successive steps were based on the ability to attract business with ever-increasing fees in ever more competitive arenas (for example sessions, circuit,

Westminster) and on the appointment to professional ranks and
offices. Together these were the signs of success. By and
large the successful barrister was the one who could win cases
in court or at least make a powerful showing there. He was the
man who would attract the notice and custom of solicitors.
Thus it was the opinion of the lower branch that largely determined the success of the members of the upper. The receipt of
honours and offices depended largely on a man's reputation in
court but as we shall see in the final chapter, political service along with connection could be decisive factors.

In this section I will examine some of the ranks and offices that constituted important stages in the careers of nineteenth-century barristers. Beginning with the low-level posts
of commissionerships of bankruptcy and revising barristerships,
we move on to the more prestigious one of municipal recorderships. We then look in some detail at the ranks of Serjeant-at-law and Queen's Counsel that were perhaps the most crucial
stages of a barrister's career since they sorted out leaders
from juniors and men with futures from those who had already
reached their peak. We then proceed to the first of the full-time judicial offices, the much-maligned judges of the County
Courts, finally arriving at the very summit of the profession:
the law officers of the crown - the Solicitor- and Attorney-General and the judges of the Supreme Court of Judicature, as
the central superior courts of Westminster became in 1875.

The ascent was filled with dangers and uncertainty and it
is not surprising that many of the starters dropped out or
nearly did so in the early stages. Lack of rapid advancement
or even initial failure tempted men, even those who would eventually reap great professional rewards, to contemplate alternative careers. Charles Russell, the future Lord Chief Justice,
related that, 'During my first years at the Bar, Gully, Herschell
and I dined together on circuit one night. Gully and Herschell
[later Speaker of the House of Commons and Lord Chancellor
respectively] were in a very despondent mood. They almost despaired of success in England. Gully...proposed going to the
Straits Settlements and Herschell to the Indian Bar...'.(74)
A few early victories in court did not dispel self-doubts or
concern about the future, as the following letter from Fitzjames Stephen amply illustrates:

> I see more & more plainly that the road to business is
> very long and very steep indeed...If I could but get two
> or three clients, or even one good & constant one, it
> would set me all right, but at present I am making a sort
> of reputation which would be very useful for an older man,
> who already had business, but is to me, glory & not gain.(75)

Even long-standing members of the bar were not automatically freed from worries about how to proceed in the profession,
if at all. In some instances the problem was lack of significant

progress after years in practice. Such was the case of George Harris, who had been called to the bar in 1843. Sixteen years later we find Harris writing in his diary, 'I might yet, I believe, retrieve my failure at the bar, but in one way only, which would be a desperate effort; and that is by obtaining a seat in Parliament and taking rank, so as to obtain employment in leading cases suitable for me to strive and come out as an orator.'(76) In others it was due to the doubts of moderately able men about how far they could go. In 1830 John Taylor Coleridge confided to his friend John May his professional prospects and dreams:

> I must by every means in my power keep my reputation for legal knowledge, and general ability as high as I can; so that if even more unsuccessful as an advocate, than I now am, I may still hold that place in the profession, which may make me eligible for any of the numerous posts of honour or retreat which our profession is well stored with. Of course my <u>dreams</u> & ambitions point to the Bench ...but these are I <u>fear dreams</u> too high for me now, and I shall be well content with a less brilliant destiny.(77)

Even less hopeful was an entry by Serjeant Thomas Talfourd in his diary in 1848 in which he resolved:

> To devote myself entirely to business; to name myself just rewards, to take an interest in any Brief or Case I receive as if I were beginning life anew, and strike onward and upward! The worst symptoms about me are dislike and indifference to my work...Against these let me struggle and pray! If the diminution of my income, should thus incline me to welcome any work I may attain, it will bring with it compensation.(78)

Their resignation notwithstanding both men, Coleridge in 1834 and Talfourd in 1849, were appointed puisne judges of the royal courts. Most barristers were not so fortunate.

Commissioners, Revising Barristers and Recorders

In 1847 Lord Chief Justice Denman wrote to a fellow judge, 'I cannot help fancying that the Bar is becoming more a stage of transition than a status - an apprenticeship exacted by custom for obtaining some office...'.(79) Among the first positions open to the junior barrister were commissionerships in bankruptcy and revising barristerships. Worth £300 - £400 and £200 per annum respectively, they served either as temporary expedients until a secure practice was established or as a permanent means of supplementing a small professional income. The commissionerships in London were abolished in 1831 with the creation of the London Bankruptcy Court, although in the provinces they continued to exist until the late 1860s. Apparently ambitious men, even in the early stages of their careers, were loath to apply for these offices, feeling that the income did not justify the investment in time that was required. Only 3 judges appointed to the bench between 1790 and 1850 ever served as bankruptcy commissioners.

With the abolition of the London commissionerships, their place as a source of additional income for underemployed members of the bar was taken by revising barristerships - created by the Reform Bill of 1832.(80) In 1831, speaking in support of the government's bill, the Attorney-General, Sir Thomas Denman, stressed the importance of these offices for fledgling counsel in particular. He told the Commons that 'unfortunately in all the Courts, there were many barristers without immediate employment in their profession; ay, hundreds of extremely accomplished and enlightened men, perfectly competent to take upon themselves the duties they would have to perform under this Act.'(81)

Revising barristers were appointed annually by the senior judge on each circuit from among the junior members, and in most instances appointments were renewed automatically from year to year.(82) Professor Hanham has suggested that these offices were often distributed on the basis of favours to relatives or friends of the judges without regard to the qualifications of the men involved.(83) While it is difficult to assess fully the validity of this charge of nepotism since the names of office-holders do not appear in the Law List, I have only found one instance of the selection of a near relative of a judge, namely Henry Coleridge, whose brother-in-law Sir John Patteson was a puisne judge in the Court of King's Bench at the time. By and large revising barristers, like bankruptcy commissioners, did not rise to the top of the profession; only four of them reached the bench of the High Court during the years 1850-1901.

Though they existed prior to the Municipal Corporation Act of 1835, the recorders or part-time borough quarter-sessions judges came into their own as a result of that legislation. By the last quarter of the nineteenth century there were approximately 100 recorderships in England and Wales. In contrast with the two offices already discussed, a barrister became a recorder once he had already begun to establish a professional reputation. Appointments usually went to juniors, but in some instances QCs were chosen, especially for larger and more prestigious boroughs. In 1880 14 per cent of the sitting recorders had taken silk prior to receiving an appointment to the municipal bench. By the terms of the Municipal Corporation Act, recorders had to be barristers of at least five years' standing, although among men in office in 1880 for example, most had been in practice for ten years or more at the time of their selection.(84) A recordership, despite its judicial character, did not disqualify a barrister from continuing to practise; on the contrary - it was a prominent landmark in the careers of rising members of the profession. A quarter of nineteenth-century QCs and of late-Victorian High and Appeals Court judges held this office at some time or another.

Serjeants and Silks

The coif of the serjeants and the silk gown of the QCs marked the barristers who wore them as senior members of the bar. These men were prohibited, at least since the mid-nineteenth century, from doing chamber work. In addition, they were briefed together with a junior barrister and they had to have chambers in London. However, the fortunes of the two orders in the second half of the century were very different (as is illustrated in Table 3.2). For the serjeants, who had lost their monopoly of practice in the Court of Common Pleas in 1846, the Judicature Acts of 1873 and 1875 sounded the death knell of their order. By contrast the QCs not only increased in numbers in accordance with the expansion of the bar but they became, as we have seen already, the almost absolute rulers of the profession through their domination of the benches of the inns of court. In the last quarter of the nineteenth century, approximately one practising barrister in six became a silk gownsman.

While taking rank became almost an essential step for a man who hoped for a judicial appointment in the courts of Westminster, there were risks involved and some men who thrived as juniors failed as leaders. The practical realities that confronted a barrister who was considering whether or not to apply for promotion were enumerated by John Taylor Coleridge in 1828:

> By taking rank I should certainly give up a thousand a year in income, by sacrificing my commission [in bankruptcy], the sessions, and certain classes of business inconsistent with that rank; this you may suppose would strain me very much for the time, especially too when the rank itself is expensive in the act of taking and it would hardly be possible to avoid some increase of general expense. I reckon that I ought to have £1500 to speculate upon, which I fear I am not in the way to lay up for the purpose.(85)

Although united by their membership in a senior professional fraternity, the QCs were far from forming a homogeneous elite. For some this was the final stop in their careers in the legal profession, while for others it was merely a springboard that would take them to the judicial bench, the woolsack or even to a senior cabinet post. There was a direct relationship between the age at which a barrister took silk and his chances of reaching high office.(86) Clearly, a man who achieved a reputation that justified his taking rank in his late

Table 3.2: QCs and Serjeants Appointed to the Judiciary 1790-1901

High Court Judges	Queen's Counsel		Serjeants	
	No.	%	No.	%
1790 - 1820	16	59	5	19
1820 - 1850	24	59	7	17
1850 - 1875	44	76	9	5
1875 - 1901	46	87	-	-
Count Court Judges				
Initial Appointments (1847)	4	10	2	5
1847 - 1874	7	23	3	10
1875 - 1901	16	36	-	-

Table 3.3: Age at Time of Becoming Queen's Counsel

	Under 42		42-46		Over 46		Unknown	
	No.	%	No.	%	No.	%	No.	%
Chief Justice/ Law Lords	14	78	3	17	1	6	0	0
Lords of Appeal/ Master of the Rolls/ President PDA	11	35	16	52	4	13	0	0
Puisne Judges	7	16	23	53	13	30	0	0
County Court Judges	2	7	7	26	16	59	2	7
Queen's Counsel 1800 - 1901	27	17	48	31	70	45	10	6

thirties or early forties, that is within fifteen years of his call, was more likely than other men to merit an appointment to the benches of the superior courts. To illustrate this point I have, in Table 3.3, compared the ages at which several groups of office-holding barristers took silk. The correlation between the age at which a man took silk and his eventual professional destination could hardly be more striking, especially in the 41 and under and the 47 and older categories. Over three-quarters of the law lords became QCs before the age of 42, compared to just over a third of appeals court judges, under a sixth of the puisnes and only a fourteenth of county court judges. The proportions for those who took silk after age 46 are almost exactly reversed.

County Court Judges

Of all the legal ranks and offices, none came under more frequent and persistent attack in the nineteenth century than the County Court judgeship. It was said that 'private and political expediency alone governs promotion' to the benches of the County Courts and that 'the profession has become thoroughly reconciled to the fact that any and every justification except learning and experience justify selection for the bench of the inferior courts'.(87) As a consequence 'from time to time men were appointed County Court Judges who not only had no reputation as lawyers, but, worse still, had the reputation of being no lawyers.'(88) As a result, it was claimed that 'the Bench itself is brought into contempt, which is peculiarly hard upon the many able judges who administer justice in those courts'.(89)

    Part of the problem can be traced to the character of these judgeships. They were described in 1847 by the Law Times as 'an office neither very lucrative nor very agreeable'.(90) In the first place most of the judges were exiled to the provinces permanently, and except in large centres, were deprived of professional society. Second, the salaries were low. Until 1850 the judges had been paid by fees and in some districts they were able to earn £2,000 or even £3,000 per annum. In 1850 the fee system was replaced by salaries that were usually £1,200 but on some circuits were £1,500. In 1865 £1,500 was fixed as a standard salary for all County Court judges.(91) That same year Lord Cairns issued an order forbidding judges to conduct arbitration for fees - hitherto a means of supplementing the low judicial salaries.(92) In 1888 Parliament imposed a general prohibition on private practice, including arbitration, on the judges.(93) Not surprisingly these conditions meant that the more successful members of the profession were loath to apply for appointment to the County Court bench.

    Despite these shortcomings there was never a dearth of candidates for these positions. Merit is often difficult to assess, as are the reasons for particular appointments, but it is possible to indicate in general terms the degree to which professional reputation was taken into consideration. Excluding the first sixty judges, who were appointed under unique conditions,(94) I have divided the men who held this office into three main categories according to their pre-judicial achievements: 1. men who had not practised law (4 per cent); 2. men who had tried to make their way at the bar but without any significant results and probably saw the security of a judicial appointment as a most attractive proposition (37 per cent); 3. men who had gained moderate success as advocates but had decided to retire from active practice (59 per cent including 35 per cent who were QCs or serjeants).

While these statistics make it possible to summarize concisely the qualifications, or lack thereof, of County Court judges in the nineteenth century, they hide almost as much as they reveal. Fortunately other evidence is available that can be used to indicate some of the motivations that were involved in these appointments. There were several reasons that may have prompted relatively successful barristers to apply for one of these judgeships. In the first place, as we shall see later, while the greatest advocates earned many times the County Court judge's salary of £1,500, the average barrister did not. Second, most of the men who became judges did so in their mid-50s or early 60s, at a time when their powers as advocates and their physical strength may have begun to decline. Third, by that stage of their careers it had become abundantly clear that they could no longer expect other more attractive promotions, and the comparative repose offered by a County Court may have seemed the best prospect available.

At this juncture a few case histories seem appropriate. In 1877 Lord Selborne wrote to Lord Cairns on behalf of Downes Griffith who was 'not long since Attorney-General at the Cape, (where he did well, but was obliged to come home on account of the climate not suiting his health)'. According to Selborne, Griffith 'is a gentleman, of kindly disposition, and conciliatory manners, and would no doubt, have been doing a good business, but for the difficulty of recovering a connexion once interrupted. He is in the prime of life and his health is, I believe quite re-established.'(95) Selborne's solicitations had their desired effect and Griffith was appointed judge of the Staffordshire County Court in that same year. In 1898 Kenneth Muir-Mackenzie, a barrister and permanent secretary of the Lord Chancellor's department, wrote to Lord Halsbury to suggest the appointment of Robert Woodfall to a County Court judgeship:

> [James Broughton] Edge has for a long time besieged you to move him to London [where there was a vacancy at the Middlesex County Court], and though I don't think him the highest class of man, he is an active and able Judge & would do very well. Then, if his court at Plymouth & in

> Devonshire were vacant, surely you might offer it to Woodfall. He is certainly entitled by abilities and practice to an appointment of that kind, and I have always understood that a South country life is what is required of his health.(96)

Apparently the Lord Chancellor, Edge and Woodfall concurred with this proposal and shortly thereafter the deal was concluded.

The final example suggests the part that personal and political considerations could play in the selection of a lower court judge. In September 1870 Lord Hatherley named Edmond Beales to the County Court bench. In 1872 Lord Salisbury criticized the appointment to which Hatherley replied:

> He [Beales] was deprived of an income of £700 or £800 a-year because he attended that meeting [Hyde Park reform riots] to which reference had been made, and deprived of it [by Lord Cockburn] on the ground that, being a revising barrister, he might be suspected of partiality. He had held that office six years, and nobody ever complained of his conduct;...Being dismissed from the post of revising barrister he lost other business in the Court of Chancery, which he had always discharged well; the deprivation of office reduced him to ruin; and I thought it only right and just, as he had been so reduced to ruin for an expression of political opinion, that he should be restored to competence.(97)

The nineteenth-century County Court judge is usually pictured as a failed barrister or a barrister in name only, who reached the bench despite the absence of professional ability. There were undoubtedly men who became County Court judges solely as a result of connection or the misuse of patronage. In part we can attribute this situation to the lack of enough qualified applicants; this might have been remedied if the financial inducements had been more generous. Furthermore, it seems likely that some suitable men chose to join the bench only after their abilities had begun to diminish due to age or illness. Nevertheless almost 60 per cent of the judges had achieved some professional success before their elevation and just over one quarter were leaders, although on average they achieved that distinction at relatively advanced ages (Tables 3.2 and 3.3). Unfortunately the more outrageous appointments and the public criticism that they justifiably engendered have resulted in the entire bench acquiring a reputation that it did not completely deserve.

The Law Officers of the Crown
Since 1814 the Attorney- and Solicitor-General have been

officially recognised as the heads of the practising bar of England and Wales. As counsel to the government they epitomised the conjunction of careers in law and politics; however, a full examination of the political character of their offices will have to wait until a later chapter. The law officers were usually rewarded for their services with a seat on the bench. In the nineteenth century 80 per cent of the Attorneys-General and 70 per cent of the Solicitors-General became judges when they left the bar and of these the vast majority (87 per cent and 69 per cent respectively) entered the judiciary at middle-ranking or senior positions. By tradition the post of the Chief Justice of the Common Pleas, and after 1881 that of the Lord Chief Justice of England, were said to be the special prerogative of the Attorney-General.(98) In conformity with the wave of earnestness that influenced the distribution of legal patronage between the mid-1860s and the mid-1880s, Gladstone tried to eliminate the practice of granting the law officers of the crown an almost inalienable right to succeed to senior judicial offices. In 1874 Lord Selborne explained the Prime Minister's policy:

> What Mr. Gladstone did, in the appointment of James & Harcourt, was, to state to them in writing...that the offices of A.G. and S.G. if accepted by them, must be accepted on the distinct understanding that they were not accompanied by any title to claim the succession to any Judicial office, on the footing either of any former usage or otherwise.(99)

Nevertheless, even after 1874 the law officers almost invariably ended their legal careers as judges. Of the 15 Attorneys- and Solicitors-General who served between 1875 and 1900, only three - Sir Frank Lockwood, Sir Henry James and Sir Edward Clarke - never graced the bench.(100)

The law offices were such well-travelled paths to the bench in the nineteenth century that apparently even an unsuccessful candidature could help a barrister qualify for a judicial appointment. In 1873, Lord Coleridge had indicated to Fitzjames Stephen that if he could win election to the House of Commons he stood a good chance of becoming Solicitor-General.(101) In the event he lost and the government selected William Harcourt instead. Shortly afterwards, while still smarting from the disappointment, he wrote 'I believe too that my chances of a judgeship would be only much improved by all that has happened. I had very much rather be a judge than a Sol^r Genl.'(102)

Superior Court Judges
The ambition to sit on the bench of one of the superior courts of Westminster must have stirred every practising English

barrister at one time or another, yet only a tiny minority (less than one in twenty) ever arrived there. In fact during the nineteenth century it became more difficult than ever to attain that objective, since the number of judgeships failed to keep pace with either the growth of the profession or of the general population. In 1800 there were 12 common law judges: 2 Chief Justices, a Chief Baron and 9 puisne judges divided into three courts - King's Bench, Common Pleas and Exchequer. At the same time the Court of Chancery had only two judges - the Lord Chancellor and the Master of the Rolls; the latter only began to preside in court in his own right beginning in 1833. The number of puisne judges in the common law courts increased to 12 in 1830 and 15 in 1868. In 1881 a reform in the judicial system resulted in the abolition of the offices of Chief Justice of the Court of Common Pleas and Chief Baron, leaving one Chief Justice and 14 puisne judges in the new Queen's Bench Division of the High Court. A vice-chancellor was appointed to the Court of Chancery in 1813 and two others were added in 1841. Thirty-five years later the vice-chancellors were re-styled Judges of the Chancery Division of the High Court and their number was increased to four in 1877 and five in 1881. In 1851 a new Appeals Court in Chancery was established with two Lords Justices. The Judicature Acts of 1873 and 1875 created a new Court of Appeal, and increased the number of judges to six; in 1881 the number declined to five on the death of Lord Justice James. In 1876 the failure of Parliament to abolish the judicial functions of the House of Lords, and the reorganisation of that body was followed by the creation of two Lords of Appeal in Ordinary - one English and one Scottish. In 1881 an Irish Lord joined them.(103) Two other senior judicial offices - one in the Prerogative Court of Canterbury and the other in the High Court of Admiralty - that had previously been filled by the civilian advocates of Doctors Commons, were opened in 1859 with the fusion of the two professions. A final category of superior court judges that must be mentioned here consisted of the four paid members of the Judicial Committee of the Privy Council, appointed in 1871. Of these men, only one remained in office in the 1880s. To summarize we find that at the beginning of the nineteenth century there were 14 royal judges; by 1850 there were 20 and by 1885, 31.

The judges whom I have just enumerated did not constitute a homogeneous elite but rather a stratified one. Significant differences in income, status and power created a clearly graduated pecking order. A judge who entered near the bottom could progress upward within the hierarchy by means of promotion or as it was known in the profession, 'translation'. There were objections to this process. Critics contended that it undermined the principles of judicial independence by encouraging ambitious judges to become subservient to the wishes of the government in return for the promise of advancement. Nevertheless it was common practice in the second half of the nineteenth century; between 1850 and 1901 85 per cent of the Lords Justices of Appeal, Presidents of the PDA Division and Masters of the Rolls and 42 per cent of the law lords, Lord Chief Justices and Lord Chancellors were appointed by means of translation.

Appointment to the bench of the Supreme Court of Judicature did not simply mark the elevation of a barrister to the elite of his profession. Rather, at the highest levels it served as one of the principal access routes leading from the professional middle classes to the heart of the governing elite. For the moment however, a full-scale examination of the convergence of law and politics must be postponed and we must content ourselves with the task of identifying the elements that made for successful careers at the bar.

THE DETERMINANTS OF SUCCESS

Recently social scientists have attempted to use sophisticated statistical methods to identify those factors in a lawyer's background, both professional and pre-professional, that contributed to a successful career. I will briefly describe two of these as useful springboards for my own work. Howard Erlanger examined national data on American lawyers in private practice for the years 1973-4.(104) As in most other studies of the legal profession in the United States he chose the size of law firms as the best indicator of a lawyer's professional status. His conclusions are that social and educational background tell only a small part of the story of success. Father's occupation, while significant in determining which men would become lawyers, only had a limited impact on the type of firm that the newly qualified attorney would join. Somewhat more significant was the law school attended and academic achievement there. He concludes that 'these findings invite the study of institutional and market forces involved in the establishment of careers and the subsequent attainment of status'.(105) The other study is concerned with British judges who sat on the benches of the superior courts between 1876 and 1972.(106) The author here defines success by the highest level of judicial office achieved: High Court (puisne and Chief judges); Court of Appeal (Masters of the Rolls and Lords Justices); House of Lords (the law lords). By comparing the social, educational and professional characteristics of the judges who sat in the Court of Appeal and in the House of Lords to the entire group of judges, he identified the ten most significant factors for predicting the success of members of the judiciary. He concludes that these factors included both 'ascription- and achievement-based characteristics' as we might well expect, but it is surprising 'to find such relatively remote ascriptive characteristics as paternal status indicators playing major roles in determining political recruitment given the social similarities characterising the...[two] groups.'(107)

Two main elements limit the application of the first (American) study to our work. Size of firm is an irrelevant factor with regard to the English bar at which all practice is individual or solo. Furthermore, we are primarily concerned with success at the end of a long career while Erlanger emphasizes the status achievement of lawyers at the beginning of their careers. While Tate has chosen indicators of success comparable to the ones I have utilised, his article is flawed both from historical and methodological points of view. By treating the entire judiciary from 1876 to 1972 as a single unit he obscures important changes that occurred in the recruitment of judges during those 96 years. Thus he obtains an average that does not accurately identify the crucial stages of a legal career either in the 1870s or in the 1970s. The other problem is that the analysis is based on a comparison between all judges and a high status subset, but this tells us only a little about those factors that determine success at the bar. What we want to compare is the characteristics of the judiciary and those of their recruitment stratum - the practising bar. This is precisely what I will be doing in the following few pages.

The task of plotting an ideal career for a nineteenth-century barrister, taking him from his entry into an inn of court to a seat in a senior judicial post, is easy enough. The father of our candidate should be a successful professional or businessman who could afford to support his son during the early lean years and also introduce him to business in order for him to show his talents. The barrister should have attended an elite public school followed by a good degree at Oxford or Cambridge, preferably in an elite college. Having been called to the bar in his mid-twenties, our ideal barrister should have established a secure and prospering junior practice within five to ten years. If he was a common law specialist he may well have become a recorder at this stage of his career. He would become a QC in his late thirties or early forties - the sooner the better. He would then in all probability begin thinking about entering politics in order to boost his professional prospects, most likely at the first general election after taking silk. Prior to 1886 his prospects would be brightest as a Liberal, but afterwards it was best to be a Conservative or Liberal-Unionist. His goal at this stage would be to combine a leading practice at the bar with an active political career and then with luck he should become a law officer by the age of 50 and finally a middle-ranking or senior judge by 60. In reality only the smallest minority of barristers followed careers that even approximated this ideal. There was no single road to the top and more than a few men arrived only after very circuitous journeys.

We must now try to discover what differentiated those men who rose to the top of the late Victorian bar from the rank and file. In assessing the determinants of success I will begin with a comparison of the social and educational backgrounds and the political careers of four groups of barristers and judges: 1. a sample of the entire bar for 1885; 2. a sample of the practising bar in 1885; 3. the elite of the bar (QCs, serjeants-at-law, law officers and judges of the superior courts) in 1885; 4. the judges appointed to the Supreme Court of Judicature from its inception in November 1875 until the death of Queen Victoria in January 1901.

The most striking aspect of the occupational section, as we noted in Chapter 1, is that at all levels barristers were recruited from an extremely narrow spectrum of English society. At the point of entry nearly half were the sons of professional men, a quarter were the sons of businessmen and urban gentlemen and a fifth were landowners and rural gentlemen.(108) Recruits from other classes that constituted the vast majority of nineteenth-century society were virtually non-existent. When we compare the occupational origins of the entire bar with those of the three groups of practising barristers, including the judges, we find only slight differences. There was an overall rise in the percentage of professionals and civil servants in the first three categories, but then this drops for the judges. The percentage of businessmen's sons rose considerably among the elite and the judges, though this may be more apparent than real since at the same time the urban gentry declined. Combining those two categories we find that they were constant for all four groups of barristers and judges. The one major exception to the general continuity among the upper-middle and middle-middle classes appears among the sons of clergymen who constituted 12 to 13 per cent of the entire bar, of all practising barristers and also of the elite practitioners, but 23 per cent of the judges.

The representation of the landed classes was far less stable than that of the professions and business: 21 per cent for the entire bar; 15 per cent for the practising bar; 9 per cent for the elite; and 15 per cent for the judges. We can probably attribute the decline among the practising barristers and the elite to the fact that within the landed classes a considerable number of eldest sons did not go to the inns of court in order to qualify for a profession but as a prelude to inheriting their paternal estates. The rise in the percentage of judges who were the sons of landowners as compared to their representation in the elite of the bar suggests that these men had some advantages over other barristers in securing top professional posts. Yet we must be careful not to exaggerate the significance of this phenomenon. In the light of all this evidence we must conclude that in Victorian England as in later twentieth-century America social origins were more important in determining who would enter the bar than who would succeed at it.(109)

Table 3.4 indicates that at least one of the educational factors, namely public school attendance, was significantly

Table 3.4: Social Origins of Late Victorian Barristers and Judges

Father's Occupation	N=725 Entire Bar 1885		N=272 Practising Bar 1885		N=54 Elite of the Bar 1885		N=53 Superior Court Judges 1875-1901	
	No.	%	No.	%	No.	%	No.	%
Bar	82	11	42	15	7	13	7	13
Solicitor	53	7	25	9	5	9	6	11
Clergy	85	12	34	13	7	13	12	23
Other Professions	83	11	29	11	10	19	4	8
Civil Service	36	5	16	6	3	6	0	0
Business	110	15	38	14	12	22	14	26
Urban Gentry	78	11	29	11	3	6	0	0
Land	117	16	27	10	4	7	8	15
Rural Gentry	37	5	15	6	1	2	0	0
Other	7	1	4	1	0	0	0	0
Unknown	37	5	13	5	2	4	2	4
			Summary					
Professions/Civil Service	339	47	146	54	32	59	29	55
Urban Middle Classes	527	73	213	78	47	87	43	81
Landed Classes	154	21	42	15	5	9	8	15

Education							
Elite Public Schools	175	24	70	26	14	26	22	42
Other Public Schools	54	7	34	13	10	19	6	11
Total Public Schools	229	32	104	38	24	44	28	53
Cambridge	200	28	85	31	20	37	15	28
Oxford	214	30	78	29	10	19	18	33
Other Universities	94	13	44	16	13	24	13	25
Total University	508	70	207	76	43	80	46	87
Trinity, Cambridge	102	14	47	17	8	15	9	17
Balliol & Christ Church	61	8	16	6	1	2	10	19
Elite Colleges	163	22	63	23	9	17	19	36

Politics							
MP	47	6	24	9	19	35	22	42
Unsuccessful candidates	18	2	11	4	5	9	8	15
Political lawyers	65	9	35	13	24	44	30	57

more important than occupational origins in affecting success at the bar. The advantage of public school old boys over other members of the bar in reaching senior offices is especially noticeable with regard to those who attended the most elite schools. These men accounted for a quarter of the entire bar, the practising bar and the elite of the profession, but for over 40 per cent of the judges. While some of the gap between the judges and the other groups was filled by other public schools, the former still retained a significant lead when the entire public school attendance record is considered. By contrast the relative size of the Oxbridge contingents in each of the four groups was almost identical; they ranged from 57 per cent to 61 per cent. Yet the percentage of total university attendance rose proportionally with success at the bar. Finally members of the judiciary were more likely than other barristers (practising and non-practising alike) to have attended elite colleges, with the greatest difference being at the two Oxford colleges - Balliol and Christ Church. Taken together the evidence suggests that the educational background, especially at school, was a significant factor in determining professional success. This may have been due to useful connections that were established in elite public schools, or to specific modes of behaviour that were instilled in pupils at these institutions, or to the fact that the elite members of the various occupational groups who were best able to promote their sons' legal careers, were also most likely to send them to these schools.

I will examine the relationship between a career at the bar and one in politics in detail in Chapter 6 but it is clear from Table 3.4 that there was a convergence between these two occupations at the upper levels of the legal profession. Only about 10 per cent of the entire bar and of the rank and file of the practising bar were politically active while nearly half of the elite members and a majority of the superior court judges had been either MPs or unsuccessful parliamentary candidates. This would suggest that a man who had already made a reputation at the bar probably increased his chances of receiving a judicial appointment if he tried his luck in politics. As we shall see later, however, there were instances, especially during Lord Halsbury's tenure of the woolsack, of political barristers who became judges despite a lack of success at the bar.

Researchers who study the causes of occupational success and mobility and career choice and development, most frequently focus their attention on social and educational determinants for the simple reason that such data are both easy to collect and eminently quantifiable.(110) From them the computer can produce vast amounts of statistics including rather precise rankings of the significance of particular characteristics. Yet such procedures despite their apparent accuracy cannot provide a satisfying answer to the question: why did certain barristers succeed in making it to the top of their highly competitive profession, when so many failed?

Even a partial solution to this riddle requires us to consider the importance of factors that are either non-quantifiable or only partially so, at least in regard to the nineteenth century. Let us begin with a consideration of the significance of connection and patronage. On the one hand we found that there was a degree of family connection among the judges that was much stronger than that dictated by mere chance. We also found that the sons of landowners and clergy - two high-status occupations - nearly doubled their representation within the judiciary as compared to the elite of the bar. In addition connections with solicitors, based on familial and occupational relationships, benefited nearly a quarter of the judges appointed in the second half of the nineteenth century. Finally the evidence suggests that useful professional connections were also to be found in the educational and political spheres - thus the preponderance in the ranks of the judiciary of old boys from the most elite public schools, of graduates of the most prestigious Oxbridge colleges, and of barristers who had entered the political lists. Yet on the other hand there were judges who succeeded despite a lack of valuable connections, as well as men who had access to patronage but nevertheless failed to make significant progress at the bar. In the light of this rather equivocal testimony it would seem reasonable to conclude that in so competitive a profession, while patronage may have given a man a headstart over others, it probably did not provide its beneficiary with an insurmountable lead over less fortunate men.

The second of the less easily quantifiable factors that we must consider is ability. The foremost components of this elusive concept - forensic skills - were unquestionably crucial elements in the making of a successful legal career, yet their assessment is extremely difficult. We can depend to some extent upon the judgements of contemporaries where these are available. Another possibility and a more practical way of looking at the relationship between ability and achievement is to plot the number of appearances made by individual barristers in the law reports and the number of cases won during an extended period of time against their receipt of professional ranks and offices. Although I have not done this yet in any comprehensive way, a few short samplings suggest that the correlation between courtroom success and official recognition is probably quite high. Of course the really crucial questions deal with the extent to which ability in court is predictive of an eventual judicial appointment, and the frequency of anomalous cases.

Interestingly enough, legal knowledge was not in itself seen as a qualification for the bench in England. This continues to the present day and is emphasized by the virtually complete division between academic and practising lawyers - the former segregated in the universities and the latter in the inns of court. There was one well-known case in the Victorian period in which a man became a judge on the basis of legal learning alone, but this was a lone exception. In 1859 Lord Campbell named Colin Blackburn to the Court of King's Bench, on the basis of his professional publications including reports of Campbell's judgements. Blackburn had little practice and was a junior at the time of his appointment. As a consequence both the profession and the public were less than enthusiastic about this unorthodox selection. Nevertheless, as Holdsworth notes, Campbell's decision was vindicated by the appointee's conduct on the bench.(111) In recognition of his abilities, Blackburn became the first English Lord of Appeal in Ordinary in 1876, an office that brought with it a life peerage.

There is one final element of professional ability that deserves mention - that is the legal equivalent of a good bed-side manner. Due to the division of labour in the legal profession and the lack of unmediated contact between barrister and litigant, this characteristic is probably of less importance for an advocate than for a general practitioner in medicine or for the family solicitor. Nevertheless what T.H.S. Escott called 'a good presence, an agreeable manner' were qualities that probably stood the advocate in good stead, especially when coupled with the ability to assure clients, both laymen and solicitors, that he was the right man for the job and the one best able to secure a favourable decision in court or to give advice on legal matters.

One prerequisite for a successful legal career that commentators constantly emphasized was good health and stamina. In the closing years of the eighteenth century Thomas Ruggles, himself a barrister, wrote, 'Perhaps no truth is fixed on a firmer base, and no assertion needs investigation less than this; that a good constitution is necessary to insure success at the Bar'.(112) This point is reinforced by legal biography with its examples of men who left the bar for less strenuous pursuits. Health was the reason that Arthur Hobhouse, a future law lord, decided to abandon his large chancery practice and accept a charity commissionership in 1866, as he explained to Sir Stafford Northcote:

> I have never properly and thoroughly recovered the shock of my health in 1863. I find myself falling again into the same state, and determined it was foolhardy to run the same amount of risk again. The question then lay between alternatives of quitting work altogether at least for a substantial time and seeking some quiet path.... the former...would probably have involved as final a farewell to the Bar as I have now made...(113)

The two last determinants are by far the hardest to evaluate; the first are psychological traits and the second is fortune or luck. Numerous theories have been developed relating personality to choice of career while occupational guidance has become an important field of psychology.(114) The application of these theories to nineteenth-century barristers might yield very interesting results, although a major problem would be the availability of enough data in the form of memoirs and letters to allow for serious psycho-historical analysis. What for example was the relationship between success at the bar and ambition, aggressiveness or self-confidence?

The most amorphous of all the determinants of professional success is luck. As we have seen, a barrister on his way up the ladder of preferment had to make quite a few choices that had far-reaching consequences for his career. Without doubt making the correct move at the right moment involved skill in self-evaluation and in analysis of career options, yet it would be idle to deny that many of the results of a particular decision could not be known in advance and were in large measure fortuitous. The choice of a circuit, the taking of silk at a particular time, the acceptance of a professional office or entrance into the political arena could each have favourable or unfavourable outcomes that were critical to a barrister's future. Success in these crucial matters depended at least in part on fortune and therefore it is natural that many authors likened the bar to a lottery.(115)

I have not tried to give unequivocal answers to the question posed at the beginning of this section. Much more work is needed on the nineteenth-century bar and by the same token on other Victorian professions before we arrive at a satisfactory evaluation of the characteristics that were most conducive to success. What I hope that I have demonstrated here is the variety of factors involved and the fact that the most easily quantifiable data do not tell the entire story.

A SINGLE-CLASS PROFESSION

In distinguishing between the rank and file and the elite of the Victorian medical profession, Jeanne Peterson has written, 'While they all belonged to one profession they did not belong to the same social class.'(116) Since medical men were among the closest professional neighbours of the barristers, this evaluation seems to provide a convenient starting-point for a brief assessment of the structure of the practising bar in the later nineteenth century. According to Peterson, the struggle for the creation of a unified and autonomous medical profession gave permanent existence to two classes of doctors. On the one hand there were the general practitioners who treated the everyday maladies of the majority of the population and who formed the backbone of provincial medical practice. On the other there were the leading London physicians and surgeons, who provided medical services to men and women of wealth and influence, held appointments in the great London hospitals and became during the second half of the nineteenth century the unchallenged rulers of the profession. The elites' power was embodied in the rulers of the two most important medical corporations - the

Royal College of Physicians and the Royal College of Surgeons. After decades of competition within the medical profession and between doctors and lay patrons, a unified professional elite emerged in the last decades of the century that imposed its control on the medical schools in the leading London hospitals from its power base in the Royal Colleges. Official recognition of the professional status and authority of this elite was granted in 1884 with the establishment of the Conjoint Board Examinations that gave the two Colleges joint responsibility for the licensing of general practitioners.(117)

The gap between the two classes of medical men was enormous and virtually unbridgeable. Those who hoped to enter the elite had to follow a very strict career pattern that included medical education at a leading London medical school, followed by junior hospital appointments in their thirties and promotion to senior ones in their early forties. Thus the vast majority of medical practitioners were excluded from ever entering the upper echelons of the professional hierarchy from the first days of their careers.(118)

The bar presents a very different picture. While the benches of the inns of court were at least as autocratic and autonomous as the governing bodies of the Royal Colleges, access to the former was much more open. According to Dr Peterson's estimates, the medical elite accounted for only one per cent of all medical men.(119) By contrast the legal elite included as much as 20 per cent of the profession if calculated on the basis of membership of the benches of the inns of court and just under five per cent if restricted to the judges of the superior courts. But perhaps even more significantly, despite its hierarchical structure the bar, unlike medicine, did not consist of two distinct classes of practitioners. While it is possible to contend that barristers and solicitors represented two classes of lawyers their segregation into independent professions each with its own governing body and privileges prevented the emergence of a situation comparable to the one that existed among medical men.

Most barristers were recruited from a narrow stratum of British society, and all of them entered the profession through the same single portal - the call to the bar at one of the inns of court. Since most barristers came from comparable backgrounds and had been socialised in an identical professional atmosphere, a stronger degree of professional consensus and esprit de corps probably existed within the bar than in most other professions.

The lack of internal conflict was also a consequence of the fact that on the day of his call, each barrister who chose to practise advocacy in the Courts of England and Wales had in theory the same opportunity to advance as every other member of the bar. Of course in reality differences of talent, drive, connections and luck, as I noted above, gave some men advantages over their colleagues. Furthermore, there was a single ladder of preferment leading to membership of the professional elite, and though only a minority of the barristers were able to travel the entire distance, no pre-determined barriers prevented any member of the profession from trying his luck to reach the top. By the later nineteenth century even men who began their careers in the provinces were not automatically excluded from reaching the highest rungs on the professional ladder.

Many barristers who began practising law never succeeded in establishing themselves. Others took one of two steps before discovering that further progress was unlikely. There were many stopping places along the road that lead to the judiciary of the superior courts. However, none of these ranks or offices ever coalesced into a distinct professional class;(120) rather together they formed a finely-graded hierarchy in which every barrister had and knew his place.(121)

NOTES

1. Duman, 'Bar in the Georgian Era', pp. 90-1.
2. Martin-Leake Papers 85848.
3. Duman, The Judicial Bench, p. 37.
4. Inns of Court Commission, p. 41.
5. Ibid., pp. 35-6.
6. LJ, 8 (May 3, 1873), p. 254.
7. Select Committee on Legal Education, p. 37; Inns of Court Commission, p. 39. This was the position taken by Blackstone in 1785, Commentaries, vol. 1, pp. 25-6, 32-3.
8. Inns of Court Commission, p. 35.
9. Witt, Life in the Law, pp. 25-7.
10. Select Committee on Legal Education, p. 24.
11. Ibid., p. 291.
12. Ibid., p. 35.
13. Robert Hazell, 'Pupilage', in Robert Hazell (ed.), The Bar on Trial (1978), p. 83.
14. LT, 58 (March 20, 1875), p. 352.
15. The popularity of crammers can be gauged from the advertisements for their services appearing on the front page of the Law Journal. A typical example finds three separate advertisements without the name of the barrister/teacher but with references via a local bookseller. Fees were 10 guineas for 20 one-and-a-half hour lessons. There were also advertisements by solicitors for similar courses. LJ, 10 (February 13, 1875), title page.
16. Wharncliffe Minuments 576-23.
17. A.G. Gardiner, The Life of Sir William Harcourt (2 vols., 1923), vol. 1, p. 75.
18. Rt. Hon. Viscount Alverstone, Reflections of the Bar and Bench, p. 4.
19. Thomas Ruggles, The Barrister, or Strictures on the Proper Education for the Bar (2 vols., 1792), vol. 2, p. 69.
20. Coleridge MS d. 128 fo. 94.

21. Traditionally a barrister's chambers was not merely his professional office but often served as his living quarters as well, especially in the early years at the bar.
22. Inns of Court Commission, pp. 9, 48. The earliest reference that I have found to barristers clubbing together in a set of chambers is 1839 in Alfred E. Gathorne-Hardy (ed.), Gathorne Hardy First Earl of Cranbrook, A Memoir (2 vols., 1910), vol. 1, p. 35.
23. Derek Walker-Smith and Edward Clarke, The Life of Sir Edward Clarke (1939), p. 43.
24. Partnerships are not allowed at the bar but it is common practice for senior barristers to employ devils - junior barristers who help him prepare the case for presentation in court. The senior is completely responsible for the conduct of the case and remuneration for the services of the devil is a matter solely between the senior and junior barristers.
25. J.E.G. De Montmorency, John Gorell Barnes, First Lord Gorell (1902), p. 50.
26. Ibid., p. 51.
27. LJ, 28 (March 11, 1893), pp. 173-4.
28. Bryce MS 5, fo. 187.
29. J.B. Atlay, The Victorian Chancellors (2 vols., 1906), vol. 1, p. 286.
30. Ruggles, The Barrister, vol. 2, p. 68.
31. Peter Campbell Scarlett, A Memoir of the Right Honourable James, First Lord Abinger (1877), p. 49.
32. Richard Harris (ed.), The Reminiscences of Sir Henry Hawkins, Baron Brampton (2 vols., 1894), vol. 1, pp. 122-3.
33. Plowden, Grain or Chaff?, pp. 101-2.
34. James Fitzjames Stephens MS 7349/7, fo. 23.
35. Circuit Tramp, Pie-Powder, pp. 3-4.
36. Plowden, Grain or Chaff?, p. 121.
37. Emily Henderson (ed.), Recollections of the Public Career and Private Life of the Late John Adolphus (1871), p. 142.
38. Duman, 'Bar in the Georgian Era', p. 97.
39. De Montmorency, John Gorell Barnes, p. 52.
40. Select Committee on County Court Jurisdiction, BPP XI (1878), p. 152.
41. Law List 1874 and 1895.
42. Hansard, 3rd series, House of Lords, 118 (1833), col. 880.
43. LT, 74 (February 24, 1883), p. 294.
44. An indication of the quality of professional life and practice in Birmingham in the late 1870s was given by James Mottram, the County Court Judge there: 'There are 12 or 13 barristers presently practising in Birmingham, and there are two of them whose income is not less than 3,000 guineas a-year, not only out of the county court alone, but using the county court as a means.' Select Committee on County Court Jurisdiction, p. 152.

45. Ibid., p. 222.
46. For example Sir John Holker, Sir John Astbury and Sir William Kennedy. See also ibid., p. 222.
47. LT, 28 (February 28, 1893), pp. 139-40.
48. James Boswell, The Life of Samuel Johnson (1970), p. 683; M. Cottu, On the Administration of Criminal Justice in England and the Spirit of English Government (1822), pp. 143-4.
49. LJ, 5 (October 20, 1870), p. 702.
50. Fred E. Katz, 'Occupational Contact Networks' in Sigmund Nosrow and William E. Form (eds.), Man, Work and Society (New York, 1962), pp. 317-21.
51. Coleridge MS c. 289, fo. 81, 133.
52. Circuit Tramp, Pie-Powder, p. 54. On this point see also Devon and Exeter Gazette (May 27, 1898) that was included in the minutes of the Western Circuit, p. 57.
53. M.S. Hardcastle (ed.), The Life of John Lord Campbell (2 vols., 1881), vol. 1, p. 294.
54. R. Barry O'Brien, The Life of Lord Russell of Killowen (1901), p. 69.
55. In his biography of his brother, Leslie Stephen wrote, 'Among his best friends was Kenneth Macaulay, who became a leader on the Midland circuit, and who did his best to introduce Fitzjames to practice.' Leslie Stephen, The Life of Sir James Fitzjames Stephen (1895), p. 140.
56. Hansard, 3rd series, House of Commons, 223 (1876), col. 345. Whether Herschell meant that one barrister actually transferred the entire conduct of the case to another member of the bar is not clear. Such practice is against the modern etiquette of the profession and was also prohibited on the Norfolk Circuit in 1820. Bolton, Conduct and Etiquette at the Bar, p. 27; Norfolk Circuit, (March 14, 1820).
57. Lord Parmoor, A Retrospect (1936), p. 40.
58. Fitzjames Stephen benefited from his friendship with Arthur Coleridge, deputy clerk of the Midland Circuit, who 'was able to suggest to the judges that Fitzjames should be appointed to defend prisoners not provided with counsel. This led by degrees to his becoming well known in the Crown Court...'. Stephen, Sir James Fitzjames Stephen, p. 140.
59. Hansard, 3rd series, House of Commons, 285 (1884), col. 1546.
60. Hansard, 3rd series, House of Commons, 353 (1891), col. 567. According to a leading article in the Law Times, 'If it is desirable to keep a son as a junior off the circuit of his father who is a leader, how much stronger is the argument in favour of keeping sons out of the courts of their judicial fathers.' LT, 91 (June 13, 1891), p. 122. The Attorney-General, Sir Richard Webster, felt that barristers should try to avoid appearing before relatives on the bench. The Times, April 11, 1892 and Bar Committee, 9th Annual Statement (1891-92), p. 2.
61. The seven sons of judges were Sir Walter Phillimore,

Alfred Thesiger, Sir Arthur Channel, Sir Roland Vaughan Williams, Sir Charles Edward Pollock, George Denman, and John Lord Coleridge. Lord Penzance was the nephew of Lord Truro; Charles Lord Russell of Killowen and Sir Robert Romer were the fathers and grandfathers of superior court judges. Sir Samuel Martin and Sir Joseph Chitty were both sons-in-law of Sir Frederick Pollock, Edward Lord Macnaghten was the son-in-law of Sir Samuel Martin, Sir George Farwell was the son-in-law of Sir John Wickens and Sir Charles Watkins Williams was the son-in-law of Sir Robert Lush.

62. Thomas N. Talfourd, 'On the Profession of the Bar', The London Magazine and Review, n.s. 1 (1825), pp. 325-6.
63. Bryce MS UB 82 January 30, 1884.
64. Sir Gervais Rentoul, This is My Case (1944), pp. 46-7.
65. T.H.S. Escott, England Its People, Polity and Pursuits (1891), p. 556. See also Warren, Introduction to Law Studies, vol. 1, p. 56; Inns of Court Commission, p. 126.
66. Thomas Sadler (ed.), Diary, Reminiscences, and Correspondence of Henry Crabb Robinson (1872), p. 186.
67. Roundell Palmer, Earl of Selborne, Memorials Family and Personal (2 vols., 1896), vol. 1, pp. 246-7.
68. Walker-Smith and Clarke, The Life of Sir Edward Clarke, p. 44; Alverstone, Reflections on the Bar and Bench, pp. 39-40.
69. Hardcastle (ed.), Life of John Campbell, vol. 1, p. 48.
70. A.C.G. Liddell, Notes from the Life of an Ordinary Mortal (1911), p. 125.
71. Ibid., pp. 138-44.
72. Ibid., p. 245.
73. Katz, 'Occupational Contact Networks', p. 319.
74. O'Brien, Life of Lord Russell of Killowen, pp. 76-7.
75. James Fitzjames Stephens MS 7349/7 fo. 11.
76. George Harris, The Autobiography of George Harris (1888), p. 245.
77. Coleridge MS c. 289 fo. 152-3.
78. Diaries of Sir Thomas Noon Talfourd, vol. 3 (September 30, 1848).
79. J. Arnould, A Memoir of Thomas, First Lord Denman (2 vols., 1873), vol. 2, p. 228. In 1872 the Law Times raised the question of the propriety of extensive patronage being in the gift of the judges. LT, 53 (August 8, 1872), p. 291.
80. Holdsworth, History of English Law, vol. 1, p. 422; Coleridge MSS c. 289, fo. 138 and d. 295, fo. 134.
81. Hansard, 3rd series, House of Commons, 6 (1831), col. 1078.
82. Coleridge MS c. 289 fo. 143,228.
83. H.J. Hanham, Elections and Party Management, Politics in the Age of Disraeli and Gladstone (1959), p. 402.
84. Debrett's Illustrated House of Commons and the Judicial Bench (1880).

85. Coleridge MS c. 289 fo. 143.
86. The importance of the age at which a barrister became a QC as a measure of his future professional prospects was suggested in C. Neal Tate, 'Paths to the Bench in Britain; A Quasi-Experimental Study of the Recruitment of a Judicial Elite', Western Political Quarterly, 28 (1975), p. 123.
87. LT, 52 (November 18, 1871), p. 38 and 92 (October 10, 1891), p. 383.
88. Hansard, 3rd series, House of Commons, 229 (1876), col. 1322.
89. LT, 92 (October 10, 1891), p. 383.
90. LT, 8 (January 30, 1847), p. 380.
91. Abel-Smith and Stevens, Lawyers and the Courts, p. 36; Hansard, 3rd series, House of Commons, 180 (1865), col. 527.
92. Norfolk Circuit (March, 1872), p. 39. See also the comments of Judge Rupert Kettle about his own arbitration work. Judicature Commission, Second Report, BPP XX (1872), p. 386.
93. 51 & 52 Victoria (1888), cap. 43, section 14. By the terms of the original act creating the County Courts with several exceptions judges were prohibited from 'practice as a Barrister within the District for which his Court is holden under this Act'. 9 and 10 Victoria (1846), cap. 95, section VIII.
94. According to the act creating the County Courts, judges of the previously existing Courts of Requests were given first claims over the new judgeships. As a result some of the first County Court judges were not even barristers, but members of the lower branch. 9 and 10 Victoria (1846), sections IX-XII. On the Courts of Requests see W.H.D. Winder, 'Courts of Requests', Law Quarterly Review, 52 (1936), pp. 369-94.
95. Cairns MS PRO 30/51/9 letter 58.
96. Halsbury Papers BL Add. MSS 56370, fo. 115-16.
97. Hansard, 3rd series, House of Lords, 209 (1872), col. 440-1. In his defence of Beales, Hatherlay minimized his association with the reform agitation. He was at the time of the riots President of the Reform Association though he did not participate in them, preferring to lead one section of the marchers to Trafalgar Square on discovering that the gates of the park had been locked. DNB, vol. II, p. 9; John Stevenson, Popular Disturbances in England 1700-1870, (1979), p. 291.
98. Duman, Judicial Bench in England, pp. 84, 87-8. A recent study has found this connection less than entirely convincing. Edwards, Law Officers of the Crown, pp. 320-1.
99. Cairns MS PRO 30/51/9 letter 47.
100. Lockwood died in 1897 before the Liberals returned to power. James refused the office of Lord Chancellor in 1886 because of his unionist sympathies. He later served as Chancellor of the Duchy of Lancaster and sat as a law lord in appeals to the House of Lords. Clarke was offered the Mastership of the Rolls, but refused the offer. On this aspect of his career see below pp. 179-81.

101. James Fitzjames Stephen MS 7349/7 fo. 80.
102. Ibid., fo. 96.
103. On the judicial functions of the House of Lords see Robert Stevens, Law and Politics, The House of Lords as a Judicial Body 1800-1976 (Chapel Hill, 1978), passim.
104. Howard S. Erlanger, 'The Allocation of Status Within Occupations: The Case of the Legal Profession', Social Forces, 58 (1980), pp. 882-903.
105. Ibid., p. 899.
106. Tate,'Paths to the Bench in Britain', pp. 108-29.
107. Ibid., p. 127.
108. On homogeneity and closure in the highest levels of modern British society see John H. Goldthorpe, Social Mobility and Class Structure in Modern Britain (Oxford, 1980), pp. 45-6, 265.
109. Erlanger, 'The Allocation of Status Within Occupations', p. 899.
110. For example see Peter M. Blau and Otis Dudley Duncan, The American Occupational Structure (New York, 1967).
111. Holdsworth, History of English Law, vol. XV, pp. 492-7.
112. Ruggles, The Barrister, vol. 1, p. 7.
113. L.T. Hobhouse and J.L. Hammond, Lord Hobhouse, A Memoir (1905), pp. 20-1. See also Caroline Emelia Stephen, The Right Honourable James Stephen K.C.B., LL.D. (Gloucester, 1906), p. 13.
114. See Samuel Osipow, Theories of Career Development (New York, 1968).
115. For example Thackeray, Pendennis, p. 317; Adam Smith, An Inquiry Into the Nature and Causes of the Wealth of Nations (New York, 1937), p. 106.
116. Peterson, The Medical Profession, p. 243.
117. Ibid., Chapter IV.
118. Ibid., p. 137.
119. Ibid.
120. The medieval bar was divided into two classes - serjeants and apprentices (the precursors of the barristers). The separation of these two orders was emphasized by the segregation of each into its own inns. But the division was not absolute and in the natural course of events the leading apprentices graduated into the ranks of serjeants.
121. The rank and file rarely disputed the rights of the traditional governors to rule, although they sometimes expressed their dissatisfactions with their governors in the pages of the Law Times and Law Journal. Yet despite the general consensus and calm, conflict could not be entirely avoided as the events of 1894/5 indicated.

Chapter Four

THE COLONIAL BAR AND BENCH

According to one frequently expressed view, the British empire served as a source of outdoor relief for unemployed members of the English upper and middle classes, most especially for the professional men.(1) Since, as we have seen, overcrowding was an endemic problem for the nineteenth-century bar, one might well expect that under-employed barristers would have flocked to the colonies in the hopes of achieving success in a less competitive arena.

In order to assess the validity of applying generalisations about the professions and imperialism to the bar, this chapter will be devoted to an examination of the colonial legal profession and the recruitment and career patterns of barristers and office-holders in the three principal divisions of the empire: 1. Crown colonies ruled directly from London by the Colonial Office; 2. colonies possessing responsible governments;(2) and 3. India. As I hope to demonstrate, not only did the relationship between the metropolitan bars of the British Isles and those of the three types of colonies differ considerably, but even within each division there were substantial geographical and temporal variations.

CROWN COLONIES AND SELF-GOVERNING COLONIES

The Barristers
Unlike in England, there was no single portal of entry into legal practice in the colonies. The most typical means in the first half of the nineteenth century was to qualify as a barrister in England or Ireland or as an advocate in Scotland. Another course was open to graduates of Oxford and Cambridge who were eligible for admission to the bars of most colonies, presumably after a period of clerkship and informal study.(3) Just before mid-century New South Wales, the oldest of the Australian colonies, established a formal system of admission to the bar for men who had not qualified in the United Kingdom.

From the 1850s the regulations in that colony required candidates to pass a bar examination that tested their classical accomplishments, their background in basic mathematics, as well as their knowledge of legal history and of the principles of the law. In most instances university graduates were exempt from all but the legal papers.(4) A similar examination system was introduced in Victoria in 1859.(5) Finally in some colonies, Newfoundland for example, serving as an apprentice in the office of a barrister was enough to qualify a man as a member of the legal profession.(6)

In the middle decades of the nineteenth century the attractions of colonial practice must have been enormous for barristers who were unable to establish themselves at home. In 1863 the Law Times virtually encouraged the emigration of members of the bar by painting a rosy picture of the prospects that awaited a diligent advocate overseas:

> It is fortunate for the Bar of England that the growing wealth of the colonies and the dependencies opens an ever-widening field of employment far more than equivalent to the decrease of the demand at home....although the prospect at home is gloomy, there is a way to speedy success abroad, if only he [the fledgling barrister] has the right stuff in him as well as upon him....It is a mistake to suppose that any man with a wig and gown will do for the colonies. The demand for ability is quite as great there as here, incapacity is as readily detected and as speedily sentenced to neglect.(7)

In the years before the colonies were producing home-grown and educated barristers, they offered a relatively open field for English, Scottish and Irish lawyers.(8) Australia and South Africa were especially attractive with their temperate climates and large Anglo-Saxon populations.(9) However, by the 1870s, prospects in the more established colonies had begun to narrow, and as in England, connection and an independent income were extremely helpful if not entirely essential assets for the prospective barrister.(10) In 1890 a correspondent to the Law Journal warned inhabitants of Britain from attempting to establish a legal practice in Australia, particularly in New South Wales and Victoria.(11) Seven years later a similar plea appeared in that journal with regard to South Africa. This concluded with the warning: 'Let the ordinary advocate pause ere he waste his money on a South African adventure. For whatever money there may be here, there is certainly none to be made in the profession of the law.'(12)

Despite such warnings, British-born, bred and trained lawyers continued to look for professional opportunities in the colonies in the latter decades of the nineteenth century, although according to our random sample of the bar in 1885, they constituted only a minority (38 per cent) of all colonial practitioners. The sample also suggests that professional failure in the United Kingdom was not a significant factor in motivating British barristers to try their luck in the empire. None of the Scotsmen or Irishmen and only four of the nineteen Englishmen included in the sample had practised law at home before emigrating. Not surprisingly, those barristers who emigrated more often than not eschewed the warnings about the lack of opportunities in the more established colonies: 42 per cent went to colonies with responsible governments; 35 per cent went to India; and only 21 per cent went to one of the other colonies.

Of course newly minted barristers who arrived in the colonies from the inns of court were not necessarily strangers to those shores. Since the 1680s when the first Americans journeyed to London for their legal education, successful colonials had sent their sons to England for university studies and a sojourn at the inns of court. Whether this rather expensive course was followed for social or professional reasons, or a combination of the two, the late-nineteenth-century inns accommodated a sizeable contingent of colonials; they accounted for almost 10 per cent of the bar in 1885. Yet the evidence strongly suggests that those men who went to England to study law were not part of a Victorian brain-drain - on the contrary, the vast majority returned home shortly after completing their studies and being called to the bar. Thus colonials constituted only about three per cent of the practising English bar in 1885, while nearly two-thirds of the colonial practitioners at that date were either born or bred in the colonies.

Colonial barristers differed from their English colleagues not only in regard to their birthplace and their professional careers, but also in terms of their social and educational backgrounds. The colonial practitioners included proportionally fewer sons of clergymen, landowners and to a lesser degree barristers, and more sons of colonial civil servants and merchants, than did their English counterparts. The explanation of these differences in occupational origins seems to be fairly straightforward. Civil servants and merchants with colonial connections were in admirable positions to aid their sons during the early years of a legal career. The absence of the sons of clergymen and landowners testifies to the comparatively low occupational status of colonial legal practice. This is borne out by the fact that while most barristers who practised in the colonies were recruited from the middle classes, as is clear from Table 4.1, members of the upper professions and gentlemen by birth were under-represented. Due in part to the predominance of colonial-born men in the colonial bars, an elite English education - public school and Oxbridge - was much less common there than among English practitioners. In addition there was a somewhat greater probability that the latter would have received a university education prior to entering the legal profession. All of this leads to the conclusion that

Table 4.1: The Social Quality of Colonial and English Barristers 1885

	Upper Professions		Gentlemen by Birth		Public School		Cambridge/ Oxford		Elite Colleges		All Universities	
	No.	%	No.	%	No.	%	No.	%	No.	%	No.	%
English Bar N=272	78	29	120	44	104	38	163	60	63	23	207	76
Colonial Bar N=72	16	22	22	31	10	14	25	35	12	17	47	65

while it would be incorrect to see the typical colonial barrister as coming from a disadvantaged background, he was less privileged than his counterparts who practised in England.

The Office-holders
Legal patronage in the Crown colonies was vested in the Colonial Secretary. Included were the junior posts of district and stipendiary magistrates and the senior ones of queen's advocates, Attorneys- and Solicitors-General and chief and puisne justices of colonial high courts. In actual fact, offices worth less than £200 were usually filled by the local governor, while more valuable appointments were made in London by the minister himself.(13) This was a daunting task if it were to be done well, and probably more difficult than the one that faced the Lord Chancellor in distributing domestic legal patronage. In the first place the Colonial Secretary, unlike his colleague on the woolsack, was hardly ever a barrister and was therefore forced to rely entirely upon the advice and judgement of others in assessing the professional qualifications of a candidate. Second, in marked contrast to the centralised bar in England and Wales, whose leaders were well-known to the judges by reputation, if not personally, there was little information about the enormous number of lawyers throughout the empire and the United Kingdom who were potential candidates for colonial legal offices. Finally, there were considerable differences between the judicial systems of the particular colonies, as a result of their varied colonial heritages. While in some instances the common law tradition alone prevailed, in others English law co-existed with or was even subordinate to Roman Dutch law or French law. Since few barristers in the empire had the training requisite for the task of administering justice within these non-English legal systems, unqualified men necessarily received important posts.(14)

Other than a formal qualification as a lawyer, no fixed standards for colonial appointments existed in the nineteenth century. Therefore the Colonial Secretary had enormous latitude in distributing his valuable patronage.(15) As a consequence, he was deluged by requests from public figures who hoped to influence his choice in favour of relatives or acquaintances. Lord Carnarvon's correspondence during the years that he headed the Colonial Office (1866-7 and 1874-8) amply illustrates the use of connections to secure colonial appointments and the motivations of the office-seekers themselves. In 1866 the Scottish Lord Advocate wrote requesting that Carnarvon consider David Peter Chalmers for a West African magistracy. The Lord Advocate described Chalmers as 'a member of the Bar [in Scotland]...and...a well educated and well principled gentleman' who had invested his own fortune and that of his mother in Overend, Gurney & Co. When that financial institution failed in 1866 he was forced to look for a secure source of income. According to his patron, 'But for that circumstance I do not think he would have been disposed to accept the situation.'(16) During Carnarvon's second term in the Colonial Office the patronage secretary to the Treasury, Sir William Hart Dyke, made a number of requests on behalf of men who were active in Conservative Party affairs. He requested the Chief Justiceship of Ceylon, one of the more lucrative of the colonial judgeships, for Henry T. Wrenfordsley who unsuccessfully contested Peterborough for the Conservatives in 1868 and 1874.(17) He also put forward Henry Burford-Hancock, Secretary to the Conservative Association in Marylebone, for Attorney-General of Jamaica, and Francis Henry Lascelles, who was said to have been recommended by 'several influential supporters of the Government', for Advocate-General of Ceylon.(18) Chalmers and Burford-Hancock received the posts that they sought. Wrenfordsley was considered unqualified professionally for so senior an appointment as the Chief Justice of Ceylon, but he was named as a puisne judge in Mauritius and eventually filled the offices of Chief Justice in Western Australia, Fiji and the Leeward Islands.(19) Although none of these four candidates for colonial legal offices had made any mark at the bar prior to their nominations, only Lascelles never received an appointment.

In the light of these examples it is no wonder that criticism of the manner in which colonial legal patronage was disbursed was rife at mid-century.(20) Commentators insisted that not only were the judges ignorant of the legal systems that they administered, but that appointments were made with an utter disregard of the abilities of the candidates.(21) According to the conclusions of one royal commission, officials were sometimes selected from among 'either untried men, or what is worse, from men who have tried and failed.'(22) This sad state of affairs was not entirely the responsibility of the officials in London. There was a general consensus that the problem stemmed from the difficulty of recruiting the most able members of the legal profession to fill posts for which the salaries were low compared to the incomes of leading barristers.(23) This was compounded by the lack of status and the difficult and unhealthy living conditions frequently encountered in the colonies.(24) The reaction of George Harris, a rather unsuccessful member of the legal fraternity, to the offer of a colonial judgeship in 1856 was perhaps typical of the attitude of English barristers towards such appointments at that time. He refused the office and suggested that a post in England worth £1,000 per annum would be much more to his liking.(25)

By the 1890s, according to a leading article in the Law Journal, the situation had changed. Just as colonial bars had in the meantime become overcrowded, so the demand by barristers for colonial legal appointments had increased.(26) However, the more successful English barristers were still not seduced by opportunities in the empire, as is suggested by Lord

Justice Bramwell's reaction on hearing the offer of the Chief Justiceship of Queensland made to John Day QC in 1880. He is reported to have said, 'Are you mad, to think of leaving your friends and burying yourself in a Colony? Stay in England, and there is nothing to prevent you from rising to the highest rank of your profession.'(27) Yet, for less talented members of the profession, the picture painted by the journal must have been almost irresistible. It contrasted 'legal life in London with its precarious successes, its constant failures, and its deferred hopes, and the sickness of heart that accompanies them' with 'life in some ancient and even infant civilization, where honour and comparative wealth awaits.'(28) The same article suggested that with the exception of the West African colonies, a barrister of less than seven years' standing could not at that time hope for a prime appointment, and that most appointees were chosen from men who had already proved their capacities within the colonial legal service.(29)

Nineteenth-century opinion about whether it was preferable to recruit colonial legal officials from local barristers or from United Kingdom practitioners, was not unanimous. In 1846 Thomas Norton, the Chief Justice of Newfoundland, told a select committee, 'I think nothing can be more objectionable, in a small community, than to elevate to a judgeship a man who has connections in the country, and has local prejudices, and knows everybody's business.'(30) In contrast to this view a correspondent to the Law Journal in 1874 complained that 'whenever any important judicial appointment, either a chief or a puisne judgeship or attorney-generalship, becomes vacant, the colonial barrister is invariably overlooked and ignored by the authorities, and a member of the English bar appointed thereto.'(31)

Two examples of the relative positions of colonial and United Kingdom barristers with regard to access to judicial offices are provided by Australia and New Zealand on the one hand and Jamaica on the other. Until the 1860s practitioners from the United Kingdom held a monopoly over judicial appointments in Australia and New Zealand. Even after the establishment of responsible government, the legal exclusion of locally trained barristers continued, though in New South Wales this anomaly was rectified in 1861(32). Nevertheless, only half of the Chief Justices who served in Australia's self-governing colonies between 1865 and 1901 were born there, while all three New Zealand chief justices during this period were born in the United Kingdom.(33) The starting point in Jamaica was exactly the opposite. In the 1840s judicial appointments on the island were restricted to locally practising barristers of at least five years' standing, and not until 1864 was an English practitioner appointed Attorney-General there.(34) Yet none of the colony's five chief justices who served between 1865 and 1901 had been born or had practised there. Three of these men had begun their careers in other colonies, and two had practised in England prior to arriving in Jamaica.

In order to assess more fully the impact of the export of professional men from the United Kingdom to the colonies on the distribution of senior legal offices, I have examined the backgrounds and careers of the 136 colonial chief justices who served in both Crown and responsible colonies between 1865 and 1901. Comparing the evidence on the geographical origins we find that while more than 60 per cent of the colonial barristers were born in the colonies, less than 40 per cent of the chief justices were born outside of the United Kingdom. This suggests rather strongly that while barristers born and raised in England, Ireland or Scotland were reluctant to go to the colonies early in their careers, at a later stage men who were only moderately successful in the United Kingdom saw the security of a colonial judgeship as preferable to the unending competition and an uncertain future at home.(35)

In fact a more detailed analysis of geographical and professional backgrounds of the colonial chief justices reveals that the picture is somewhat more complex than the preceding description would suggest. When the judges are divided according to the political status of the colonies in which they served, as in Table 4.2, we find that in those instances where judicial appointments rested with the authorities in London, barristers who were born, trained and practised in England were particularly favoured. By contrast, in the colonies with responsible governments, a majority of chief justices were local men who practised in the colonies, half of whom had acquired their legal qualifications outside of Britain. Even among the Crown colonies there were differences in the geographical origins of the chief justices. Englishmen dominated the benches of the African and Asian colonies, were less well-represented in the Caribbean region and were a rarity in Malta and Mauritius.(36)

The division between Crown colonies and those with responsible governments is also evident in regard to the career patterns of the chief justices. A few examples should suffice to make this distinction clear. Joseph Hutchinson was born in England and practised there for nine years before receiving an appointment as Queen's Advocate of the Gold Coast in 1888. In the following year he was promoted to the post of Chief Justice in that colony and he remained there until 1895 when he became Chief Justice of Granada. In 1897 he was transferred to Cyprus and ended his career as Chief Justice of Ceylon in 1906.(37) William Sheriff, son of the President of Nevis, was called to the bar at the Middle Temple and practised at the Antiguan bar from 1868 to 1872. In the latter year he became Attorney-General of the Bahamas. He was named Chief Justice of British Honduras in 1882. Four years later he accepted an appointment as a puisne judge in the Straits Settlements and finally in 1887 he became Chief Justice of British Guiana.(38)

Table 4.2: Backgrounds and Careers of Colonial Chief Justices 1865 - 1901

	N=112 Crown Colonies		N=24 Responsible Governments		N=136 Total	
	No.	%	No.	%	No.	%
Place of Birth						
England	55	49	2	8	57	42
Ireland	8	7	7	29	15	11
Scotland	7	6	2	8	9	7
Colonies	40	36	13	54	53	39
Unknown	2	2	0	0	2	1
Legal Qualification						
Inns of Court	89	79	9	38	98	72
Scots or Irish Bar	9	8	3	13	12	9
In Colonies	14	13	12	50	26	19
Pre-judicial Career						
English Practice	47	42	2	8	49	36
Scottish or Irish Practice	6	5	1	4	7	5
Colonial Practice	29	26	17	71	46	34
Colonial and U.K. Practice	3	3	2	8	5	4
Administrative Career	6	5	0	0	6	4
Unknown	21	19	2	8	23	17

Source: Colonial Office List 1865-1901.

John de Villiers was born in the Cape Colony and was called to the bar at the Inner Temple. He then returned home to practise, became Attorney-General of the Cape Colony in 1872, and a year later Chief Justice. In 1901 he became the first Chief Justice of the Union of South Africa.(39) Samuel W. Griffith was born in Wales but emigrated to Brisbane at age nine with his family. He qualified for the bars of New South Wales, Victoria and Queensland in the late 1860s. In 1876 he became a QC and the Attorney-General of Queensland. He held a number of ministerial posts in that colony between 1876 and 1893, and served as Premier in the years 1883-8 and 1890-3. In 1893 he became Chief Justice of Queensland and ten years later Chief Justice of Australia.(40) Frederick Darley was born and called to the bar in Ireland. He practised there for nine years and then in 1862 emigrated to New South Wales. He was a leading practitioner in the colony for twenty years. In 1878 he was made a QC and in 1886 he was appointed Chief Justice of New South Wales.(41)

In summary then we find that the men who were chief justices of the Crown colonies were more or less equally divided between those who had practised in the colonies and those who had practised in the United Kingdom. Once they were appointed to office, they rarely remained in a single colony for the rest of their careers, and were frequently transferred from one region to another. In most cases, a transfer signified a promotion in the colonial legal hierarchy as indicated by an increase in salary. By contrast, in the colonies with responsible governments, and in several Crown colonies as well, especially Mauritius, Malta and Natal, most chief justices either began their practice in the colonies or continued their professional careers there after practising briefly in the United Kingdom. In most instances they remained in that colony throughout their entire careers, though occasionally they spent some time in a neighbouring colony, especially in Australia and South Africa.

The evidence presented in the preceding pages indicates rather conclusively that the more developed colonies, those with established professional infrastructures, were less open to the influx of legal practitioners and office-holders from the United Kingdom than were newer colonies. Yet it would be premature to draw any final conclusions about the colonial legal profession before examining the largest of the imperial bars - namely that of the Indian subcontinent.

INDIA

The Barristers
While India was an integral part of the British empire, I have chosen to examine the legal profession there separately for several reasons. First, India was neither under the jurisdiction

of the Colonial Office nor did it have a responsible government; rather it was ruled by its own administrative establishment in the India Office, presided over by the Secretary for India. Second, Indian legal offices were by far the most valuable ones in the empire. Third, from the 1860s India was the most important example of a colony in which European and non-European barristers practised side by side. Finally, Indians were the first major group of non-Europeans to enter the inns of court as students and to qualify for the bar.

Advocates who practised in India in the nineteenth century were divided into two classes - barristers and vakils.(42) The barristers all qualified in the United Kingdom, predominantly at the inns of court, though some had been trained in Ireland or Scotland. They were the superior branch and had an absolute monopoly over practice before the Supreme Courts located in the three Presidency towns - Calcutta, Madras and Bombay. Furthermore, prior to 1862, barristers were exclusively Europeans; however in that year the first Indian, G.M. Tagore, was called to the bar at Lincoln's Inn.(43) By contrast the vakils or Indian-trained advocates were predominantly non-Europeans. They greatly outnumbered the barristers but were inferior to them in respect both to prestige and income.(44)

Until 1862 the vakils only practised in the courts established by the East India Company in the late eighteenth century, headed by Sudder Courts in each Presidency. In that year the old Supreme and Sudder Courts in Calcutta, Madras and Bengal were each amalgamated into a single High Court, and shortly afterwards a fourth High Court was permanently established in Allahabad. Vakils could practise in the new High Courts though still not on terms of complete equality with the barristers. Therefore, while this reform added considerably to the status and incomes of the vakils, they remained inferior to the barristers.(45)

Advocacy was the premier profession in nineteenth- and early twentieth-century India.(46) The law was particularly attractive because of its high status and the glittering prizes of wealth, influence and political power that accrued to its most successful practitioners. Once the English universities and the inns of court began to admit Indians, it was natural for them to want to take advantage of this opportunity.(47) Professional education in England became the ideal for those who were ambitious and could afford the considerable expense. To a certain extent this was probably due to a desire to emulate their colonial masters, but there were also more practical reasons. An English legal qualification was more prestigious, less demanding educationally and more remunerative than an Indian one, so that naturally those who were offered the choice went to London.(48)

Not only were many Indians anxious to obtain an English legal education, but they were encouraged to pursue this goal by the Government of India and by the relevant authorities in

London. According to one recent study, this policy emanated from the belief that an English-educated Indian legal intelligentsia would be pro-British.(49) In the long run the results were just the opposite, as Indian barristers became instrumental in the establishment and leadership of the Indian National Congress.(50) In order to foster their attendance at the inns of court, Indians were granted concessions by the Council of Legal Education in order to facilitate their call to the bar, while the inns allowed Indians and other colonial barristers to be called after eating eight terms of dinners instead of the standard twelve.(51)

Training in England was expensive, and an Indian who wanted to be a barrister either had to have a well-to-do father, find himself a generous benefactor or work to save the money out of his income. Despite the financial and cultural difficulties inherent in this course, hundreds of Indians went to London during the second half of the nineteenth century to join the inns of court, in much the same way that American colonists did a century and a quarter earlier. By 1885, at the end of the first generation of Indian barristers, there were 108 men from the sub-continent who were members of the profession, and of these almost two-thirds were practising in India.(52)

The social and occupational background of these men is displayed in Table 4.3. Indian barristers were recruited almost exclusively from the nation's social elite, though it is possible that a considerable number of men from far less illustrious origins, including 'scholarship boys', are concealed in the large number (21 per cent) with unknown origins. The social background of the Indian barristers resembled that of contemporary English barristers, except for the high percentage of men from the landed and official classes, which mirrored the structure of the English bar more than a century later.

The sons of lawyers did not hold a dominant position at the Indian bar. There were more landowners' sons and almost as many businessmen's sons. Furthermore the sons of landowners were even more successful than those of lawyers in establishing legal practices. In India, as in Britain, landowners, lawyers and businessmen were in enviable positions to help their sons during the early years of a career at the bar, both with the necessary financial aid and perhaps more importantly with connections and introductions to business.(53) Especially in the closing decades of the nineteenth century when the bar in India became increasingly overcrowded, connections became even more crucial both for native and European barristers. In these circumstances it is not surprising that the majority of Britons who practised in India at this time were not 'carpetbaggers' who came to exploit lucrative professional opportunities.(54) On the contrary, they were mostly men with Indian backgrounds, either having been raised there or having fathers whose careers in the military, the civil service or in the business had taken them to the sub-continent.

Table 4.3: The Social Origins of Indian Barristers 1885

Father's Occupation	Titled and Official Classes	Landowners	Lawyers	Civil Servants/ Other Professionals	Businessmen	Unknown	Total
No.	12	19	18	19	17	23	108
%	11	18	17	18	16	21	

Source: Foster, Men-at-the-Bar.

Although Indians were able to achieve parity with Englishmen in regard to their professional qualifications by going to London for training, real equality of opportunity was more elusive. As demonstrated in recent studies, Indians were at a distinct disadvantage. Not only did Europeans receive most of the plum briefs on the original side of the High Courts but they were preferred by both British and Indian solicitors alike. This was apparently due to the belief that Indian barristers were less likely to win cases in the High Court. While the professional opportunities began to improve in the 1880s, most Indians who tried their luck at the bar were not successful.(55) However for the minority who did crack the profession, as we shall see in the next chapter, the sky was the limit.

The Office-holders
Despite the similarities between the English and Indian legal systems, there was one striking difference with regard to the qualifications for judicial office. In England the benches of the superior courts and of some local ones, such as the county courts, were the absolute monopoly of members of the bar. The usual procedure was for a man to begin his career as a practising barrister and then to be promoted to the bench at a latter stage after having proved his ability. While as we have seen a barrister who had not practised or had failed in trying was sometimes given inferior court appointments, this did not vitiate the basic premiss that judicial posts were the perquisites of the practising bar. In this way England differed from most of continental Europe where a lawyer upon qualifying chose either to be an advocate or to enter the separate career of judicial service. Only men who chose the latter course could become judges. The advocates were destined to remain advocates for their entire professional careers.

In India, after 1861, elements of both of these systems were combined. According to the India High Courts Act of that year, at least one third of the High Court judges, including all of the chief justices, were to be chosen from men who had qualified at the bars of England, Ireland or Scotland. In addition, another third of the appointments was to be given to members of the Indian Civil Service, and the ICS also retained its monopoly over the higher subordinate court offices, such as district judgeships. Finally, other men, namely vakils, who were not qualified barristers but who had practised before the High Court for at least ten years, were eligible for appointment to its bench.(56)

Due to the central position of the Indian Civil Service in the administration of justice, it was not unusual for civil servants also to be members of the bar. In some instances these men already arrived in India with legal qualifications, while in others they spent years in India and only then returned to London on leave for the statutory period of residence at one of the inns of court in order to qualify for the bar. Presumably these detours were taken as a means of advancing the candidate's prospects for a judicial appointment or promotion once he returned to the sub-continent.

One of the best-known examples of a member of the ICS who was called to the bar at an advanced stage in his career was George Campbell, nephew of Lord Chief Justice Campbell. George Campbell entered Haileybury in 1840 and after two years there he went to India.(57) In 1843 he was appointed assistant magistrate and collector at Budaon. After serving subsequently in a variety of other judicial and non-judicial posts, he returned to England in 1851 due to ill health. During his furlough, which lasted for three years, he entered the Inner Temple and was called to the bar there in 1854. Upon his return to India in 1854 he was named Magistrate and Collector at Azinghur in the North-West Provinces and in 1862 he was made an acting judge of the newly created Bengal High Court by Lord Elgin.(58) In fact Campbell's ambitions were not directed towards judicial service and he only accepted the judgeship as a temporary measure.(59) He later refused an offer by the Governor-General, Sir John Lawrence, that his name be put forward for the office of Chief Justice of the North-West Provinces.(60)

The division of judicial appointments between members of the practising bar and members of the ICS was a cause of jealousy and conflict. On the one hand the civilians resented their exclusion from the chief justiceships of the High Courts. As Campbell wrote in his autobiography:

> I have always thought it an abominable injustice and blot, that since the establishment of the High Courts in which English and Indian judges sit together, the Chief Justice must by law be a barrister, and the Indian civilian judges, however distinguished are positively excluded. An Indian soldier may be Commander-in-Chief, an Indian civilian may be Governor-General, but he cannot be Chief of a High Court. It is degrading to the judicial service and must tend to keep the best men out of it. I do not believe in the clap-trap about 'trained lawyers', meaning only those who have passed the Inns of Court.(61)

On the other, barristers were anxious to protect their monopoly with regard to chief justiceships and to extend it if possible. In the years 1900 to 1902 the issue of barrister versus civil servant came to the fore in respect to the appointment of the Chief Judge of the Chief Court of Lower Burma, which was part of India at the time.(62) Upon learning that a member of the ICS was to be named to the post, the Rangoon Bar Association turned to the Bar Council in London to support its contention that Sir William Agnew, recorder of Rangoon, be given the post. However since the appointment had already been made, there was little that the Bar Council could do.(63) In the following year, the newly appointed Chief Judge resigned and the controversy flared up once again as the name of another civil servant was submitted for the position. This time the Bar Council acted promptly and wrote to the Secretary for India to press the claims of the Rangoon bar. In the event, their appeal was to no avail. The Secretary stated that it was not a professional but an executive matter that depended upon personal fitness and knowledge of local conditions that were outside of the competence of the Bar Council.(64)

Compared to the members of other colonial judiciaries, the superior court judges in India were a kind of professional aristocracy. When the Supreme Court was established in Calcutta in 1773 the Chief Justice was given a salary of £10,000 per annum and the three puisne judges £6,000 each.(65) Thus with the exception of the Lord Chancellor and the chiefs of the three common law courts in England, they were the most highly paid judges in all of Great Britain and the empire. The size of the emoluments in India was a source of great concern to Lord Eldon in the 1820s. He warned George IV that unless measures were taken to correct the imbalance in the salaries of judges in England and India, the situation might well arise 'which would induce the gentlemen in the profession to accept Puisne Judgeships in your Majesty's Courts in Westminster Hall; not with a view of retaining their judicial seats there but in order the more readily to pave the way to their becoming Chiefs in India.'(66)

In fact Eldon's forebodings proved to be unfounded and no judge ever gave up a puisne judgeship in England for a seat on the Indian bench. Despite the salary differential and the other benefits that existed in India, no barrister who felt that he was in the ascendancy in his profession would give up a career in England for India. For this was tantamount to an admission of professional failure.(67) In July 1823 Christopher Puller was offered the office of Chief Justice of Calcutta. He justified accepting the appointment in a letter to his wife on the grounds that there was little more that he could expect to accomplish in his profession at home. His assessment of his future prospects was not rosy: 'after fifty the labour of an advocate unless gifted in an extraordinary manner is far from agreeable & every year he discovers more & more the want of that spring & energy which as it enabled him to pass others so it enables others to pass him.'(68)

Puller agreed to go to India, but others with brighter futures did not. In 1845 both Roundell Palmer, a future Lord Chancellor and John Rolt, a future Attorney-General and Lord Justice of Appeal, rejected appointments as Advocate-General of Calcutta, an office with a salary of £4,000 per annum plus whatever the office-holder could earn at the local bar.(69) While the financial inducements were considerable for these two men in the early stages of their professional careers, the prevailing assessment was made by Palmer's father who wrote his son, 'Perhaps if you were to accept it you would succeed. But here at home I think, Deo Volente, you have a sure game.'(70)

Even after the reduction of Indian judicial salaries in the nineteenth century, they were by far the most impressive in the empire, and the chief justices there continued to earn more than puisne judges in England. The Chief Justice of Bengal had an income of 72,000 Rs (about £7,000), the three other Chief Justices 60,000 Rs each and the puisnes 45,000 Rs, raised to 48,000 Rs in 1899.(71) At this time a puisne judge in England earned £5,000 and the Chief Justice of the King's Bench £8,000, while the highest-paid colonial chief justices outside of India at the end of the century received £3,500 in New South Wales, Queensland and Victoria, followed by £3,000 in the Cape Colony and about £2,700 in Ceylon, Hong Kong and the Straits Settlements.(72) By now the problem of recruiting Indian High Court judges was exacerbated by the enormous difference between barristers' incomes and judges' salaries in the sub-continent, without the moderating effects of prestige that encouraged the most successful advocates in England to abandon lucrative practices for the bench at home.(73) Furthermore, Englishmen were loath to go to India as much for social, climatic and health reasons as for professional ones.

Despite the reluctance of the more distinguished British barristers to accept an Indian appointment, most candidates (85 per cent) for the four Indian chief justiceships were recruited from the practising bars in the United Kingdom; 15 of the 20 office-holders had spent their entire pre-judicial careers in England, and one each in Scotland and Ireland. Only three had practised in India prior to taking professional office, and needless to say, none was an Indian.(74) Socially the Indian chief justices came from middling backgrounds similar to those of the other colonial chief justices. The same was true of their educational backgrounds: four (20 per cent) had been to public schools, nine (45 per cent) had attended Oxford or Cambridge and in all, fifteen (75 per cent) were university graduates. None of these men had achieved more than moderate success at the bar. Under half had taken silk during their pre-judicial careers and nine (45 per cent) reached the office of chief justice by means of translation from a puisne judgeship. Finally, we find that the Indian chief judiciary stood in splendid isolation from the remainder of the imperial legal profession; only one man, Charles Serjeant, served as a chief justice of another colony before arriving in India.

PROFESSIONAL IMPERIALISM AND THE LAW

I began this chapter by referring to the commonplace assumption that the colonies served as a haven for men who had failed to establish themselves at home. As the preceding examination of the colonial bars and benches suggests, it is an oversimplification to describe the recruitment process of barristers and judges as a function of professional imperialism.

As we have seen, the majority of colonial barristers were either born or bred in the colonies. Furthermore, most of those born and raised in the United Kingdom emigrated to the colonies within a few years after their calls to the bar without having tried their luck at home first. Thus it seems fair to describe the colonial bars not as refuges for men who failed in Britian but rather as alternative careers for less ambitious and competitive English, Scots and Irish lawyers.

By contrast the choice of colonial chief justices presents a very different picture in which British and more particularly English practitioners had a distinct advantage over their colonial counterparts. This was especially true in the less developed Crown colonies on the one hand and in India, whose judicial offices were by far the most valuable ones in the empire, on the other. In fact it is not surprising that officials in London turned as a matter of course to the English bar when searching for suitable candidates for colonial chief justiceships. These were the barristers who were best known to the men responsible for colonial judicial appointments or to their advisors. However, this is not to deny that other factors, such as the repayment of political debts, influenced the choice, as the correspondence of Lord Carnarvon reveals.

There is some basis to the claim that the empire provided a haven for less successful professional men. For a barrister who was not of the first rank and possibly not even of the second, the later years of a career in England could be frustrating and demoralising as he was constantly passed by rising young men, knowing full well that he had little or no chance for anything better than a County Court judgeship and perhaps not even that. Not surprisingly such a man might well find a senior colonial judgeship attractive with its security, status and even power, albeit in a much smaller pond. But by no stretch of the imagination could the colonial judiciary be described as poor relief for members of the upper or upper middle classes. In fact less than 30 per cent of the chief justices were the sons of landowners or of members of the gentlemanly professions.(75) But then this is only to be expected; well-connected men, even those with only average abilities, could find much more comfortable situations considerably closer to home than those afforded by the colonial judiciary.

Without doubt, elements of favouritism, political patronage, discrimination and even of racism influenced the appointment of colonial chief justices.(76) Nevertheless, it seems doubtful that on the whole the over-representation of barristers from the United Kingdom on the colonial benches was the consequence of a deliberate policy of professional imperialism. Rather this phenomenon was more likely the result of less nefarious factors, such as the availability of suitable candidates and the fact that English barristers were closer to the decision-making process.

NOTES

1. O'Boyle, 'The Problem of an Excess of Educated Men in Western Europe', pp. 480-2; R.S. Neale, Class and Ideology in the Nineteenth Century (1972), p. 97; Terence Johnson, 'Imperialism and the Professions' in Paul Halmos (ed.), Professionalisation and Social Change (Keele, 1973), pp. 287-8.
2. The colonies with responsible governments and the years in which this status was granted are as follows: New South Wales (1842); Tasmania (1850); South Australia (1850); Victoria (1850); Newfoundland (1855); New Zealand (1856); Queensland (1859); Cape Colony (1872); Natal (1893). I have included neither Canada, that became a dominion in 1867, nor any of its constituent provinces, except for Newfoundland which only became a part of Canada in 1949.
3. Select Committee on Legal Education, p. 256.
4. J.M. Bennett (ed.), A History of the New South Wales Bar (Sydney, 1969), pp. 62, 220-1.
5. Sir Arthur Dean, A Multitude of Counsellors, A History of the Bar of Victoria (Melbourne, 1968), p. 1.
6. Select Committee on Legal Education, pp. 257-8.
7. LT, 38 (February 7, 1863), pp. 189-90.
8. R.B. Mowat, The Life of Lord Pauncefote (1929), p. 15.
9. Dean, Multitude of Counsellors, pp. 25-6.
10. Bennett (ed.), History of the New South Wales Bar, p. 97.
11. LJ, 25 (August 30, 1890), p. 523.
12. LJ, 32 (November 13, 1897), pp. 550-1.
13. LJ, 29 (September 29, 1894), p. 567.
14. Select Committee on Legal Education, p. 254-5.
15. Ibid., p. 253.
16. Carnarvon MS PRO 39/6/134, fo. 98-9.
17. Ibid., PRO 30/6/17 fo. 68.
18. Ibid., fo. 38-9, 35-6.
19. Ibid., fo. 68.
20. Select Committee on Legal Education, pp. 279-80; F. Condé Williams, From Journalism to Judge (Edinburgh, 1903), pp. 309-10.
21. A blatant example of this was the career of R.C. Woods who was appointed Attorney-General of the Straits Settlements 'under the auspices of the noble Earl Carnarvon'. He 'had no knowledge of the law, and...had been specially passed through Gray's Inn within one year, as he was only to practise in a colony'. C. Northcote Parkinson, British Intervention in Malaya 1867-77 (Singapore, 1960), p. 191.
22. Inns of Court Commission, p. 14.
23. David Kimble, A Political History of Ghana, The Rise of Gold Coast Nationalism (Oxford, 1963), p. 96.
24. Williams, From Journalism to Judge, pp. 312, 234-5.

25. Harris, Autobiography, p. 208.
26. LJ, 28 (July 3, 1893), p. 481. See also the National Review for March, 1892 quoted in Williams, From Journalism to Judge, pp. 311-2.
27. Arthur Day, John C.P.S. Day: His Forebearers and Himself (1916), p. 93.
28. LJ, 28 (July 3, 1893), p. 481.
29. Ibid.
30. Select Committee on Legal Education, p. 256. A substantiation of this claim that also demonstrates the importance of connection is found in LJ, 5 (June 3, 1870), pp. 309-10.
31. LJ, 9 (March 14, 1874), pp. 143-4.
32. Bennett (ed.), History of the New South Wales Bar, pp. 72, 1.
33. Robin Cooke QC, Portrait of a Profession: The Centennial Book of the New Zealand Law Society (Wellington, 1969), p. 47.
34. Martin-Leake Papers 85686 (April 18, 1841); LJ, 6 (February 3, 1871), p. 78.
35. For a description of the life-style of a colonial judge, see L.H. Gann and Peter Duignan, The Rulers of British Africa 1870-1914 (Stanford, 1978), p. 237.
36. There was one black colonial chief justice in this period, namely William C. Reeves, the mulatto son of a white doctor from Barbados and a negro slave. He began to practise at the Barbados bar and in 1867 he became Attorney-General of St. Vincent. He returned to the bar of his home island after a short time and in 1882 he was appointed Attorney-General of Barbados. In 1886 he was promoted to the office of chief justice, a post he held until 1902. In the West African colonies, Africans ceased to be advanced to senior administrative and judicial ranks beginning in the last decades of the nineteenth century. Gann and Duignan, Rulers of British Africa, pp. 257-8.
37. Foster, Men-at-the-Bar; Who Was Who 1916-28, p. 535.
38. Foster, Men-at-the-Bar; Frederick Boase, Modern English Biography (6 vols., 1965 reprinted), vol. VI, p. 552.
39. DNB 1912-22, pp. 155-6.
40. Australian Dictionary of Biography.
41. Ibid.
42. Johnson, 'Imperialism and the Professions', p. 293.
43. Ralph Braibanti (ed.), Asian Bureaucratic Systems Emergent from the British Imperial Tradition (Durham, 1966), p. 65.
44. B.B. Misra, The Indian Middle Classes, Their Growth in Modern Times (1961), pp. 328-9.
45. Samuel Schmitthener, 'A Sketch of the Development of the Legal Profession in India', Law and Society Review, III (1968-9), pp. 356 and 359. This article has been used throughout this section.
46. Charles Morrison, 'Kinship in Professional Relations:

A Study of Northern Indian District Lawyers', Comparative Studies in Society and History, 14 (1972), p. 124; Braibanti (ed.), 'Asian Bureaucratic Systems', p. 65; Schmitthener, 'Legal Profession in India', p. 339; Misra, Indian Middle Classes, p. 307.

47. G.F.M. Buckee, 'An Examination of the Development and Structure of the Legal Profession in Allahabad 1866-1935', unpublished PhD thesis, University of London, 1972; foreword by Professor Edward Shils in Amar Kumar Singh, Indian Students in Britain (New York, 1963), pp. xii-xiii.

48. T. Johnson, 'Imperialism and the Professions', p. 302; Schmitthener, 'Legal Profession in India', p. 365; D.V. Tahmankar, Sardar Patel (1970), p. 39; Mohondas K. Gandhi, Autobiography (Boston, 1957), p. 36.

49. Buckee, 'Legal Profession in Allahabad', p. 297.

50. On this see p. 190.

51. Buckee, 'Legal Profession in Allahabad', p. 300; LJ, 3 (January 10, 1868), p. 41.

52. Schmitthener, 'Legal Profession in India', p. 375.

53. Ibid.

54. On Europeans without Indian connections, see Buckee, 'Legal Profession in Allahabad', pp. 164, 244.

55. Schmitthener, 'Legal Profession in India', pp. 367-9; John R. MacLane, Indian Nationalism and the Early Congress (Princeton, 1977), pp. 57-9.

56. Buckee, 'Legal Profession in Allahabad', pp. 43-4.

57. This refers to the East India Company's college Haileybury and not the public school of the same name.

58. DNB.

59. Sir George Campbell, Memoirs of My Indian Career (2 vols., 1893), vol. II, pp. 95-6.

60. Ibid., p. 113.

61. Ibid.

62. Since the office was of Chief Judge and not Chief Justice of one of the High Courts, it was not restricted to members of the bar.

63. Bar Council, Annual Statement (1900-1), pp. 13-14.

64. Bar Council, Annual Statement (1901-2), pp. 9-10.

65. Peter Brown, The Chathamites (1967), p. 265.

66. Arthur Aspinall (ed.), The Letters of King George IV 1812-1830 (3 vols., Cambridge, 1938), vol. 3, p. 94.

67. On English attitudes towards the Indian service see Bradford Spangenberg, 'The Problem of Recruitment of the Indian Civil Service During the Late Nineteenth Century', Journal of Asian Studies, 30 (1971), pp. 353-4.

68. Papers of Christopher Puller D/E GP C. 10.

69. Sir John Rolt, Memoirs of the Right Honourable Sir John Rolt (1939), pp. 99-100; Papers of Roundell Palmer, Earl of Selborne 1878 fo. 92.

70. Papers of Roundell Palmer 1878 fo. 92-3.

71. India List.

72. Colonial Office List.
73. Buckee, 'Legal Profession in Allahabad', pp. 64, 261-2. On top incomes at the Indian bar see pp. 147-8.
74. On Indians raised to the High Court bench, see Buckee, 'Legal Profession in Allahabad', pp. 67-9, 259-60.
75. This suggests that a recent assessment of the social quality of colonial barristers and judges was overly optimistic. Gann and Duignan, The Rulers of British Africa, p. 237.
76. Ibid., pp. 257-8; Kimble, Political History of Ghana, pp. 98-9.

Chapter Five

WEALTH-HOLDERS, LANDOWNERS AND COMPANY DIRECTORS

In this chapter I will deal with three topics: the incomes and wealth of barristers, their investments in land and securities and their involvement in the world of business. Despite their diversity, these three topics are all connected by a common economic thread. They lead us away from exclusively professional concerns and help us to begin to place the barrister in a wider social context.

INCOMES AND FORTUNES

In the early 1850s young Fitzjames Stephen was considering which of the three learned professions - divinity, law or physic - was most suitable for him. He set down his thoughts in an essay that weighed the advantages and disadvantages of each one. With regard to the financial prospects at the bar he wrote:

> It is a profession the entrance to which is more expensive than the entrance to the Church...it is one which entails celibacy on its members for a longer period of time than the Church, its profits are more uncertain and for longer delay. Judging from what I have heard then on this subject I should not think myself unfortunate if at the end of 10 years after being called to the bar my professional income was large enough to support a family.(1)

Three-quarters of a century later, the fictional Lewis Eliot at a similar stage in his career listed the attractions of the bar that made the intendent risks worthwhile:

> In favour of the gamble, there was just one thing to say. If my luck held at every point and I came through, there were rewards, not only money, though I wanted that. It gave me a chance, so I thought then, of the paraphernalia of success, luxury and a name...(2)

In attempting to go beyond these speculations by young men embarking on a career at the bar and arrive at an estimate of the incomes of nineteenth-century barristers, we are confronted by an unpromising mixture of fact, rumour and guesswork. Despite the very evident limitations in both the quantity and quality of the data, I hope to be able to construct a scale of incomes at the bar. The most natural starting point is Sir John Jervis's testimony on barristers' earnings presented to a parliamentary select committee in 1850. According to the Attorney-General there were five men at the head of the profession with incomes in excess of £11,000 per annum, though none of them was said to be earning as much as £20,000. They were followed by three men who had annual incomes of between £8,000 and £11,000 and another fifteen or sixteen men with fees that ranged from £5,000 to £8,000.(3) By the end of the 1850s, according to H. Byerley Thomson, only a small percentage of QCs earned as much as £3,000 annually, even after fees had begun to rise in response to the mid-Victorian economic boom. A few of the most able junior barristers at this time could hope to earn as much as £2,000, although the more usual income from the rank and file was in the region of £500 to £1,200 yearly.(4)

Unfortunately we possess no comparable synopsis of incomes for the latter decades of the nineteenth century. Nevertheless, the scattered evidence that does exist strongly suggests that a pronounced upward drift occurred in the real incomes of the most successful members of the profession. For example, in a generally gloomy description of the prospects of rank and file barristers c. 1894, a correspondent to the Law Journal indicated with little satisfaction that £4,000 was the most that a common law junior could hope to earn.(5) In absolute terms this represents a doubling of the £2,000 attributed above to leading juniors a quarter of a century earlier. When these figures are adjusted to changes in the cost of living the rise is even more striking; in real terms there was a three-fold increase between the 1850s and 1890s, from £1,800 to £5,400.

A similar though less pronounced trend is evident in Table 5.1. Here we find a steady rise in the real incomes of men who stood at the head of the profession with the exception of the years between 1830 and 1850. While this hiatus may be more apparent than real due to the absence of sufficient data, evidence given to the Select Committee on Official Salaries in 1850 indicated a contemporary recognition of the fact that incomes at the bar had declined in the preceding decades as a consequence of the general economic depression.(6)

While the great wealth of leading barristers may be more fascinating than the poverty of the many briefless ones, concentrating our attention on the former while ignoring the latter distorts historical reality. Nineteenth-century observers were well aware that the range of incomes at the bar was enormous.(7) While no measurement of the distribution of barristers' earnings exists for the nineteenth century, data for the

Table 5.1: The Incomes of Barristers 1796-1913

	Date of Maximum Income	Reported Income	Weighted Income
John Scott	1796	E £12,140[a]	£8,300
Samuel Romilly	c. 1815	A £18,000[b]	£10,000
Edward Sugden	c. 1830	A £17,000[c]	£15,600
John Jervis	1847-9	A £10,000[d]	£10,000
Richard Bethell	1860	A £24,000[e]	£20,000
George Jessel	1871	A £29,000[f]	£25,200
Judah P. Benjamin	c. 1880	A £25,000[g]	£24,500
Charles Russell	1893	E £22,517[h]	£27,500
Edward Clarke	1902	E £27,000[i]	£31,400
Stanley Buckmaster	1913	A £40,000[j]	£37,700

Notes: The letter E or A in front of the income of each barrister refers to the quality of the income data, i.e. whether it is exact (E) or approximate (A). The exact data are derived from the fee books, while the approximate data come either from estimates made by the men themselves, from well-informed contemporaries or from biographers. The indices used to weight the incomes are as follows: for 1796 the average of consumer and producer goods in the Schumpeter-Gilboy Price Indices; for the remainder of the table the overall index from the Rousseaux Price Indices. The fit between these two indices is very close for 1800 so I have used them as if they were one continual series. There are of course difficulties in weighting money wages in this way using the less than completely satisfactory data that are available. The weighted incomes are not meant to be taken as exact calculations of real incomes, rather what is significant is the relationship between them, which provides a picture of the rise and fall of professional earnings over more than a century. The indices are found in R.B. Mitchell and Phyllis Deane, Abstract of British Historical Statistics (Cambridge, 1971), pp. 469, 471-3. For a discussion of some of the problems with the Rousseaux Indices see Dean and Cole, British Economic Growth, p. 282.

Sources: a J.C. Jeafferson, A Book About Lawyers (2 vols., 1867), vol. I, p. 296; b Patrick Mead, Romilly: A Life of Samuel Romilly, Lawyer and Reformer (1968), p. 294; c Report of

Sources, Table 5.1 (cont'd)

the Select Committee on Official Salaries, p. 164; d Ibid., p. 183; e Thomas A. Nash, The Life of Richard Lord Westbury, (2 vols., 1888), vol. I, p. 132; f Sir Elwyn Jones, 'The Office of Attorney-General', Cambridge Law Journal, 27 (1969), pp. 45-6; g Law Times, 74 (1883), p. 274; h R. Barry O'Brien, The Life of Lord Russel of Killowen (1901), pp. 267-8; i Derek Walker-Smith, Edward Clarke, The Life of Sir Edward Clarke (1939), p. 279; j R.F.V. Heuston, Lives of the Lord Chancellors (Oxford, 1964), p. 260.

early twentieth indicate that the spread of incomes at the bar was wider than in any other profession. While in 1913/14 the emoluments of barristers at the highest decile amounted to £1,820 per annum compared with £1,410 for solicitors and £1,200 for doctors, at the lowest quartile it was a mere £155 for barristers compared to £185 for solicitors and £197 for doctors.(8)

The discrepancy between these estimates and those of Byerley Thomson (£500-£1,200 yearly) are considerable and the difference calls for some explanation. While the gap may simply be the result of exaggerated estimates of the earnings of junior barristers in the 1850s it seems more likely that it is due to whom was counted. Many of those at the lower end of the profession in terms of income probably left the bar after a few unfruitful years. We cannot measure the dimensions of this phenomenon for the nineteenth century but thanks to the data published recently by the Royal Commission on Legal Services we do know the extent of the outflow from the profession for the years 1964 to 1978.(9) Thomson may well not have considered these transients as fully-fledged members of the practising bar, and so the depressing effects of their low incomes on the professional average would have been ignored. The figure of £500 probably referred to men who had established permanent practices, though even given this limitation he may have overestimated the minimum income.

The extremely wide spread of incomes at the bar was not a characteristic that was limited to the second half of the nineteenth century. A recent study of the bar in the 1970s reveals that the situation today is identical.(10) Furthermore, in the last quarter of the eighteenth century Adam Smith justified the extraordinarily high remuneration of the most successful barristers as compensation to the few for the many who earned little or nothing in the profession.(11) The extremely uneven and unequal distribution of legal incomes was probably a necessary consequence of the division of professional labour and function between barrister and solicitor. The prohibition against counsel entering into direct consultations with lay clients and his resulting dependence upon the lower branch undoubtedly served to depress the earnings of the fledgling

barrister, while at the same time inflating the emoluments of
the leaders whose services were most in demand.
    The barrister was also among the most vulnerable of all
professional men with regard to his income. The decision to
take silk could be the key to the great riches that the bar had
to offer, on the other hand it could spell the virtual end to
the career of a successful junior who did not have the talents
necessary to make the transition to leader. Furthermore a reputation at the bar needed constant nurture and the solicitors
were sure to note any decline in a barrister's stamina or his
intellectual powers. One of the most dramatic examples of the
rapidity with which a barrister could fall from the top of his
profession is found in the career of James Stuart Wortley.
A younger son of the first Baron Wharncliffe, he rose steadily
in his profession, taking silk in 1841 and serving successively
as Solicitor-General to the dowager Queen Adelaide, Judge Advocate General, Recorder of London and Solicitor-General to the
Crown. Due to ill health he was forced to abandon his practice
and within a relatively short time was reduced to eating into
his capital and borrowing from his nephew, 3rd Baron and 1st
Earl Wharncliffe.(12) While no doubt Wortley's was a very extreme case it represents the obverse side of the great wealth
that is recorded in Table 5.1.
    Turning for a moment from England to the empire we find
that by comparison with the few scattered examples of the incomes of colonial barristers that I have located, the English
data look like a mine of information. The earliest comes from
the Caribbean region. In 1841 a very junior member of the
Jamaican bar reported to his former pupil master in London that
one of the leading practitioners on the island was earning
£3,000. The young man himself had earned £700 in his first
year and near to £1,000 in his second.(13) Incomes of this order for a man in his first years of practice were virtually unknown in England where the fees of fledgling barristers, even
those who were later to rise to prominence, were miniscule.
One explanation for this difference is that in a comparatively
insular society a well-connected man might be able to secure a
sizeable clientele more quickly than his counterparts in the
more open and competitive world of the English bar. At about
the same time, leading practitioners in British Guiana were
earning as much as £5,000 or even £6,000 per annum.(14) No
wonder then that the Chief Justice of that colony received one
of the highest judicial salaries in the empire.
    The remaining data on incomes of colonial barristers come
from Australia and South Asia during an extended period from
the 1860s to the 1920s. According to a report in the Law Times
in 1861 the fees of the 13 leading members of the Melbourne bar
ranged from £2,000 to £6,000, while in the middle of the following decade their counterparts in New South Wales were earning
as much as £5,000.(15) In India of the mid-1860s the newly
established salary for puisne judges of the High Courts, Rs 3500,

monthly (£4,200 per annum), was said to represent a substantial income for members of the bar in the sub-continent. However, by the beginning of the twentieth century it was a mere pittance compared with the Rs 15,000 per month (£13,000 annually) then being earned by leading Indian barristers.(16) Within two decades even incomes of this amount, substantial by English standards at the time, paled in comparison to the fees earned by C.R. Das. In 1920 his professional remuneration amounted to Rs 50,000 monthly, which surpassed the £46,541 earned contemporaneously in England by Douglas Hogg, the future Lord Hailsham. Despite the enormous dimensions of the top Indian incomes, the early years of a barrister's career, especially for an Indian trying to break into a profession dominated and controlled by Englishmen, were at least as barren as those of fledgling barristers in England.(17)

Much of the evidence presented here is second- and third-hand at best and constitutes only an estimate of professional incomes in the nineteenth century rather than a precise reconstruction. Nevertheless, the data leave little doubt that elite practitioners, both at home and in the colonies, were among the best remunerated professional men in the realm and that they could certainly have afforded to adopt a life style which included most of those symbols of economic and social status that Professor Banks has called the 'paraphernalia of gentility,' and perhaps even more as well.(18)

By contrast, at the lower end of the profession, barristers were engaged in a constant struggle for existence. If Routh's data for 1913/14 are typical of the late Victorian period, then the lower three-quarters of the bar would have been hard pressed to cover their minimum professional and personal expenses even if they were bachelors.(19) Undoubtedly, there was a heavy turnover in personnel at this level with newly called barristers continually replacing both the men who left the profession for greener pastures and those who began to climb the ladder of success after a few barren years. Unfortunately, we shall probably never know how many barristers spent their lives as practising advocates earning several hundred pounds a year which they supplemented by law reporting, journalism, giving legal tuition, or other peripheral endeavours.

Judging by the data on the personal estates left by members of the bar, few remained at these low income levels for long - even if this meant leaving the practising bar.(20) An examination of the probates of barristers practising and non-practising in 1835 and 1885 reveals that at the lowest quartile their personal estates were valued £4,000 and £3,800 and at the lowest decile £1,000 and £600 respectively, unadjusted for changing prices.

The comparison between the personal estates of all practising barristers and QCs (Table 5.2) confirms the impression given by the data on incomes at the bar that the leaders of

Table 5.2: The Wealth of Practising Barristers and Queen's Counsel

	Practising Bar		Queen's Counsel	
	N=91 1835	N=202 1885	N=26 1800-1850	N=105 1851-1901
% of estates over £200,000	2%	1%	0%	6%
% of estates over £100,000	3%	7%	0%	19%
highest decile	£48,000	£86,200	£80,000	£148,200
highest quartile	£25,000	£43,300	£52,500	£70,700
median	£14,000	£15,100	£30,000	£30,300
lowest quartile	£4,000	£4,200	£11,200	£8,200

the profession became wealthier during the course of the nineteenth century. Estates at the upper decile and quartile increased by more than 70 per cent for the barristers in 1885 as compared with their predecessors in 1835. By contrast little change occurred during this fifty-year period in the size of median and lower quartile fortunes. The probates of a random sample of nineteenth-century QCs, taking 1850 as the dividing line, all show a significant rise in the wealth of barristers during the century. The first indication of change is the appearance in the sample of post-1850 QCs of a significant number of men who left large estates of more than £100,000 where there had been none in the pre-1851 sample. Furthermore the highest decile increased by 85 per cent, while the highest quartile had a more modest rise of 35 per cent. Clearly the rich were getting richer while the less well off were more or less standing still. Had we calculated the value of the personal estates in real rather than absolute terms, the gap between the wealth of the early and late Victorian barristers would appear to be even wider, since prices were considerably higher in the third quarter of the century when the majority of 1835 barristers and pre-1851 QCs died, than in the closing decades of the nineteenth and opening ones of the twentieth century when most of the 1885 barristers and post-1850 QCs died. Taken together, the data on incomes and on the estates of barristers indicate that professional remuneration at all levels was rising, though the pace was rather faster the closer we get to the summit. Concomitantly an increasingly large share of professional business was being monopolised by the relatively tiny group of leading advocates.

There seems little doubt that the leading members of the bar, including the judges, were by far the wealthiest of all practising professional men in the nineteenth century. For example we find that the fortunes of the post-1850 QCs were considerably larger than those of the presidents, censors and vice-presidents of the Royal Colleges of Physicians and Surgeons who died between 1858 and 1928. Furthermore when we juxtapose the personal estates of these medical men and those of judges of the superior courts we find that at the top decile the judges left 70 per cent more than the officers of the RCP, while the median fortune among judges was higher than the top decile among the physicians.(21) Another indication of the exceptional character of the wealth of lawyers in general compared to other professional men is found in a recent study of English wealth-holders. Between 1860 and 1919 there were 13 professional men who left estates worth between £500,000 and £999,999. Of these 10 (77 per cent) were members of the legal profession, taken in its widest sense.(22)

The data presented in Table 5.3 permit us to compare the relative wealth of barristers who belonged to four elite groups. However before proceeding there are two caveats that we must bear in mind. First, only the judges were a true occupational category. For example while some of the company directors were full-time businessmen, a considerable proportion were either landowners or practising barristers. In fact a single barrister could in theory belong to all four groups listed in the table. Second, some of the categories were more exclusive than others. Thus while the judges and cabinet ministers were national legal and political elites respectively, the company directors did not constitute a business elite, comparable to the one made up of directors or better still chairmen of the largest industrial concerns, the leading banks and the most important mercantile firms.

The exceptional financial rewards that accrued to the most successful Victorian barristers are illustrated by the probate data for the judges appointed to the bench between 1850 and 1901. In fact the fortunes amassed by these men could not rival those of the wealthiest of their pre-reform predecessors, such as Lords Hardwicke and Eldon, who derived immense profits from the legal sinecures in their gifts.(23) The great increase in barristers' earnings during the nineteenth century, which we traced above, partially compensated the profession for the abolition of these 'excess profits'. Consequently, the judges who graced the benches of the superior courts during the last 25 years of the reign of Queen Victoria left personal estates that were comparable at all but the highest level to those of the last generation of judges who benefited from the

Table 5.3: The Wealth of Barristers Belonging to Various Professional, Economic and Political Elites

	N=111 Judges 1850-1901	N=287 Company Directors (1889)
% of estates over £200,000	10%	8%
% of estates over £100,000	27%	24%
highest decile	£201,400	£186,400
highest quartile	£119,100	£96,900
median	£60,000	£47,400
lowest quartile	£26,500	£17,900
	N=117 MPs in 1880	N=35 Cabinet Ministers 1850-1901
% of estates over £200,000	9%	20%
% of estates over £100,000	27%	46%
highest decile	£186,900	£285,700
highest quartile	£134,800	£186,900
median	£41,200	£75,400
lowest quartile	£10,000	£36,200

'old corruption', namely those appointed between 1790 and 1820.(24)

The company directors had the smallest fortunes of the four elite groups, but they included the wealthiest of all the nineteenth-century barristers; in my research I have found only two millionaire barristers and both of these men were businessmen. Conversely, despite the fact that the average wealth of the cabinet ministers exceeded that of any other group of gentlemen of the long robe, none had a personal estate larger than £356,000. They were distinguished by a comparatively narrow spread in wealth and by the high concentration of men who left fortunes of between £200,000 and £300,000 (17 per cent) and between £100,000 and £200,000 (26 per cent).

The last of the four elite groups - the barrister/MPs - constituted the recruitment stratum for the cabinet ministers. Perhaps not surprisingly these MPs were less wealthy than barristers who sat in the Cabinet. This difference in wealth can be ascribed primarily to two factors. Among the practising barristers, those who were most likely to be selected for top political offices, especially the Lord Chancellorship, were usually men with outstanding professional reputations whose incomes and fortunes were naturally larger than those of their colleagues who remained on the back-benches. In addition there were several barristers who reached cabinet rank who had independent incomes that permitted them to enter Parliament in their early thirties and devote their full energies to politics. These men, such as Charles Villiers, Edward Marjoribanks and Arnold Morley, either never practised at the bar or abandoned advocacy for a career in politics after only a few years.

Not only were barrister/MPs less wealthy than the ministers but their fortunes were smaller than those of other members of the House of Commons. Taking the data compiled by William Rubinstein on the wealth of MPs in 1895 as the basis of comparison, we find striking differences. For example, while none of the barrister/MPs in 1880 were millionaires, 6 per cent of the 1895 MPs were. Similarly there were three times as many MPs in 1895 as there were barrister/MPs who left fortunes in excess of £300,000 and 50 per cent more whose estates were greater than £100,000.(25)

To summarize briefly the results of this survey of the income and wealth of Victorian barristers, we find that they were far and away the best remunerated and the wealthiest of all nineteenth-century professional men. However the economic gap between the most and least successful practitioners was significantly wider than in other professions. I have also suggested that many of the men at the bottom end of the income scale left the bar to take advantage of the alternative sources of employment that were open to members of the bar, especially in the latter part of the century. Between the 1850s and the outbreak of the First World War the earnings of leading barristers doubled in real terms and this increased prosperity filtered down at least to the middle ranks of the profession.

Before concluding this section it is essential that we place the financial portrait of the barristers that I have just sketched into a wider social context. While the bar was nineteenth-century Britain's most affluent profession, few if any of its members were part of the national economic elite and only a small minority could rank as wealthy, even when we take a personal estate of £100,000 as the lower limit of that category. The professions in general and the bar in particular provided their more able practitioners with an extremely comfortable existence. Nevertheless, these were most certainly not occupations in which men would amass great fortunes comparable to those of great landowners, leading merchants, bankers or industrialists - at least in post-reform Britain.(26)

THE BARRISTER AS LANDOWNER

The landed members of the nineteenth-century bar can be divided into two main sub-groups: those whose principal occupation and source of income was landowning, and those for whom it was only a secondary concern. Taking the 73 full-time landowners in the random sample of the 1885 bar as examples of the former group in the late Victorian period, we find that they were typical members of the gentry, whose professional qualifications seem rather incidental. Among the 68 for whom I have found exact data on estate rentals, just under 60 per cent owned landed property that made them members of the greater gentry (£3,000-£10,000 p.a.) or of the squirearchy (£1,000-£3,000 p.a.). Furthermore, just under 10 per cent presided over estates worth more than £10,000 a year, while nearly one third owned property with annual rentals of less than £1,000. Given this breakdown in the size of their holdings it is not surprising to find that only a few of these barrister/landowners were titled. Three were peers of whom two inherited their titles and four others were baronets.(27)

The large majority of these men (nearly 90 per cent) were either first sons and heirs or younger sons who eventually inherited their paternal estates or land from near relatives. At most seven men (10 per cent) were first-generation gentry who purchased their estates. In none of these instances was the land worth more than £2,000 per annum and in most cases its value was considerably less than that.

The pre-professional education received by these land-owning barristers was typical of their class. Forty-two per cent attended a major public school and nearly four-fifths were university graduates, primarily from Oxford and Cambridge. Not surprisingly the most popular colleges among the Oxbridge men were, in order of preference, Trinity, Cambridge, Christ Church and Balliol. Entry into the inns of court formed a fitting conclusion to a gentlemanly education that would provide future landowners, some of whom would enter Parliament, with a useful, albeit not particularly rigorous introduction to the law. The evidence suggests, however, that more professionally oriented considerations were not entirely absent. A third of these barrister/landowners exhibited some interest in practising their profession primarily in the first years after their call to the bar, as indicated by the fact that they took the trouble to include their names on the circuit lists found in the Law List. Yet one suspects that they did not pursue their professional activities with any particular intensity or seriousness. It seems likely that many merely attended the local assizes and sessions for a few years in a desultory fashion, devoting little effort to building up a practice.

There were other landowners who became committed and successful members of the bar. Seven per cent of the practising bar in 1885 were landowners, as were 15 per cent of a sample of nineteenth-century QCs and 35 per cent of the high court judges appointed between 1850 and 1901. An examination of the value of the property of practising barristers reveals that they owned considerably smaller estates than did the full-time landowners. None possessed land worth as much as £10,000 per annum: 90 per cent of these men owned estates valued at under £3,000 per year and almost half had landed incomes of less than £1,000 annually.

For the practising barristers, landed incomes could be useful supplements to their professional earnings. In some instances this addition was considerable; in others it amounted to no more than a pittance of several hundred pounds per annum or even less. Furthermore, in the case of the smallest estates the owners may well have retained their entire property as park, woods or home farm, without renting any of it out to tenants.

Traditionally the purchase of a landed estate was the means by which socially pretentious members of the upper middle classes made their entry into gentry and even aristocratic society. In this respect members of the legal profession were no exceptions and numerous examples of this process of social transformation can be found among the professional elite in the eighteenth and early nineteenth centuries. As I have shown elsewhere a decline in the desire of members of the royal judiciary to establish landed families began among the men appointed to the bench after 1820, in part as a result of the administrative reforms of the courts and the abolition of lucrative sinecures that had enriched the most senior judges.(28) This change was already well advanced by 1875 and it became even more pronounced during the last quarter of the nineteenth century. The percentage of judges who were landowners dropped from 55 per cent for the cohort appointed to the bench between 1850 and 1875 to 27 per cent for the 1875 to 1901 cohort. Moreover while only 33 per cent of judicial peers (36 per cent of those with hereditary titles) were non-landed in the earlier period, this rose to 69 per cent (75 per cent of the hereditary peers) in the latter one. Not only do we find a decline in landowning among the judges, but this phenomenon was accompanied by a significant decrease in the average rentals of judicial estates. While half of the estates in the earlier period were valued at £1,000 per annum or more, this was true of only a quarter of the estates in the latter one.

Similarly, while the percentage of landowners among the QCs and the rank and file of the bar remained more or less constant during the nineteenth century, the value of their estates dropped considerably. While a majority of landed barristers in both groups who practised before 1850 had annual rentals of more than £1,000, this was true of only a minority of their post-1850 counterparts. Further evidence of the loosening of the ties between the bar and landed society is found in the decrease in the proportion of judges who purchased land and a decline in the value of the estates that they acquired.

The nineteenth century witnessed a significant decline in the connection between the upper branch of the legal profession and landed society. Most nineteenth-century barrister/landowners were men who had inherited land, and the earlier propensity of successful advocates to purchase land as a means of founding a family or for investment purposes virtually disappeared. The relatively small size of their estates suggests that barristers who bought land apparently did so in order to establish retreats for themselves away from the hectic metropolitan world of law and politics. The reasons for this change are clear: by the later nineteenth century land had lost much of its social attraction for leading professional men, while as we shall see next business provided a much more fertile field for profitable investments.

INVESTMENTS AND DIRECTORSHIPS IN BUSINESS

In studying the investment patterns in nineteenth-century England we must abandon any thought of quantification. Unlike the case in the early modern period, inventories of personal estates were not made at this time, so it is impossible to build up a comprehensive picture of the distribution and value of investments. While occasionally the wills themselves provide information about the stocks, bonds and cash belonging to deceased persons, a detailed examination of these documents was not possible in the case of nineteenth-century barristers. Therefore it is necessary to fall back on two sources which together provide a few clues about this subject. There are private papers that sometimes include lists of investments; there are also wills probated in Scotland which do include inventories of personal wealth. I have been able to compile data on seven barristers, and from these I have tried to build a composite picture of the investments of members of the profession.(29) Naturally we are treading on treacherous ground in trying to apply the data derived from a few exemplary cases to an entire occupation. Furthermore the seven men who left us their inventories are by no stretch of the imagination typical of the bar as a whole; they include two cabinet ministers and five Scotsmen. Finally each of the portfolios has a distinct character of its own. In 1873 John G. Dodson, the future Lord Monk Bretton, had about £40,000 in English and foreign railways, £15,000 in English government stocks, and £27,000 in foreign government stocks. Lord Blackburn who died in 1896, had £111,000 invested in English and Scottish railways and £21,000 in the Grand Junction Canal. Not surprisingly James Bryce, who was an expert on American politics and future Ambassador to Washington, had a majority of his investments in 1898 in American railways - £8,000 - and by 1904 this had risen to nearly £20,000. In addition he had almost £4,000 in British rails, £6,000 in canals, £2,000 in mining and £1,000 in India. Charles J. Pearson, who died in 1910 had £12,000 in consols, £3,600 in Scottish company shares, £2,000 in an India rubber plantation and £3,000 in English railways. John D. Inverarity (d. 1923), whose estate was the largest of the seven men, had the bulk - £195,000 - in government war bonds, £43,000 in colonial and foreign government bonds, £43,000 in Latin American railways, £9,000 in Canada (Hudson's Bay Company and Canadian Pacific Railway), £4,000 in British rails, and £3,800 in the Mortgage Company of Egypt. Mark John Stewart, who died the same year, had invested £9,200 in government stocks, £11,500 in Latin American railways and £10,300 in other Latin American shares, £8,500 in English rails, nearly £5,000 in Indian stocks, £4,100 in the Hudson's Bay Company and £3,500 in mining and plantations. Finally George Watson (d. 1927) had £12,000 in various investment trusts, £3,200 in war bonds, and just under £1,000 in the Canadian Pacific. Combining the seven portfolios we find that the vast majority of investments were placed in British, colonial and foreign government stocks and in British, American and Latin American railways. Other sectors including mining and land companies, investment trusts, utilities and industrial stocks only accounted for a small percentage of the total. The pattern of investment found among these seven men mirrors rather closely the general distribution of stocks in the British market - with the rank order being consols, foreign government stocks, British railways and American railways.(30)

The stockmarket was not the only point of contact between the bar and the world of business. Though the connection between the lower branch of the legal profession and business may seem more natural, the involvement by members of the upper branch, most notably as company directors, was far from nominal. In order to measure its extent more precisely I have crossreferenced the men listed in Foster's Men-at-the-Bar (1885) with the Directory of Directors (1889). This procedure yielded the names of 439 barristers who were directors of 781 companies. While there may have been some underenumeration, it seems safe to conclude that between six and seven per cent of late Victorian barristers sat on one or more boards of directors. Naturally there were enormous differences in the level of participation in business affairs by these men. Some were non-executive directors who furnished a name on a company's letterhead in return for a courtesy fee. The only legal requirement in the appointment of directors was that from 1878 they had to possess company shares with a nominal value of £500.(31) Other barristers, as we shall see, were active businessmen who served as chairmen, managing directors and promoters of investment opportunities.

Table 5.4: Social Origins and Occupations of Barrister/Directors

	Social Origins		Occupation or Status	
	No.	%	No.	%
Landowners	110	25	64	15
Businessmen	92	21	71	16
Barristers	47	11	164	37
Other Professional Men and Government Officials	117	27	39	9
Younger sons of greater gentry and peers	-	-	26	6
Urban Gentry	23	5	-	-
Rural Gentry	17	4	-	-
Other Occupations	3	1	-	-
Unknown	30	7	75	17

Barrister/directors by no means formed a random sample of the profession. More than 40 per cent were recruited from the sons of landowners and businessmen - 25 per cent and 21 per cent respectively; alone these two occupational groups may have contributed as much as half of the total if we add to their number the rural gentry and a portion of the urban gentry. The dominant position of land and business was a natural consequence of the fact that family succession and local landed connections were two of the most frequently travelled paths to the boardroom. There were few self-made men among the barristers in business, not an unexpected situation in a profession like the bar in which lower-middle and working-class recruits were a rarity. While these barristers were drawn from a representative cross-section of middle and upper class English society, their occupational choices reveal the same bias in favour of land and business that characterised their social origins. Thus the proportion of landowners and unoccupied younger sons of the landed elite and of businessmen was respectively two and three times as large among the directors as it was within the rank and file of the profession.

Although the participation of barristers in business extended to every continent and to enterprises of nearly every variety, their endeavours were primarily concentrated in British companies, (70 per cent), while the three most popular fields were rails and trams, insurance, and banking and investment companies (57 per cent). The distribution of the 781 directorships both by geography and by type of company is displayed in Table 5.5.(32) In the succeeding pages I intend to elaborate on the data that appear there by examining in some detail the place of the gentlemen of the long robe in Victorian commerce and industry.

In surveying the careers of these men no general patterns are apparent. One would be hard put to show that barristers formed a coherent or even loosely related sub-stratum within the business community. In many instances their professional qualifications were incidental to their business activities. Nevertheless, there were individual firms as well as groups of inter-related companies in which members of the bar played significant roles both in their establishment and management.

Insurance provides an example of a field in which barristers were numerically significant without playing a central role in company affairs. More than a fifth of the barristers who were involved in insurance directed five companies whose appeal was oriented primarily towards lawyers and university graduates: Legal and General Life, Law Life, Equity and Law Life, Law Fire and University Life.(33) Many of these directors were successful advocates and more than a few were high court judges. The most distinguished board - Legal and General Life - numbered among its members justices Bacon, Kekewich, Lopes, Mathew and Smith. One cannot help but suspect that the most important service that these men provided in return for their directors' fees was the use of their names in attracting clients and investors.(34)

After insurance the next largest contingent of barrister/directors was involved in British railways. Most of these men had interests in local lines as a result of regional landed business or professional connections. In a few instances directors of large trunk lines also sat on the boards of several local ones. For example Sir Charles Wood, deputy chairman of the Great Western from 1860 to 1890 was a director of six local railways, five of which were situated in South Wales or Devon.

Table 5.5: Distribution of Directorships by Location and Type

	Rail-ways/ Trams	Insur-ance	Banks/ Invest-ment Companies	Utili-ties	Mining	Land Develop-ment	Indus-try	Commercial and Mercantile	Others/ Unknown	Total	
United Kingdom	115	153	86	48	6	40	57	7	34	546	70%
Latin America	39	0	2	8	15	5	0	1	3	73	9%
North America	5	0	5	1	14	16	1	0	0	42	5%
Rest of Europe including Asia Minor	11	0	5	8	5	1	1	0	7	38	5%
India/ South and East Asia	7	0	4	4	4	0	0	10	0	29	4%
Austral-asia	2	0	6	1	9	2	0	1	0	21	3%
Africa	0	0	1	1	9	1	0	1	2	15	2%
Unknown	0	0	1	0	8	0	0	2	6	17	2%
Total	179	153	110	71	70	65	59	22	52	781	
	23%	20%	14%	9%	9%	8%	8%	3%	7%		

Of all the British lines, the London, Brighton and South Coast Railway had the largest number of barrister/directors - five in all. Although there were no apparent professional relationships between these men, their business contacts went beyond that particular railway; four were directors of the Newhaven Harbour Company and two were on the board of the Eagle Insurance Company. The most prominent of the directors of the London, Brighton and South Coast was Samuel Laing. His involvement with railways began in 1842 when he was appointed secretary to the railway department of the Board of Trade. In 1848 he became chairman and managing director of the line and remained in that office until he temporarily retired from the company in 1854. During the late 1850s and early 1860s, while an MP, he served successively as financial secretary of the treasury and financial minister in India. In 1867 he returned to head the London, Brighton and South Coast and he also served as chairman of the Newhaven Harbour Company. In the 1870s Laing founded the Railway Debenture Investment Trust and the Railway Share Investment Trust, which were concerned with floating and managing railway shares and bonds as well as speculating in these issues. Both of these investment trusts were active in the American securities market, a subject that I will return to later.(35) After his retirement from these concerns in c. 1890, Laing was succeeded as managing director by his son-in-law, Charles Macrae, who was also a member of the bar.

While I will not go into further detail here about directorships in English banks, investment companies and in the land development business, there is one company that falls somewhere between these discrete categories that is deserving of separate notice. Beginning in the 1840s the capital requirements of improving landlords fostered the growth of private loan companies established for this purpose under private acts of Parliament. In terms of the amount out on loan the most successful of these concerns was the Lands Improvement Company, formed in 1853.(36) In 1889 three members of the board, including the managing director Granville Richard Ryder, were barristers, Inner Templars and former MPs.

By comparison with most other fields there were relatively few barrister/directors of industrial firms, a phenomenon mirrored by the investment patterns of the profession. Nevertheless, the depth of the involvement by members of the bar in industry can be seen as compensation for their small numbers. Industrial directorships were concentrated largely in three sectors - metals, engineering and brewing - which together accounted for nearly three-quarters of the English industrial group. Ten barristers were directors of companies that ranked among the 50 largest industrial concerns in Britain in 1905, and six of these men served either as chairmen, managing directors or partners.(37) The connection was particularly strong between the legal profession (both branches) and the steel industry, as Dr Erickson has noted.(38) This fact was eloquently demonstrated by the dominant position of lawyers in the management of Sir W.G. Armstrong, Whitworth & Company and John Brown & Company.

South American directorships formed a distinct second place after those in the United Kingdom, but the British capital investment and economic control that they represented were significant factors in the development of the continent. The vast majority of companies with barrister/directors were located in three countries - Argentina, Uruguay and Brazil. Argentina, the most important of the three, began to foster and encourage British investments in the 1860s. The 1880s were particularly prosperous and they saw the burgeoning of British participation in the economy.(39) Railway directorships formed the largest single category by far in the Latin American group. (40) In a number of cases lines were connected through a series of interlocking directorates located in London. The dominant position of the railway, the key to the economic development of the continent, among barrister/directors was mirrored in the general pattern of direct British investment there. But the business interests of members of the bar in Latin America were not limited to railways or to only a few major countries. Rather they included mining, tramways, utilities and land development companies in virtually every part of South America as well as in Central America, Mexico and the Caribbean islands. There were a number of barristers who specialised in the direction of Latin American concerns, and their holdings are illustrative of the economic involvement of Britain in the region. A few of the leading members of this contingent were: Edward Pearce-Edgcumbe, banker and barrister of Lincoln's Inn, who sat on the boards of several railways in both Argentina and Uruguay and on the board of a land development company in the latter as well; Sir George Russell, a former County Court judge and heir to a family estate worth £3,000 a year, was the director of three railways in Costa Rica, Argentina and Venezuela; and Emmanuel Underdown QC MP was associated with five railway companies, a tramway, a railway construction firm and a bondholders' investment trust that were located in both South America and the Caribbean.

The character of British participation, including that by members of the bar, in the United States' economy was very different from the situation in Latin America. In contrast to the British control of the railways in the southern continent, Britons had virtually no share in the management of railways in the northern one, despite the large amounts of stock they owned there.(41) There was only one major exception to this rule - the Alabama Great Southern Railway; members of the bar played an extremely pivotal role in that venture. Two barristers, Augustus B. Abraham, a leader of the Melbourne bar from 1854 to 1862, and Thomas Snagge, later a County Court judge, were influential not only in directing the railway but also its associated land company - the Alabama Coal, Iron and

Colonization Company. The latter venture was established on 500,000 acres of land granted by the State of Alabama to settle claims made by English bondholders; Snagge led the protracted negotiations.(42) Abraham who was chairman of the land company also sat on the boards of the Alabama, New Orleans, Texas Railway and of two important investment trusts - Foreign and Colonial Government Trust Company and the Foreign, American and General Investment Trust Company, on which Laing modeled his own investment companies. In this latter project one of Abraham's co-directors was Francis H. Jeune, a leading practitioner in the ecclesiastical courts who became judge of the Probate, Divorce and Admiralty Division of the High Court in 1891 and President in 1892. Upon his retirement from the bench in 1905 he was raised to the peerage as Baron St. Helier.(43)

If the involvement of barristers in managing American companies was typical, then the main sectors of British interest were land development, ranching and mining.(44) These were located primarily in the Mid-West in a strip extending from Manitoba south to Arkansas, in the Gulf states from Alabama to Texas, in Colorado and California. Among the barristers with major interests in the United States were: William Austin of Lincoln's Inn, who was the chairman of two land companies in Kansas and one in Minnesota; George Readman, a Scots advocate and Inner Templar, who was director of a land company and a cattle company in Missouri; and Sir John Irving Courtney of Lincoln's Inn who had holdings in land and cattle companies in Arkansas and Colorado; Henry Seton-Karr, also of Lincoln's Inn, who was a director of a California mining company and chairman of the Detroit Breweries and the Chicago and North-West Granaries Company; and Samuel Pope, a Middle Templar, who was on the board of mining companies in Colorado and Missouri and chairman of the England Association of American Bond and Share Holders and of the New York Belting and Packing Company. In general British participation in these ventures was motivated by the high rate of return. In addition American promoters made use of the names of distinguished English personalities including barristers in order to encourage participation by the British investing public.(45) For example Judah P. Benjamin, a very successful member of the bar after his short tenure as Secretary of State of the Confederacy in the American Civil War, lent his support to the Flagstaff Mining Company.(46)

While most of the North and South American companies were perfectly respectable concerns there were a fair number that were of questionable character. Often the selection of British directors served simply as a means of hiding financial blemishes. In commenting upon schemes of this sort the Pall Mall Gazette wrote, 'The small English capitalist dearly loves a lord or M.P. as a director, and with the name of one or other on a prospectus his gullibility knows no limit but the length of his purse.'(47) According to Henry Hess, one of the most vociferous critics of these practices, there were public men who, though wealthy and not dependent upon 'directors' fees voted them, join the Boards of companies with no legitimate objects and no prospects of success, and who do so with the object of manipulating the share-market and pocketing enormous sums which a 'rig' in worthless pieces of paper brings them.(48)

Hess, who nicknamed these men 'guinea pigs', lists 44 barristers among hundreds of others in the 1902 edition of his <u>Critic Black Book</u>. These men sat on the boards of hundreds of mining and land companies primarily in the Americas but also in Africa and Asia. There is no doubt that the swindles among the American companies with British directors were a minority, nevertheless the disreputable concerns were already legend by the mid-1870s when Trollope created Augustus Melmotte as the quintessential corrupt promoter.(49)

In the 1880s British involvement in Asian, African and Australasian colonies had a much lower profile than in the Americas. In fact barristers held more directorships in Latin America than in all British colonies combined. The main sectors of imperial enterprise were as follows: mining - Africa, Australasia and to a lesser degree India; commerce including plantations - India; banks and investment companies - Australasia and India; and railways - India. Undoubtedly the most dramatic event in this period related to the colonial economies was the discovery of gold in the Transvaal.(50) The British public naturally enough invested large sums in the numerous mining companies that were established there and several barrister/directors were quick to recognise the opportunities in South Africa. Among them was Leigh Hoskyns who was a director of three mining concerns - two gold and one diamond - in 1889. The third son of a baronet, he was called to the bar at Lincoln's Inn in 1875, served as a prosecutor in Griqualand West in 1880, and three years later became acting crown prosecutor there. Hoskyns's career contained one element that typically distinguished barristers involved in colonial ventures from those with interests in North and South America; he lived and worked in the colonies and this was his entry card to business there.

ECONOMICS AND THE BAR - A SUMMARY

Barristers and judges in the second half of the nineteenth century earned and accumulated as large if not larger fortunes in real terms than had their predecessors, with the single exception of the wealthiest of the pre-reform Lord Chancellors and Chief Justices. Yet these men lived at a time when the relatively new professional ideal which asserted that a gentleman need not be a landowner was gaining currency.(51) This change was coupled with a decline in the rate of return on landed property and in its social attractiveness especially in the last quarter of the century.(52) As a consequence, after 1830 or so the most successful lawyers were loath to sink a significant part of their wealth in landed estates or in the founding of landed families. Rather they were content to be known as England's leading professional men and they preferred to invest their fortunes in the share and bond markets that promised considerably higher interest and the possibility of more substantial capital appreciation, albeit at a somewhat greater risk.

While most barristers were content with this rather passive economic role, a minority - less than 10 per cent - took a more direct part in business by sitting on the board of directors of at least one company. Some of these men were full-time businessmen but others combined directorships with careers in the law, in other professions, in government service or as landowners. These men, despite their small numbers, were at the centre of the economic life of late-nineteenth- and early-twentieth-century Britain, her colonies and certain foreign nations as well. In fact their involvement here represents the late Victorian world of business in miniature.

Scholars have often portrayed the professional man and the businessman as two distinct species with diametrically opposed motivations and goals.(53) However, just as historians during the past generation have demonstrated that landowning and business were not incompatible activities, but rather complementary ones, so it was with the professions, even the so-called gentlemanly ones.(54) An able professional could also be a capable entrepreneur both in his private practice and in wider spheres as well.(55) As this survey of barristers in business has suggested, there was no contradiction between advocacy and participation in commerce and industry. Perhaps the most eloquent proof of the compatibility of these two worlds was the ability of the most distinguished of the gentlemen of the long robe - the judges of the Supreme Court of Judicature - to inhabit both of them simultaneously.

NOTES

    1. James Fitzjames Stephen Papers 7349/18 f. 23.
    2. C.P. Snow, <u>Time of Hope</u> (Harmondsworth, 1962), p. 111.
    3. <u>Select Committee on Official Salaries</u>, BPP <u>X</u> (1850), pp. 173-4.
    4. Thomson, <u>The Choice of a Profession</u>, pp. 94, 97-8.
    5. <u>LJ</u>, <u>29</u> (September 15, 1894), p. 523. The incomes of leading provincial barristers were comparable to those of London juniors, according to the testimony of James Mottram, Judge of the Birmingham County Court in 1878. He told a parliamentary select committee that two of the twelve or thirteen local Birmingham counsel were earning at least 3,000 guineas a year. <u>Select Committee on the County Courts</u>, p. 152.
    6. In order to give the reader some benchmarks with which

to compare the fees of nineteenth-century barristers, here are a few representative incomes after mid-century: the greater gentry from £3,000 to £10,000 per annum; a successful provincial doctor around £1,000 per annum; Chief Clerks in the Civil Service from £1,000; a senior clerk in a legal or insurance office £600. According to R.D. Baxter, a statistician who wrote in the late 1860s, a typical upper class family required an income of £5,000 per annum, and that of a professional or tradesman with a house rental of £50 and three servants needed at least £500 yearly. Thompson, English Landed Society, p. 114; Peterson, The Medical Profession, p. 99; Geoffrey Best, Mid-Victorian Britain, 1851-75 (St. Albans, 1973), pp. 109-10.

7. Select Committee on Official Salaries, p.175.

8. Guy Routh, Occupations and Pay in Britain 1906-60 (Cambridge, 1965), pp. 62-3. Even in 1972 thirty per cent of barristers earned less than £1,000 per annum and the median income was £2,300. Hazell, 'Clerks and Fees' in Hazell (ed.), The Bar on Trial, p. 100.

9. The Royal Commission on Legal Services (2 vols., 1979), vol. 2, p. 55.

10. Ibid., p. 601.

11. Smith, Wealth of Nations, p. 106.

12. Wharncliffe Minuments 605 (January 24, 1861 and November 12, 1876).

13. Martin Leake Papers 85868 (April 18, 1841).

14. Select Committee on Legal Education, p. 256.

15. LT, 36 (January 12, 1861), p. 130; Bennett, The New South Wales Bar, pp. 96-7.

16. Buckee, 'Legal Profession in Allahabad', p. 64.

17. Schmitthener, 'Legal Profession in India', p. 370; R.F.V. Heuston, Lives of the Lord Chancellors 1885-1940 (1964), pp. 445-6; MacLane, Indian Nationalism, p. 60.

18. J.A. Banks, Prosperity and Parenthood: A Study of Family Planning Among the Victorian Middle Classes (1954), pp. 86-102.

19. Duman, The Judicial Bench, pp. 55-7. J.C. Jeafferson estimated that a barrister would be reckless to marry on an annual income of less than £1,500. Jeafferson, A Book About Lawyers (New York, 1868), p. 91.

20. On the issue of probate data see W.D. Rubinstein and D.H. Duman, 'Probate Valuations, A Tool for the Historian', The Local Historian, 11 (1974), pp. 68-71. All the figures given here have been rounded off to the nearest £100.

21. Peterson, The Medical Profession, p. 208.

22. W.D. Rubinstein, Men of Property, The Very Wealthy in Britain Since the Industrial Revolution (1981), p. 65. It should be noted that these men were not all barristers. What it does indicate is the wealth that accrued to men of law of all kinds.

23. Lord Hardwicke, according to a contemporary, was worth £800,000 at the time of his death in 1764, while Lord Eldon

left a personal estate of £700,000 and landed property estimated at £600,000 when he died in 1838. George Harris, The Life of Lord Chancellor Hardwicke (3 vols., 1847), vol. 3, p. 513; Duman, The Judicial Bench, p. 143. On pre-reform legal sinecures see the previously cited work, pp. 116-26.

24. This does not agree with the conclusions of W.D. Rubinstein on the general pattern of professional fortunes. W.D. Rubinstein, 'Wealth, Elites, and the Class Structure of Modern Britain', Past and Present, 76 (1977), p. 122, note 54.

25. W.D. Rubinstein, 'Men of Property: Some Aspects of Occupation, Inheritance and Power Among Top British Wealth-holders', in Philip Stanworth and Anthony Giddens (eds.), Elites and Power in British Society (Cambridge, 1974), p. 167.

26. The number of professional millionaires and half-millionaires was negligible next to other occupational groups. Rubinstein, Men of Property, pp. 62-5.

27. Professor William Aydelotte's research on the gentry MPs in the 1840s indicates that of the 166 heads of families he investigated, 28 (17 per cent) were barristers. W.O. Aydelotte, 'The Business Interests of the Gentry in the Parliament of 1841-47' in G. Kitson Clark, The Making of Victorian England (1962), p. 297.

28. Duman, The Judicial Bench, pp. 139, 144.

29. These are based on the probate records of Lord Blackburn d. January 1896; John Duncan Inverarity d. December 1923; Charles John Pearson d. August 1910; Mark John McTaggart Stewart d. September 1923; and George Watson d. February 1927, deposited in the Principal Probate Registry, Somerset House; and on the private papers of Viscount Bryce, Bryce MS UB 75 for 1898; Lord Monk Bretton, Monk Bretton Papers 69 for 1871-4.

30. See A.R. Hall, The London Capital Market and Australia 1870-1914 (Canberra, 1963), pp. 4-6, 11; Matthew Simon, 'The Pattern of New British Portfolio Foreign Investment, 1865-1914', in A.R. Hall (ed.), The Export of Capital From Britain 1870-1914 (1968), pp. 18, 25, 27.

31. LT, 87 (September 21, 1889), p. 343.

32. On the geographical distribution of British overseas investments in 1913 see Hall, The London Capital Market, p. 11.

33. H.A.L. Cockerell and Edwin Green, The British Insurance Business 1547-1970 (1976), p. 37.

34. Lord Monk Bretton's annual fee as a director of the Rock Life Assurance Company was just under £53 in 1874. Monk Bretton Papers 69. At the same time the Sun Insurance Office paid its directors £330 per annum. There were several barristers on the board of that company. P.G.M. Dickson, The Sun Insurance Office 1710-1960 (1960), pp. 266, 280-8.

35. Dorothy R. Adler, British Investment in American Railways 1834-1898 (Charlottesville, 1970), pp. 92, 150-1.

36. David Spring, The English Landed Estate in the Nineteenth Century: Its Administration (Baltimore, 1963), pp. 151-8.

37. The companies were Sir W.G. Armstrong, Mitchell & Co. and Sir Joseph Whitworth & Co. (These were merged in 1897 to form Sir W.G. Armstrong, Whitworth & Co.); Bass, Ratcliff & Gretton; John Brown; Salt Union; and Threlfall's Brewery. The men who served as either chairmen or managing directors or partners were: Stuart Rendel; Richard G. Christie; Charles Benjamin Bright McLaren; Sir Charles E. Ellis; Herman John Falk; and Thomas Threlfall. For a list of the largest industrial firms in Britain in 1905 see P.L. Payne, 'The Emergence of the Large-scale Company in Great Britain, 1870-1914', Economic History Review, XX (1967), pp. 539-40.

38. Charlotte Erickson, British Industrialists, Steel and Hosiery 1850-1950 (Cambridge, 1959), p. 61. On the business connections between Lord Armstrong and Lord Rendel see F.E. Hamer (ed.), The Personal Papers of Lord Rendel (1931), passim.

39. H.S. Ferns, Britain and Argentina in the Nineteenth Century (Oxford, 1960), pp. 326-7, 397.

40. On British involvement in the economy of South America see ibid; Richard Graham, Britain and the Onset of Modernization in Brazil (Cambridge, 1968); Leland H. Jenks, 'Britain and American Railway Development', Journal of Economic History, XI (1951); Irving Stone, 'British Direct and Portfolio Investment in Latin America Before 1914', Journal of Economic History, XXXVII (1977).

41. Jenks, 'Britain and American Railway Development', pp. 378-9.

42. Adler, British Investments in American Railways, pp. 129-31, 150-1; Jenks, 'Britain and American Railway Development', p. 379.

43. Another barrister who was involved with Abraham in the former of these was Thomas Freemantle, 2nd Baron Cottlesloe who succeeded to his father's title in 1890 and to the family estate of 2,683 acres worth £5,675 per annum. Cottlesloe was also a director of Samuel Laing's London, Brighton and South Coast Railway and Newhaven Harbour Company.

44. On British investments in America see Adler, British Investments in American Railways; W. Turrentine Jackson, The Enterprising Scot: Investors in the American West After 1873 (Edinburgh, 1968); Clarke G. Spence, British Investments and the American Mining Frontier 1860-1901 (Ithaca, 1958).

45. Jackson, The Enterprising Scot, pp. 44-5.

46. Spence, The American Mining Frontier, p. 67.

47. Pall Mall Gazette, August 11, 1892. Taken from a clipping so the page number is not known.

48. Henry Hess, The Critic Black Book (1902). See also Spence, The American Mining Frontier, pp. 52-3, 56.

49. Melmotte was a less than reputable businessman who helped promote a railway that was supposed to run from Salt Lake City to Vera Cruz. The scheme eventually failed but not before involving a number of gullible gentlemen and peers. Anthony Trollope, The Way We Live Now (1969). First published

in 1875.

50. Ronald Robinson and John Gallagher, Africa and the Victorians (New York, 1968), pp. 210-11; Jenks, 'Britain and American Railway Development', p. 337.

51. On the professional ideal of the nineteenth century see Duman, The Judicial Bench, pp. 173-82.

52. On the decline of the social attractiveness of land see W.D. Rubinstein, 'New Men of Wealth and the Purchase of Land in Nineteenth-Century England', Past and Present, 92 (1981), pp. 125-38; Thompson, English Landed Society, pp. 292-326; Rubinstein, 'Wealth, Elites and the Class Structure', p. 120; Rubinstein, Men of Property, pp. 214-18. As this last work makes clear the disinterest of barristers in land was typical of the middle classes at least from the 1850s.

53. See Carr-Saunders and Wilson, The Professions, p. 471; R.H. Tawney, The Acquisitive Society (New York, 1967), pp. 92-5, first published in 1920; S. and B. Webb, 'Special Supplement on Professional Associations' part II, The New Statesman, IX (1917), p. 40, 48. For an analysis of this dichotomy see Daniel Duman, 'The Creation and Diffusion of a Professional Ideology in Nineteenth Century England', Sociological Review, 27 (1979), pp. 113-38.

54. For example see Lawrence Stone, Crisis of the Aristocracy (Oxford, 1965), Chapter VII; David Spring, 'The English Landed Estate in the Age of Iron and Coal', Journal of Economic History, 11 (1951), pp. 3-24; J.T. Ward and R.G. Wilson (eds.), Land and Industry, The Landed Estate and the Industrial Revolution (Newton Abbott, 1971), passim.

55. On the doctor as entrepreneur see Peterson, The Medical Profession, pp. 244-82.

Chapter Six

POLITICS AND THE BAR

When David Maxwell Fyfe entered Parliament in 1935 his friend, fellow barrister and newly appointed Home Secretary, Sir John Simon, told him that the British House of Commons is 'the one legislative assembly in the world where lawyers as such are not popular.'(1) Nonetheless there can be little doubt that barristers were more numerous in Parliament than any other occupational group in nineteenth-century England, except for the country gentlemen. The prevalence of lawyers in Parliament has elicited considerable comment from scholars including Sir Lewis Namier, Harold Laski, John Vincent, W.L. Guttsman and David Podmore.(2) In venturing into this much-explored territory, I intend to examine the relationship between careers in law and in politics from the barrister's perspective, rather than just as one aspect of a general analysis of the composition and structure of the political elite.

BARRISTERS IN THE HOUSE OF COMMONS

We can begin simply by counting the MPs who were members of the bar. In Table 6.1 I have listed the number and percentage of lawyers in the Parliaments of 1832 to 1886. With the exception of the elections of 1880 and 1885 for which I have arrived at complete counts of the number of English barristers, all the other data must be taken as estimates. Certainly between 1832 and 1865 the percentages are somewhat inflated by the inclusion of solicitors and Irish and Scots barristers and advocates. On the other hand, the total for the entire period 1832-1885 is an underenumeration since the main source, Dod's, invariably omits the legal qualifications of some of the non-practising members of the bar who sat in the House of Commons. Despite these limitations, it seems clear that the percentage of barrister/MPs increased considerably during these fifty years and may have actually doubled. The peak in the number of parliamentary barristers was apparently reached in the late Victorian era with the gentlemen of the long robe accounting

Table 6.1: Lawyers in the House of Commons 1832 to 1886

Election Years	No.	%	Notes
1832[a]	71	11	Thomas counted interests, not individuals, so that a barrister who was also a landowner would appear in both categories. The total includes practising and non-practising barristers and solicitors in England, Scotland and Ireland.
1835[a]	75	11	"
1837[a]	80	12	"
1841[a]	77	12	"
1847[a]	80	12	"
1852[a]	102	16	"
1857[a]	99	15	"
1859[a]	101	15	"
1865[a]	94	14	"
1868[b]	99	15	For the year 1872. Only barristers are enumerated here, but there were 8 solicitors as well.
1874[b]	104	16	Barristers only. There were also 11 solicitors.
1880[c]	130	20	Includes all men who were called to the bar, but not Irish barristers or Scots advocates.
1885[d]	131	20	"
1832-86[e]	309	10	Includes only men called to the English bar according to the biographies listed in Dod's Parliamentary Companion.

Sources: a. J.A. Thomas, The House of Commons, 1832-1901: A Study of its Economic and Functional Character (Cardiff, 1939), pp. 4-7. b. Vincent, The Formation of the British Liberal Party, p. 77. c. Debrett's Illustrated House of Commons and Judicial Bench (1880), corrected to June 1880. d. LT, 80 (December 26, 1885), pp. 129-30; LJ, 20, pp. 734-9. e. M. Stenton (ed.), Who's Who of British Members of Parliament 1886-1914 (1976).

for a fifth of the total membership of the House of Commons.

Political Affiliations
Barristers did not form a random sample of nineteenth-century parliamentarians with regard to their party affiliations. From 1832 until the Irish home rule crisis of 1886 the majority of lawyer/MPs were Liberals in every general election except for Sir Robert Peel's victory in 1841. Between 1852 and 1885 Liberal lawyers never accounted for less than 57 per cent of the total legal contingent, even after the Conservative victory of 1874, and four times they exceeded 60 per cent. The Liberal dominance of the legal profession ended in 1886 as the number of lawyers sitting as Conservatives increased, while others transferred their allegiance from Gladstone's party to the new Liberal-Unionists. In the Home Rule election of 1886 only 36 per cent of the lawyers were official Liberals. With the Liberal victory in 1892 this increased to 47 per cent, before declining to 32 per cent in both 1895 and 1902. By the inter-war years the Conservative Party had become the natural home of the majority of barrister/MPs, as it was for much of upper-middle-class Britain.(3)

There seem to be three possible explanations for the great affinity of lawyers for the Liberal Party between 1832 and 1886 and the subsequent gradual decline. The degree of affiliation of lawyers with the Liberals may have been simply a reflection of that party's electoral fortunes. But this explanation alone is not sufficient; as we have seen, even in 1874 a majority of barristers in the Commons were Liberals. Furthermore, the percentage of barristers adhering to the Liberal Party exceeded the percentage of Liberal MPs during the second half of the nineteenth century even in 1886, 1895 and 1900 when a majority of barristers sat as Conservatives or Liberal-Unionists. Another factor that may have attracted barristers to the Liberals was opportunism. Since the Liberal Party dominated national politics between 1832 and 1886, it was in a position to dispense vast amounts of patronage to its supporters, including not only professional offices but junior and senior ministerial portfolios and peerages as well. With the decline in Liberal fortunes after 1886, Conservative barrister/MPs now had access to these offices. The final possibility is that until the 1880s, barristers felt that they had a greater chance to advance to the front-benches in the socially heterogeneous Liberal Party. Between the 1850s and 1880s about half of the Liberal MPs were from business and professional origins and the other half from the landed classes, especially the old Whig aristocracy. By contrast the Conservatives were predominantly landowning, with the addition from the 1870s of bankers and merchants. This preference for the Liberals began to decline as a result of the Irish Home Rule crises that brought in their wake a social and political realignment of forces during the last decade and a half of the nineteenth century. At that time barristers, along with other business and professional groups, began to shift their loyalties from the Liberals to the Conservatives and their Liberal-Unionist allies.(4)

The attachment of barristers to the Liberal Party was probably due to the confluence of all three factors discussed above. At a later stage we will return to examine the relationship between a career in politics and professional advancement, but first we must consider the social quality and educational backgrounds of the late-Victorian barristers who sat in the House of Commons.

Occupational and Educational Backgrounds

In his brilliant study of the Liberal Party, John Vincent has sketched a concise portrait of the place of the barristers in the world of mid-Victorian politics.(5) There he raised several questions concerning the barrister/MPs' social origins, their access to patronage and their reasons for embarking upon a political career. In the following pages I hope to add details to his sketch through a social and career analysis of these men, in particular those barristers who won seats in the election of 1880. This will allow us to take a closer look at the social quality, professional socialisation and the motivations of politically active members of the bar.

In Table 6.2 I have divided the barristers elected to Parliament in 1880 into twelve status and occupational categories, including five categories of men from landed origins, according to status and wealth. Aristocratic connections in the second degree have been included both in order to allow easier comparison with other studies of English members of Parliament and because they help to make the relationship between political and social elites more explicit. Likewise I have sub-divided both the professionals and the businessmen into two groups each, the former according to status and the latter by the type of activity.

A comparison between the social origins of barrister/MPs and those of the entire late Victorian bar (Table 1.6) reveals striking contrasts. Among the MPs the sons of aristocrats, the greater gentry and successful businessmen were over-represented, while the professions, squirearchy and lesser landowners, and small businessmen were under-represented. For example only a third of the members of the bar in 1885 from landowning families were the sons of landowners with annual rentals of £3,000 or more, compared with nearly three-quarters of the barristers with landed origins in the 1880 Parliament. Similarly, the businessmen whose sons sat in the Commons included a higher proportion of wealthy and successful individuals than did the entire bar. Among the fathers of the barristers elected to the lower house in 1880 were Thomas Brassey, the millionaire rail-

Table 6.2: The Social and Occupational Origins of Barrister/MPs (1880)

	No.	%
Aristocratic Sons	14	11
Aristocratic Grandsons	8	6
Gentry over £3,000 p.a.	15	12
Gentry under £3,000 p.a.	11	8
Rural Gent. and Esq.	4	3
Upper Professions	20	15
Lower Professions	17	13
Banking/Commerce/Publishing	19	15
Industry	11	8
Urban Gent. and Esq.	4	3
Artisan	1	1
Unknown	6	5
Total Aristocrats and Gentry	52	40
Total Professions and Government Service	37	28
Total Middle Class	71	55

way contractor, Sir Dudley Coutts Marjoribanks MP, a partner in Meux's Brewery, Samuel Morley MP, who made a fortune in the hosiery business, Sir William Jackson Bart., an African merchant who left a personal estate of £700,000, and Baron de Worms, whose interests included banking at home and coffee plantations in Ceylon.

Data on the educational backgrounds of the barristers in the 1880 House of Commons strengthen the conclusion that the men were largely recruited from among the social and economic elite of the bar. A considerably higher proportion of barrister/MPs attended elite public schools, all public schools, Oxbridge and selected elite colleges at the two ancient universities than had rank and file members of the bar. Thus both in his social and educational profiles the typical barrister/MP in 1880 resembled his fellow politicians much more closely than he did other inns of court men.

Converging Careers in Law and Politics
Two-thirds of the barrister/MPs in 1880 had had active careers

in the professions, government service or business before entering Parliament(6) and many of these men were able to combine work in those fields with their political activities. As we shall see, nowhere was the opportunity for a dual career greater than at the practising bar.

Advocacy has traditionally been recognised as one of the few occupations that allows practitioners the freedom to enter the world of politics. The compatibility is usually ascribed to the fact that membership in a successful law partnership affords the lawyer the possibility of indulging in politics and perhaps even continuing to receive some of his former income as well as having the knowledge that he has a place to return to in the event of electoral defeat. Similar advantages are available to businessmen.(7) But this explanation of the conjunction between political and legal careers does not fit the case of the English barrister, at least not in the nineteenth and early twentieth centuries before the rise of large sets of chambers. Since the barrister was essentially an independent practitioner, he did not have the luxury of depending on partners to reserve a place for him while he devoted his energies to politics. A barrister had to endeavour to keep his name before members of the lower branch and in consequence it was unusual for him to try to re-establish himself in practice after having retired. There were of course exceptions, most notably H.H. Asquith, who returned to the bar after having served as Home Secretary in Lord Rosebury's cabinet between 1892 and 1895. Furthermore, barristers who entered Parliament with an eye to a judicial appointment were virtually required to continue to practise, since both the profession and public opinion frowned upon the selection of judges, especially for the Superior Court, from among unsuccessful or inactive members of the bar.

Unless a barrister had independent means or non-professional sources of income, he would invariably have to live on the fees he derived from practice at the bar while a back-bencher. Until 1911 MPs were unpaid for their services and between then and 1937 they received only £400 per annum. As a consequence, most practising barristers in the late nineteenth century did not have the opportunity available to Gervais Rentoul in 1927. After some five years of combining law and politics, 'I had very largely to let my practice at the Bar go; but that did not trouble me much at the time, as my ideas were fixed more or less on a political career, and I was also engaged in certain business activities.'(8)

Of the 54 practising barristers elected to Parliament in 1880, as many as 46 may have continued in the profession for at least a few years, while 27 of these men pursued active and successful careers as advocates concurrently with their membership in the House of Commons. Not surprisingly, the dual careers of these barrister/MPs were sometimes a subject for criticism. For example in 1841 during a debate about the request for a leave of absence to enable Robert Ingham to attend the meeting of the assize courts on the Northern circuit of which he was a member, Sir Robert Peel told the Commons:

> that, if lawyers found their duties as Members of the House, onerous, they were not obliged to retain their seats. If there was a pressure of business in the House requiring the attendance of Members, he did not see why lawyers should be exempted more than others, for in such cases they ought take their fair share of duties as Members.(9)

The fact that parliamentary sittings were held in the evenings facilitated the combination of the two careers, at least for those men whose legal business was concentrated in the capital. Yet according to the Law Times, the inevitable result was that barrister/MPs neglected their legislative duties.

> For some reason or other lawyers very rarely succeed in achieving distinction in the Legislature. But the temptation to enter Parliament is too strong for most men to resist...If the object of entering the House is to serve the country and not merely to promote a man's career, there may be doubts whether lawyers who have much practice can serve the country as others members who have no absorbing professional avocation...
> There are many who think that the practice of law is more absorbing, more exciting, than it was fifty years or even twenty years ago. It is more difficult for a busy lawyer to achieve and maintain a first-rate position in the House of Commons, and lawyers cannot and will not sacrifice their private practice to the public service. The constituencies know this, and are becoming less and less anxious for legal candidates who are seldom rich and never rich fools.(10)

In the following section I will take a detailed look at the relationship between a political career and professional success. At this juncture, however, it is sufficient to note that many of the practising barristers had achieved professional prominence prior to their entry into the House of Commons; almost half had taken silk before seeking election.(11) As a consequence of the time it took to establish a position as a leader, practising barristers were considerably older than the average MP when they entered the House. This phenomenon was noted by J.P. Cornford in his examination of the late-Victorian Conservative Party.(12) Half of the MPs in his study entered Parliament at age 40 or under and this is similar to the percentage for all barrister/MPs elected in 1880. By contrast, 70 per cent of the practising barristers were over 40 when first elected to the Commons and 46 per cent were between 41 and 50 years old. Yet this age difference did not mean that barristers had relatively shorter parliamentary careers than other groups. On the contrary, 44 per cent of all barristers and 36 per cent of practising ones sat in Parliament for more than 16 years compared to 34 per cent of the Conservative MPs elected between 1885 and 1900. The reason that so many members of the bar had long political careers despite their relatively late age of entry into the Commons can best be explained by the fact that barristers, practising and non-practising alike, entered Parliament as professionals and not amateurs. As we shall see shortly, they were not content to sit on the back-benches. Their goals were to achieve office, either ministerial or judicial, and this required persistence and encouraged them to remain active in the political arena for many years.

In summary we have found that in the late nineteenth century, barrister/MPs were recruited by and large from among the social and economic elite of the profession, and that until 1886 they were primarily allied with the Liberal Party. Furthermore, the majority of all barristers continued to follow their original occupation after election to the House of Commons and this was especially true of the practising barristers. Finally, these practitioners were latecomers to Parliament; nevertheless their careers in the Commons were relatively long. This leaves unexplained two related problems in regard to the bar and politics, namely the ubiquity of barristers in the Victorian political world and the forces that motivated barristers to enter that world. In the remainder of this chapter I hope to throw some light on these questions by examining the relationship between politics and professional advancement and the place of the barrister within the national political elite.

POLITICS AND PROFESSIONAL ADVANCEMENT

Few students of the English legal profession would take issue with the assessment that barristers 'all too frequently...are in the House more to serve their professional ambitions than from any great regard for the interests of their country.'(13) Yet with the exception of Professor Vincent's survey of the mid-Victorian bar, no-one has yet tried to 'trace a flow of lawyers from Parliament to lucrative Crown offices.'(14) In order to remedy this omission I propose to examine the extent to which political considerations influenced the bestowal of professional rewards. I have divided the major ranks and offices into junior and senior groups: included in the first are recorders, County Court judges and Queen's Counsel, and in the second, law officers of the crown and judges of the superior courts.

The office of recorder was, as we have seen, one of the

lesser professional plums; nevertheless, since it was only a part-time judicial office it was tenable with a seat in the House of Commons. In 1880 103 men served as recorders in England and Wales of whom 16 per cent could be considered political barristers: four were current members of the lower house, seven had been members and five were unsuccessful parliamentary candidates. Yet less than a third of the recorder/politicians were members of the Commons or had been candidates at the time of their appointments. Clearly politically active barristers (MPs and candidates) were not favoured in appointments to recorderships. Furthermore in the minority of cases in which they were chosen, more often than not it was a prelude to a political career rather than a reward for services rendered.(15)

The picture of political activity among the County Court judges was much the same, although these members were prohibited from sitting concurrently on the bench and in the House of Commons. Only 14 men (12 per cent) out of a random sample of 116 judges appointed between 1847 and 1901 were ever MPs or parliamentary candidates. Of these, 12 were elevated to the bench subsequently to having sat in the House of Commons and 10 were appointed when their own party was in power. While most County Court judges were either non-political or at most rank and file party supporters, a political barrister who wanted a secure if not particularly prestigious or highly remunerative professional office could probably have had one of these judgeships for the asking. In actual fact ambitious barrister/MPs were not usually attracted either to recorderships that required time that busy men were unwilling to spare, or to County Court judgeships which spelled the end to any real hopes of advancement, either political or professional.

These limitations did not apply to the office of Queen's Counsel. Taking rank opened the door not only to the material rewards of the profession but also to future promotions. It was, as we have seen, almost an inevitable step for a successful barrister. Analysis of a random sample of 118 QCs who took silk between 1850 and 1901 reveals that nearly half (54 men) were at some time in their careers either MPs or had stood unsuccessfully for election to the House of Commons. Of these, just under three-quarters were granted silk by their own party and 18 (15 per cent) were MPs or had been candidates at the time of their appointments. Finally 22 of the 36 QCs who took rank before they ran for Parliament contested a seat either at the first general election after they took silk or prior to that at a by-election.(16) Thus it appears that in many instances a barrister with political ambitions was granted a silk gown as a means of grooming him for the House of Commons.

The evidence strongly suggests that the purely political QC, chosen solely on account of his parliamentary service without any regard to his professional suitability, was a rarity in the second half of the nineteenth century and I have discovered only a few barristers who may have taken rank in this manner. A prime example was Rowland Blennerhasset, the first son of an Irish country gentleman with an annual rent roll of £2,145. He entered the Commons as a Liberal MP for County Kerry in 1872 at the age of 22 and served there until 1885 when his parliamentary career ended. Blennerhasset was called to the bar at the Inner Temple in 1878 when already an MP, and the only reference to his legal career that I have found is his inclusion on the circuit list of the North-Eastern circuit in 1895. Despite his apparent lack of achievement at the bar, he was made a QC in 1894 at the age of 44.

One likely explanation for the absence of silks whose only claims were political was that the office of QC was the bar's most important rank and a symbol of professional achievement. Its politicisation would not only have debased the rank, but may also have undermined the organisational foundations of the bar. Of course a seat in Parliament could on occasion hasten the receipt of a silk gown, but in most instances where this did occur the men were professionally qualified for the honour. There can be little doubt that men like Robert Reid (Lord Loreburn) and Henry James (Lord James of Hereford), who took rank at the ages of 36 and 41 respectively, did not become QCs simply as a result of their political activities.

One of the more curious instances of an MP taking silk is found in the career of Edward Macnaghten who, after serving in the House of Commons for seven years, ended his professional career in the House of Lords as a Lord of Appeal in Ordinary. Macnaghten practised as an equity junior for 23 years until he was made a QC in April 1880 even before the meeting of the new Parliament to which he had been elected as a Conservative member for Antrim. At the time he was already 50 years old - an advanced age for a future law lord to take silk.(17) This does not seem to have been simply a political promotion. Macnaghten showed himself to be a reasonably able appeals judge and in addition, although he had been appointed to the Lords during Lord Halsbury's tenure of the woolsack, he was by no means a rubber stamp for the Conservative Lord Chancellor. In the controversial trade union case of <u>Allen v. Flood</u> (1898), he sided with the majority to overturn the decision of the Court of Appeal contrary to the stand taken by Halsbury.(18)

The high proportion of barrister/MPs who were also QCs was not due simply to favouritism in the appointment of silks. These men did not constitute a random sample of the bar, but rather a select cohort who were drawn into Parliament in the vast majority of cases after their promotion. This was due to four main reasons: 1. a successful silk has a far easier time of sustaining his practice while actively participating in politics than does a junior; 2. a barrister whose professional mettle had already been tested would probably be more attractive to politicians and perhaps to constituents than a man who was only beginning to make his way at the bar; 3. QCs whose ambitions were directed towards the bench often saw service in the House of Commons as a way of increasing their chances of obtaining a judgeship; 4. finally there were those men for whom the bar was not an end in itself but a means of entry into the political elite. Some of them at least must have felt it was best to establish their professional credentials and secure a comfortable income before trying their luck in politics.

Of all the official positions that were open to members of the bar, none, with the possible exception of the Lord Chancellorship, better epitomised the conjuncture of careers in law and politics than the law offices of the crown - the Solicitor- and Attorney-Generalships. While these offices were often bestowed on lawyers of note, political considerations weighed heavily in the selection of candidates for these positions. In most instances, the men chosen as Attorneys- and Solicitors-General were already members of the House of Commons and had only to win re-election in consequence of their appointments. However, in the last quarter of the nineteenth century there were several instances in which candidates were chosen for a law officership without having a seat in Parliament. Naturally this created impediments for the ministry that could not be tolerated for long, as Lord Cairns explained to Sir Hardinge Giffard, the Solicitor-General, in 1876:

> It has been a matter of much regret & no small inconvenience to the Government that owing to the difficulty you have found in obtaining a seat in the Ho. of Commons, they have been during the past session deprived of the advantages of your aid in Parliament. They would deeply regret that a continuance of this state of things should lead to a severance of their official connection with you; but it would be absolutely necessary, if this connection is to continue, that you should be able to meet Parliament at the commencement of the coming session with a seat in the House.(19)

Giffard was eventually successful in securing a safe seat for himself as member for Launceston, and in 1885 when the Conservative Party returned to power, he succeeded to the Lord Chancellorship.

The complex relationship between political and professional considerations in the choice of law officers of the crown is usefully illustrated by the selection of Conservative nominees in the 1880s and 1890s. In June 1885, Lord Salisbury began to form his first administration and the name of Richard Webster QC was put forward as a likely candidate for the post of Attorney-General. In reaction to this Edward Clarke QC MP wrote to the new Prime Minister in order to warn him that efforts had to be made not to offend party stalwarts among members of the bar. Clarke reminded him that in 1880 Cairns had offered a vacant puisne judgeship to two Liberal barristers, Herschell and Bowen. Now the man chosen as Attorney-General was not only without a seat in the House of Commons, but younger and with fewer years of practice than all the QCs in Parliament. Clarke concluded, 'I think it would be extremely unfortunate that a public announcement should be made to the Bar that services rendered to the Party inside the House of Commons and outside its walls, are to be treated as an actual disqualification for professional promotion.'(20) Salisbury rejected the advice and replied that seniority and political service alone could not determine the distribution of senior legal patronage.(21)

Clarke was far from being a disinterested party; in fact he was putting forth his claims for the job of Attorney-General. Nevertheless there was probably an element of truth in what he wrote, and this was recognised by the Prime Minister in his selection of a Solicitor-General. Once again Clarke was passed over, but this time no-one could claim that political considerations had been ignored. The appointee, John Eldon Gorst, had been the Principal Agent of the Conservative Party in the early 1870s and in this capacity contributed significantly to the party's election victory in 1874. After failing to reap immediate political rewards for his efforts, Gorst returned to his legal practice and in 1875, shortly after his election to the Commons, took silk. Disaffected from the Party establishment, he joined with Lord Randolph Churchill, Henry Drummond Wolff and Arthur Balfour in 1881 to form the 'fourth party'. His appointment as Solicitor-General in 1885 was due largely to the influence of Churchill who became Indian Secretary. In 1886 Gorst was again offered the Solicitor-Generalship, but with the understanding that this was only a temporary expedient until he could be 'promoted' to a seat on the bench. Gorst, whose political ambitions were far from satisfied by this arrangement, rejected it and was appointed instead Under-Secretary of State for India,(22) while Clarke became Solicitor-General.

When the Conservatives returned to power in 1895, the Prime Minister offered Webster and Clarke their previously held posts of Attorney- and Solicitor-General - but on new terms: they had to become full-time law officers and give up their private legal practices. Webster accepted, but Clarke refused, and returned to the back-benches from where he attacked his own leadership.(23) Nevertheless, with the retirement of Lord Esher from the Rolls in 1897, Clarke was considered in the arrangements to fill that vacancy. Questions were raised concerning Clarke's legal knowledge and he was described by Salisbury as 'our chief difficulty'. The Prime Minister summed up the situation to Lord Chancellor Halsbury as follows:

...I had rather see Clarke M.R. than Attorney: without

taking into account that if he is made attorney he has a
claim which could not be passed over to higher possible
vacancies. There remains the third course - to throw
Clarke over altogether & tell him that the highest point
of his career has been reached.
    I confess that the more I consider this alternative
the more I dislike it. It is at variance with the unwritten law of our party system: & there is no clearer
stricture than that unwritten law, than the rule that
party claims should always weigh heavily in the disposal
of the highest legal appointments.(24)

Clarke himself provided the solution to his dilemma: Salisbury salved his political conscience by offering him the Mastership of the Rolls, but Clarke rejected the offer, as the
Prime Minister had probably hoped he would, in order to remain
in the Commons.(25)
    Quite naturally, the judgeships of the superior courts at
Westminster had been scrutinised in greater detail than any
other legal office with regard to the connection between politics and professional appointments.(26) Beginning with Professor Laski, numerous commentators have measured and assessed
the influence of political participation on a barrister's chances of promotion to the bench.(27) The last of the nineteenth-
century Lord Chancellors, Lord Halsbury, had a particularly in-
famous reputation for making political appointments to the judiciary.(28) Recently J.A.G. Griffith, commenting on Professor Heuston's evaluation of Halsbury, has suggested that the
Lord Chancellor's six 'bad' appointments were the result of
his predilection for choosing 'political associates' for the
bench.(29) In fact the proportion of political appointees -
MPs and candidates - elevated to the bench by their own party,
was considerably lower during Halsbury's tenure of the woolsack (1:3), than during the entire period 1850-1901 when it
was 1:2. Seen within the context of the nineteenth-century
system of legal patronage, there was nothing unusual in Halsbury's choice of politically active barristers. For example
in 1868 Lord Chelmsford gave Lord Cairns the following advice
with regard to the suitability of W.R. Grove and Anthony Cleas-
by for a vacant judgeship:

> I have the highest opinion of Grove...but from what I
> have seen of him I should not be disposed to rank him be-
> fore Cleasby who I have always taken to be a well read
> Lawyer - upon the whole if I were myself called upon to
> make the choice I should prefer Cleasby, & I quite agree
> that if the scales hang equally between him & Grove, his
> services to the party act to incline them in his favour.(30)

I would suggest that in fact Halsbury's 'bad' appointments stemmed from his inability or unwillingness to ensure

that barrister/MPs who were selected as judges were not only politicians but competent lawyers as well.(31) Salisbury was more sensitive than his Lord Chancellor to the demands of public and legal opinion in this regard. In 1897 the Prime Minister cautioned, 'The judicial salad requires both legal oil and political vinegar; but disastrous effects will follow if due proportion is not observed.'(32) In appointing men like William Grantham, Charles Darling and Edward Ridley to the High Court bench, Halsbury violated this guiding principle by favouring political expediency over professional quality. For example in 1897 the Law Journal commented upon the occasion of Ridley's elevation:

> The appointment of Mr. Edward Ridley Q.C. to the Bench... is something more than a surprise. It is certain to be described as a political job, and indeed it is difficult to disassociate it from the parliamentary position of his brother [Sir Matthew Ridley, the Home Secretary]. Neither his practice at the bar nor his experience as an official referee gives him any claim on the Bench of the High Court....The appointment can be defended on no ground whatsoever. It would be easy to name fifty members of the Bar with a better claim.(33)

The Halsbury-Salisbury judicial creations were not the only ones that aroused public and professional indignation in the second half of the nineteenth century. But other Lord Chancellors and Prime Ministers were less guilty of placing really incompetent lawyers on the bench. An examination of four appointments that elicited criticism between 1859 and 1882 should suffice to establish this claim. As we saw earlier, despite the attacks on Lord Campbell's appointment of Colin Blackburn in 1859, later events justified this choice.(34) In 1871 Gladstone came under severe fire for naming Robert Collier, the Attorney-General, to the Court of Common Pleas in order to qualify him for one of the newly created salaried positions on the Judicial Committee of the Privy Council. There was no question of Collier's professional suitability for office. Instead, criticism revolved around the cynical manner in which Gladstone manipulated circumstances to suit his plans. (35) Another much debated appointment was that of Alfred Thesiger, son of former Lord Chancellor Chelmsford, to the Court of Appeal in 1877 at the age of 39. The main charge levelled against this choice was that Thesiger was promoted over the head of his seniors at the bar because of his legal connections. However, even his harshest critics never denied his ability. The Law Times sprang to Thesiger's defence, rejecting the contention that his age or his comparatively few years of practice should have barred his elevation to the Appeals bench.(36) Finally, in 1832 the Law Times came out in favour of the promotion of Charles Bowen from a puisne judgeship to the Court

Table 6.3: Legal Officeholding Among Practising Barrister/MPs Elected in 1880   (N = 54)

	Superior Court Judges	Crown Law Officers	Judge Advocate General	Queen's Counsel	County Court Judges	Recorders	Colonial Law Officers	Department Counsel	Total
No.	13	3	4	4	3	4	1	3	35
%	24	6	7	7	6	7	2	6	65

of Appeal. While noting that Lord Coleridge's patronage had contributed to Bowen's professional progress, it concluded that, 'it is satisfactory to know that in the opinion of the Profession the appointment is the best which could have been made.'(37)

We can now measure the global importance of Parliament as a path to legal offices and honours in the late Victorian period more precisely by examining the frequency with which the 54 practising barristers elected to the House of 1880 were appointed to the positions discussed above and several others as well. I have counted each man only once, according to the highest post he held, and the results are displayed in Table 6.3. They could hardly be more striking. Nearly two-thirds of the barrister/politicians who were members of the 1880 Parliament subsequently received at least one professional appointment. In the light of this overwhelming evidence there can be little doubt that 'legal careerists' were entirely correct in viewing the House of Commons as the high road to office, to profit and to power.(38)

BARRISTERS AND THE POLITICAL ELITE

Members of the bar were well represented in the nineteenth-century political elite. Of the 289 cabinet ministers who held office between 1815 and 1914, sixty (21 per cent) had been called to the bar. Of these, two men - Melbourne and Asquith - served as Prime Minister, while a third, Spencer Perceval, was filling that post when he was assassinated in 1812. In addition, many other leading political figures of the age, including Peel, Disraeli and Gladstone (all of Lincoln's Inn), had been students at an inn, although they were never called to the bar. All of these men - students and barristers alike - had inhaled the legal atmosphere in the chambers and dining halls of the inns of court, and therefore we are justified in ranking these institutions with the great public schools and Oxford and Cambridge as the principal socialising agents of the nineteenth-century political establishment.

The size of the legal contribution to the many cabinets formed between the Battle of Waterloo and World War One was not constant. The wide fluctuations are clearly visible in Table 6.4. Before commenting on the data displayed there, we must realise that every government had to have at least one barrister in the cabinet since the profession had, as it were, a reserved ministerial seat in the person of the Lord Chancellor. We can divide the table into three sections. During the first three ministries, barristers accounted for between 23 and 33 per cent of the total number of ministers. Wellington's government of 1828 contained only one barrister, and with the exception of Lord John Russell's cabinet of 1846 the number of barrister/ministers did not exceed two (15 per cent) until 1859.

Table 6.4: Barristers in British Cabinets 1815-1914

Date	Party	No. of Ministers	Barristers No.	Barristers %	Date	Party	No. of Ministers	Barristers No.	Barristers %
1815	Tory	13	3	23	1865	Lib.	15	6	40
1827	-	13	4	31	1866	Cons.	15	4	27
1827	-	15	5	33	1868	Cons.	15	5	33
1828	-	13	1	8	1868	Lib.	15	4	27
1830	Lib.	13	2	15	1874	Cons.	12	5	42
1834	Lib.	16	2	13	1880	Lib.	14	3	21
1834	Cons.	14	1	7	1885	Cons.	16	4	25
1835	Lib.	14	2	14	1886	Lib.	14	3	21
1841	Cons.	16	1	7	1886	Cons.	14	5	36
1846	Lib.	16	5	31	1892	Lib.	17	7	41
1852	Cons.	13	2	15	1894	Lib.	16	8	50
1852	Lib.	13	1	8	1895	Cons.	19	4	21
1855	Lib.	14	2	14	1902	Cons.	20	3	15
1858	Cons.	13	2	15	1905	Lib.	19	7	37
1859	Lib.	15	4	27	1908	Lib.	21	7	33

Note: I have used the names Lib. (Liberal) and Cons. (Conservative) in years before they are strictly applicable for convenience. Because of the fluid situation in the political system in the late 1820s, I have not used any party designations for that period.

Here began the third phase that lasted until 1914; only once
(1902) did the proportion of barristers fall below one-fifth,
and it rose above 40 per cent four times. The most lawyer-do-
minated of all the cabinets was Lord Rosebery's administration
that included Lord Herschell (Lord Chancellor), Lord Tweedmouth (Lord Privy Seal and Chancellor of the Duchy of Lancaster),
Sir William Vernon Harcourt (Exchequer), H.H. Asquith (Home
Secretary), John Morley (Chief Secretary for Ireland), James
Bryce (President of the Board of Trade), G.J. Shaw-Lefevre
(Local Government Board) and Arnold Morley (Postmaster-General).
No great difference in the number of barrister/ministers according to party is evident, with the possible exception of the
years 1894-1908 in which the percentage in Conservative cabi-
nets was less than half of that in Liberal ones.

What interests us most here is the relationship between
careers in the law and those in politics. As we have already
seen, a seat in Parliament was a favoured path to senior legal
posts. For some men, ministerial office was a substitute for
the professional honours that eluded them. Finally there were
men for whom the law was primarily a means by which to enter
the world of high politics.

We have already looked in some detail at the first of the
motivations for entering Parliament, namely to advance a man's
prospects in his profession. The second, in which politics
served as a consolation prize for barristers whose legal ambitions had been thwarted at least for the moment, was exemplified by the career of Sir William Harcourt. According to Sir
Charles Dilke, Harcourt had his hopes set on the woolsack, but
these were frustrated by the re-appointment of Sir Henry James
as Attorney-General. Having seen his principal goal evaporate,
he then accepted Gladstone's offer of the Home Secretaryship.
(39) Six years later, in 1880, under similar circumstances
Lord Salisbury explained to Lord Halsbury the arguments that
could be used, in this instance unsuccessfully, to convince
Sir Edward Macnaghten to accept the office of Home Secretary.

> I hope you will not mind seeing Mr. Macnaghten for me.
> He might be pressed by very different arguments from those
> which could be used to Webster [the Attorney-General]. He
> is not in the running now [for a senior legal office]. If
> he took the Home Office it would put him in the running
> for the highest prizes of his profession....I believe the
> application is not so hopeless in his case for his prac-
> tice is not so large; & his private income is larger.(40)

The Home Office and other non-legal ministerial posts in
general were not invariably seen as professional side-tracks.
In fact, according to recent research, a majority of mid-twen-
tieth-century barrister/MPs would have agreed with the comments
of John Simon when he was chosen to fill the post of Attorney-
General in 1908:(41) 'If the choice had been mine, I should

not have wished to get a legal post, for to me the main attraction of the profession was that it might provide the means of pursuing politics in the broader sense.'(42) In 1915 Simon refused Asquith's offer of the woolsack. In his memoirs he wrote of this decision:

> The prospect of leaving the House of Commons and becoming Lord Chancellor at the age of forty-two did not attract me. This was not a call to war-work that I was bound to undertake, but a removal at too early an age from the centre of parliamentary life to a bourne from which no politician returns, with the prospects at best, of unnumbered years of dignified but unexciting judicial duty while my contemporaries would still be in the thick of the fight.(43)

Instead Simon preferred the Home Office.

In fact the Home Secretaryship was the second most frequently held Cabinet office among members of the bar between 1815 and 1914.(44) Only the Lord Chancellorship, the legal profession's reserved seat in the government, surpassed it in popularity. Among the 60 barristers who attained Cabinet rank between the Congress of Vienna and the First World War, 17 (29 per cent) served as Lord Chancellor and 13 (22 per cent) as Home Secretary. But barristers were by no means restricted to those two posts. They held nearly every cabinet office at least once during the century under consideration, with the only major exception being that of Foreign Secretary; the first barrister to head the Foreign Office was the Marquess of Reading in 1931. Other portfolios that were frequently held by members of the bar were War (8), Duchy of Lancaster (7) and Exchequer (6).(45)

Both in terms of their social origins and occupations, barrister/ministers were the cuckoos in the nineteenth-century political nest. Few of them were what Sir Lewis Namier described as 'inevitable Parliament men' - the scions of the aristocracy who were born to rule.(46) As we see in Table 6.5, only slightly more than ten per cent were the sons or grandsons of peers or baronets during the entire period 1815 to 1914, although this group accounted for nearly 20 per cent of the barrister/ministers during the first fifty years. In addition, approximately five per cent were sons of great nontitled landowners with annual incomes of £10,000 or more. By comparison the sons of peers accounted for 68 per cent of all ministers who served between 1801 and 1866, and for 56 per cent in the years 1867-1916.(47) Even if we broaden the definition of aristocratic to include all those landowners with annual incomes of at least £2,000, the landed contingent rose only to 36 per cent. By contrast, the urban middle classes accounted for 62 per cent of the barrister/ministers.

Turning to the occupations of these men, we find a very

Table 6.5: The Social Origins of Barrister/Cabinet Ministers 1815-1914

	Aristocracy		Landed Gentry		Professions/Business		Other		Total	
	No.	%	No.	%	No.	%	No.	%	No.	
1815-1864	5	19	6	23	14	54	1	4	26	
1865-1914	3	9	8	24	23	68	0	0	34	
1815-1914	8	13	14	23	37	62	1	2	60	

Table 6.6: The Occupations of Barristers/Cabinet Ministers 1815-1914

	Landowners		Barristers		Businessmen		Government Officials		Other Professionals		No. Occupation	
	No.	%	No.	%	No.	%	No.	%	No.	%	No.	%
1815-1864	4	15	12	46	0	0	4	15	3	12	3	12
1865-1914	5	15	20	59	3	9	0	0	3	9	3	9
1815-1914	9	15	32	53	3	5	4	7	6	10	6	10

similar situation. Most of the barristers in Parliament had to secure a steady source of income and only then could they look to a political career to fulfil their higher ambitions. As we see in Table 6.6, no more than a quarter of the barristers who sat in the Cabinet were landowners or rentiers with assured incomes (this includes men categorised as having no occupation). The remaining 75 per cent had to earn their living in the professions or business. The circumstances of other ministers were very different. Of the men who held cabinet rank between 1868 and 1914, 55 per cent had independent means while 45 per cent had to work to support themselves.(48) By far the most common occupation among barrister/ministers was the law itself. In fact it was a much more frequent choice among politicians than among the rank and file of the bar. The inevitable consequence of the social and occupational backgrounds of the barristers who held ministerial office was that they were considerably older when they first entered Parliament than their cabinet colleagues. On the other hand, they were on average younger than other middle-class MPs.(49) This may be due to the special circumstances of the bar, especially the high incomes that accrued to its most successful members and the desire of the parties to recruit able lawyers for their side.

Compared to non-lawyer parliamentarians, barrister/MPs had inordinately successful political careers as measured by their rate of entry into the cabinet, into all ministerial posts and into the peerage.(50) In Table 6.7 I have compared the number and percentage of ministerial appointments among the barristers elected to the Commons in 1880 to those of all Conservative MPs who sat in the House between 1885 and 1900. The results could hardly be more unequivocal. The percentage of barristers who served as ministers exceeded that of the Conservative MPs in every category, except for the law officers who were of necessity members of the bar. The gentlemen of the long robe entered the cabinet three times as frequently as did the Tory MPs; they held non-cabinet ministerial portfolios two and a half times as often, were junior ministers four times as often, while overall they outdistanced the Conservative politicians by a ratio of 3:1.

A similar picture emerges when we examine the acquisition of peerages by barrister/MPs. Twenty-six barristers elected to the House of Commons in 1880 were created peers during their careers, of whom 23 were given hereditary titles. These men account for 20 and 18 per cent respectively of the entire inns of court contingent. By contrast, Professor Thompson estimates that between 1886 and 1914, 200 individuals received titles of nobility for the first time, of whom two-thirds were politicians.(51) These new peers represent six or seven per cent of the 2,000 or so MPs who sat in the Commons during these years.(52) Thus once again, using the most conservative estimates, barristers were two and a half times more successful

Table 6.7: Frequency of Ministerial Appointments Among Barrister and Lay MPs*

	n=130 Barrister/MPs 1880		n=701 Conservative Ministers 1885-1906	
	No.	%	No.	%
Cabinet Minister	20	15	35	5
Minister not in Cabinet	6	5	12	2
Junior Minister	16	12	21	3
Law Officer	3	2	17	2
Total	45	35	85	12

*By highest office only.

Source: The data for the Conservative MPs are found in Cornford, 'Hotel Cecil', p. 311, Table E.

in securing peerages than were their lay contemporaries.

Participation by the gentlemen of the long robe in politics was by no means limited to Britain. Just as lawyers, some of whom had been trained in England, were instrumental in directing American efforts towards independence, so their late-nineteenth- and early-twentieth-century counterparts in Africa and Asia were crucial in the establishment of nationalist political movements.(53) The most important example of this phenomenon was undoubtedly the contribution by barristers to the founding of the Indian National Congress, whose early history has recently been chronicled. All eight of the young men who formed the core of the Congress leadership had been called to the bar at one of the inns of court.(54) Furthermore, of the 16 men who held the Congress presidency between 1885 and 1909, 11 were lawyers and two others had been called to the bar although they did not practise.(55) Lower down in the hierarchy of the movement, members of the legal profession were also prominent; of the 86 most active congressmen, 60 were lawyers.(56)

While the legal training and the influence of London may have been responsible for pushing these men towards the nationalist cause, it also dampened their effectiveness in the subcontinent by impressing upon them an English outlook and the desire to emulate English customs and life-styles.(57) But anglicisation was not an inevitable consequence of a sojourn at the inns of court, as the careers of the second generation of nationalists illustrates so clearly. Men like Mahatma Gandhi and C.R. Das rejected the luxurious life of a successful Indian barrister and became the leaders of a radical and popular Congress that aimed at ending British rule in India.(58)

In the preceding pages, I have tried to demonstrate that not only were barristers ubiquitous in British and colonial politics, especially in the late Victorian period, but that they were notably successful in rising to positions of power and status. During the past 25 years, many scholars have attempted to explain the reasons that in numerous countries lawyers are so prevalent within legislative bodies.(59) In the final section of this chapter I will summarize some of the factors that motivated English barristers to follow political careers, and politically ambitious individuals to enter the inns of court, during the final decades of the nineteenth century.

THE INNS OF COURT: PORTALS TO POWER

In classifying the motivations that led the gentlemen of the long robe to enter the world of politics, I have adopted the categories suggested by Guttsman, that were themselves revisions of those utilised by Namier for the eighteenth century. (60) The first category - the 'inevitable Parliament men' (pure Namier) - included members of the greater gentry and younger sons of the aristocracy for whom a seat in Parliament was a family tradition.(61) Their principal reason for embarking on a political career was neither profit nor mobility, but rather the opportunity to stand at the centre of affairs and the possibility of achieving personal power and glory if they succeeded in securing a senior ministerial appointment or a peerage. One of the leading representatives of this class of MPs was Lord Edmund Petty-Fitzmaurice, 2nd son of the 4th Marquess of Landsdowne and scion of one of the foremost Whig families. Lord Edmund was created Baron Fitzmaurice in 1906 after two terms as Under Secretary for Foreign Affairs, and ended his political career as Chancellor of the Duchy of Lancaster from 1908 to 1909. Somewhat later, from the other side of the political fence we find Lord Robert Cecil, son of the late Conservative Prime Minister Lord Salisbury. After a career at the bar he entered politics and served successively as Minister of the Blockade 1916-17, Assistant Secretary for Foreign Affairs 1918-19, Lord Privy Seal 1923, and Chancellor of the Duchy of Lancaster 1923-7. In 1923 Lord Robert was raised to the peerage with the title of Lord Cecil of Chelwood.

The second category - 'the intellectuals' - were the middle-class counterparts of the first. For them, politics served primarily as a means of influencing the formulation of public policy and as an entry card into high and sophisticated society.(62) There can be little doubt that this is the most problematic group of all, since the line that divided them from the profit and status seekers we shall discuss next was rather thin. Guttsman has discussed the men in this category in some detail and I will not review his evidence here. It is sufficient to note that the principal representatives - James Bryce, Richard Haldane and H.H. Asquith - were all barristers whose interests and activities extended far beyond the world of law.

The motivations of the final two groups - the 'status seekers' and the 'legal careerists' - were the exact opposite of the two categories we have already mentioned.(63) Here the drive for status, recognition and upward mobility was paramount. The 'status seekers' were primarily businessmen and newly endowed landowners and rentiers from entrepreneurial backgrounds for whom a seat in Parliament, a ministerial post and a title added a fitting gentlemanly touch to the wealth accumulated by their fathers and grandfathers. Among the most successful of the barrister 'status seekers' were Dudley Marjoribanks and his son Edward, both Liberal MPs in 1880. Edward Marjoribanks senior was a partner in the banking firm of Coutts and left a fortune of £600,000. His son Dudley in due course became a partner in Meux's Brewery, left a personal estate of £749,000 and land with an annual rental of £9,146. In 1866 he became a baronet and in 1881 was promoted to the peerage as Baron Tweedmouth. His son and heir Edward had no connection with business, and after a short career at the bar, he settled down to the life of a first son and devoted himself entirely to politics. He served as chief Liberal whip from 1892 to 1894, and in the latter year, after succeeding to his father's estates, he entered the cabinet as Chancellor of the Duchy of Lancaster and Lord Privy Seal. When the Liberals returned to power in 1905, he first became Lord of the Admiralty and then in 1908 became Lord President. Other businessmen's sons who gained ministerial posts, peerages, or both, were Arnold Morley, son of Samuel Morley, the hosiery manufacturer, Thomas Lord Brassey, son of the multi-millionaire railway contractor, Cyril Lord Battersea, son of Philip Flower, a London merchant, and Charles McLaren, a chancery barrister who later became a chairman of John Brown & Co. The son of Duncan McLaren MP, an Edinburgh manufacturer and nephew of John Bright, McLaren became a baronet in 1902 and received a promotion to the peerage in 1911.

Another group of men on the way up who were much less numerous than those from business origins but worthy of notice nonetheless, were the sons of successful professional men. Here the sons completed the ascent begun by their fathers. For example, John G. Dodson, son of Sir John Dodson (Judge of the Prerogative Court of Canterbury and owner of a landed estate worth in excess of £3,000 per annum), was successively deputy speaker of the House 1865-72, financial secretary to the Treasury 1873-4, President of the Local Government Board with a seat in the cabinet 1880-2 and Chancellor of the Duchy of

Lancaster 1882-4. In the latter year he retired from politics and was raised to the peerage as Baron Monk Bretton. Henry T. Holland was the son of Sir Henry Holland Bart., physician to the Royal Family. The younger Holland was a member of the Northern circuit. He declined a County Court judgeship in 1860 and in 1869-70 served as legal adviser to the Colonial Office. After holding a number of junior ministerial posts, he entered the cabinet as Colonial Secretary in 1887 and retained that post until 1892. In 1888 he was created Baron Knutsford and in 1895 was advanced to a viscountcy.

This brings us to the last group and the most central one of all for this study - the 'legal careerists'. Included here are most of the individuals whose professional achievements were charted in Table 6.3. We have already looked at the careers of a few of these men, namely John Gorst and Edward Clarke, but a few more examples may be useful to complete the picture. Richard Webster, a contemporary of Gorst and Clarke, was the son of Thomas Webster QC. He went the Home circuit and took silk in 1878 at the age of 36. As we saw earlier, he entered the Commons only after he was appointed Attorney-General. He served in that post in 1885-6 and 1886-92, and then again in Salisbury's third administration from 1895 to 1900. In 1900 he was appointed Master of the Rolls and the office was sweetened with a baronetcy; later that year he became Lord Chief Justice and a peer with the title Baron Alverstone. In 1913 upon resigning from the bench, he was advanced to a viscountcy. Robert Reid was the son of the Chief Justice of the Ionian Islands. He went the Oxford circuit and entered Parliament in 1880. In 1882 he took silk and two years later served in quick succession as Solicitor-General and Attorney-General. Although he was not a first-class advocate according to the DNB, he became Lord Chancellor in Campbell-Bannerman's cabinet and remained in that post until 1912.(64) He took the title of Baron Loreburn upon entering the Lord Chancellorship and in 1911 was promoted to an earldom. For a final example I have chosen Charles Darling, one of Halsbury's political judges. The son of an estate agent and farmer, he began his legal career as the articled clerk of a Birmingham solicitor. He went the Oxford circuit and became a QC in 1885. In 1888 he entered Parliament as a Conservative MP for Deptford, a far from safe seat. He was not a particularly successful advocate, and the appointment was subjected to almost universal condemnation as being politically motivated in the extreme. On the bench, he was neither popular nor did he exhibit great skill, nevertheless upon his retirement as the senior judge in the King's Bench Division in 1924 he was raised to the peerage. (65)

The vast majority of barrister/MPs were 'status seekers' and 'legal careerists'. They were neither born into the ruling class nor were they self-made men, rather they were members of the substantial middle and upper middle classes. Many of them had received an elite education at a public school and Oxbridge, followed of course by the inns of court. Through their parliamentary careers these men were able to build on their rather considerable patrimony and ultimately give it a finishing touch with the addition of a ministerial post, a judgeship, a knighthood or a coronet.

The achievements of barrister/MPs are undeniable and it is hoped that some light has been thrown on their motivations for participating in politics, but one crucial question remains unanswered: why did these men enter the inns of court? As we have seen, only 54 men out of 130 barrister/MPs in 1880 spent the major part of their lives as practising barristers, and to these can be added another 26 men who tried their luck at the bar for a few years. These 80 men clearly went to the inns for professional reasons, but for the remaining 50 men (38 per cent) we must look for an alternative explanation. In order to understand the motivations of these landowners, rentiers and businessmen, we must see the inns of court as much more than just one of the many professional qualifying associations that existed in nineteenth-century England. These societies had once been described as 'the nurserie for the greater part of the gentry of the realme.'(66) While they could not hope to regain that standing in modern English society, they were one of the principal channels of recruitment for the political and social elite especially in the late Victorian period. They constituted one of the 'switch-board' institutions described by Anthony Giddens, that guided individuals into elite positions, 'regardless of prior class background or prior class educational experience'.(67) The inns were of course ideally suited for this purpose, being located in close proximity to the Royal Courts of Justice, the Houses of Parliament, Whitehall and the fashionable London clubs. Yet until now they have been invariably overlooked by students of English society and politics who have preferred to concentrate on the so-called Clarendon schools and on Oxford and Cambridge.(68) In fact the relative invisibility of the inns is not altogether surprising since they were assumed to be schools for lawyers. What was ignored was the large number of men on the way to the top who passed through their gates.

For their aristocratic and greater gentry members the inns served as fashionable colleges in central London, that provided a gentleman with the opportunity to learn some law and to qualify as a member of a high-prestige profession if he were so inclined, while at the same time mixing with men of quality, education and ambition. But these societies were of far greater importance for the upwardly mobile men of the upper middle class and squirearchy, who had to make their own way in the world of national politics. Here ambitious men gained entrance to a high-status professional fraternity, became masters of specialised legal knowledge and of skills that would be invaluable assets in the House of Commons, were inculcated with the norms of the governing classes and made potentially useful social and political connections.

The late Victorian inns of court were one of the doors that led to the world of high society and high politics. This helps to explain why in an age of professionalisation they continued to attract so many men who had no intention of pursuing a career at the bar. It may not be too much to rephrase the description quoted earlier to read: in the late nineteenth century the inns of court were one of the principal nurseries of the governing elite.

NOTES

1. Anthony Sampson, Anatomy of Britain Today (New York, 1965), p. 172.

2. Lewis Namier, The Structure of Politics at the Accession of George III; Harold Laski, 'The Techniques of Judicial Appointment', in Studies in Law and Politics (New York, 1968), reprint; John Vincent, The Formation of the British Liberal Party 1857-68 (Harmondsworth, 1972); W.L. Guttsman, The British Political Elite (1963); David Podmore, 'Lawyers and Politics', British Journal of Law and Society, 4 (1977), pp. 155-85.

3. J.A. Thomas, The House of Commons, 1832-1901: A Study of its Economic and Functional Character (Cardiff, 1939), pp. 4-5, 14-15; H.R.G. Greaves, 'Personal Origins and Interrelations of the Houses of Parliament', Economica, 9 (1929), p. 178.

4. Vincent, The Formation of the British Liberal Party, pp. 40-3; Thomas, The House of Commons, pp. 4-5, 14-15. Guttsman contends that 'new men' were much more common in the elite of the Liberal Party than they were in the Conservative Party. Guttsman, British Political Elite, p. 91. By contrast Feuchtwanger points to the 'new men' among Conservative leaders. E.J. Feuchtwanger, Disraeli, Democracy and the Tory Party (Oxford, 1968), p. 52.

5. Vincent, The Formation of the British Liberal Party, pp. 76-84.

6. The principal occupations of the 130 barrister/MPS in 1880 were as follows: 54 practising barristers (42 per cent); 10 members of other professions or government officials (8 per cent); 24 businessmen (18 per cent); 29 landowners (22 per cent); and 13 men with no known occupations, of whom some were living on private incomes (10 per cent). On the occupations of all MPs in 1880 see Guttsman, British Political Elite, p. 82.

7. See for example H.H. Gerth and C. Wright Mills (eds.), From Max Weber, pp. 85, 94-5; Mattei Dogan, 'Political Ascent in Class Society: French Deputies 1870-1958' in Dwaine Marvick (ed.), Political Decision Makers (New York, 1961), pp. 69-70. For a general discussion on the convergence between law and politics see Heinz Eulau and John D. Sprague, Lawyers in

Politics (Indianapolis, 1964).

8. Rentoul, This is my Case, p. 82. Another barrister wrote in his memoirs about his reasons for refusing an offer to run for Parliament, '...what I could not afford to do was to run the risk of winning...I was too poor to fill with credit the position of County Member...I was forced to turn my eyes away from a prize I had always coveted, and which might almost be said to be within my grasp.' Plowden, Grain or Chaff?, p. 198.

9. Hansard, 3rd series, House of Commons, 57, col. 76.
10. LT, 92 (April 9, 1892), p. 404.
11. See also Vincent, The Formation of the British Liberal Party, p. 78.
12. J.P. Cornford, 'The Parliamentary Foundations of the Hotel Cecil' in R. Robson (ed.), Ideas and Institutions of Victorian Britain (1967), p. 280.
13. J.F.S. Ross, Parliamentary Representation (2nd edition, 1948), pp. 140-1.
14. Vincent, The Formation of the British Liberal Party, p. 79.
15. P.G. Richards, Patronage in British Government (1963), pp. 132-3. See also Armin David Rosencranz, 'The Role of Lawyers in the House of Commons', unpublished PhD Thesis, Stanford University, 1970, pp. 201-3.
16. Podmore, 'Lawyers and Politics', pp. 178-9; Rosencranz, 'Lawyers in the House of Commons', pp. 197-9.
17. DNB 1912-22, pp. 361-2.
18. Robert Stevens, Law and Politics, The House of Lords as a Judicial Body 1800-1976 (Chapel Hill, 1978), p. 93.
19. Halsbury Papers BL Add. MS 56373, vol. VII, fo. 7-9; see also Heuston, Lives of the Lord Chancellors, p. 104.
20. Walker-Smith and Clarke, The Life of Edward Clarke, p. 160.
21. Ibid., p. 160-1.
22. DNB 1912-22, pp. 218-19; Hanham, Elections and Party Management, p. 361; E.J. Feuchtwanger, Disraeli, Democracy and the Tory Party, p. 146.
23. DNB 1931-40, pp. 179-80.
24. Halsbury Papers, BL Add. MS 56371, vol. V, fo. 49-54.
25. R.F.V. Heuston, 'Lord Halsbury's Judicial Appointments', Law Quarterly Review, 78 (1962), pp. 521-3.
26. A.A. Paterson, 'Judges: A Political Elite?', British Journal of Law and Society, 1 (1974), p. 120.
27. Laski, 'The Techniques of Judicial Appointment'.
28. Heuston, 'Lord Halsbury's Judicial Appointments', pp. 504-32.
29. J.A.G. Griffith, The Politics of the Judiciary (1978), pp. 21-2.
30. Cairns MS, PRO 30/51/9, letter 12.
31. Stevens, Law and Politics, pp. 84-5.
32. Heuston, Lives of the Lord Chancellors, p. 57.

33. LJ, 32 (April 17, 1897), p. 215.
34. See above p. 112.
35. Holdsworth, A History of English Law, XVI, p. 167.
36. LT, 63 (November 11, 1877), p. 1. On his father's lack of enthusiasm for the appointment see a letter from Lord Chelmsford to Lord Cairns, Cairns MS, PRO 30/51/9, letter 16.
37. LT, 73 (June 3, 1882), p. 73.
38. Guttsman, The British Political Elite, p. 177. See also Vincent, The Formation of the British Liberal Party, p. 84. He wrote, 'there was an atmosphere of search for private advantage about the lawyer M.P.s which distinguished them from other Parliamentary groups, however discreetly they gained their ends.'
39. Gardiner, Life of Harcourt, vol. I, p. 362.
40. Halsbury Papers, BL Add. MS 56371, vol. V, fo. 29.
41. Rosencranz, 'Lawyers in the House of Commons', pp. 84, 91-2.
42. Viscount Simon, Retrospect, The Memoirs of the Rt. Hon. Viscount Simon (1952), p. 75.
43. Ibid., p. 103.
44. A.V. Dicey for one opposed barristers becoming Home Secretary. In 1892 he wrote to James Bryce: 'No lawyer ought ever to be appointed to that post. His habits of mind are sure to make him alternatively rash and timid. He is moreover deprived of the great advantages of throwing himself back on the opinion of the Law Officers.
Lastly I very much deprecate the connection with the Home Office of a man who may practice [sic] again at the Bar. I believe the more this is thought over the more clearly it will be seen to be objectionable.' Bryce MS 2, fo. 141-3. In fact this prediction was correct and in 1895 Asquith returned from the Home Office to the practising bar.
45. On the mode of entry of middle-class men into the Cabinet see Guttsman, British Political Elite, p. 77.
46. Namier, Structure of Politics, pp. 2-4.
47. Harold Laski, 'The Personnel of the British Cabinet, 1801-1924' in Laski, Studies in Law and Politics, pp. 186-8; see also Guttsman, British Political Elite, pp. 78-9. Guttsman only counted men as aristocrats who had grandfathers who were either peers or baronets, p. 77.
48. Ibid., p. 84.
49. Of the 34 barristers who were first appointed to Cabinet offices between 1868 and 1914, three (9 per cent) were between 21 and 30 when they entered the House of Commons, 21 (62 per cent) were between 31 and 40 and ten (29 per cent) were over 40. For comparative data on Conservative MPs 1885-1905 see Cornford, 'Hotel Cecil', p. 311.
50. Of the 145 'new men' in British Cabinets between 1868 and 1955, 34 were barristers. Guttsman, British Political Elite, p. 57. The same author has also written (p. 57), 'Victorian Lord Chancellors and other legal luminaries provide some

of the little explored success stories of the period; indeed they have done so ever since.' See also F.M.G. Wilson, 'The Route of Entry for New Members of the British Cabinet 1868-1958', Political Studies, VII (1959), pp. 229-30.

51. Thompson, English Landed Society, p. 294.
52. These percentages are based on the fact that between 1886 and 1914 approximately 140 political peers were created out of the MPs who sat in Parliament during those years. Stenton (ed.), Who's Who of British Members of Parliament 1886-1914 (1978).
53. Kimble, Political History of Ghana, p. 96.
54. MacLane, Indian Nationalism, pp. 52-3.
55. Ibid., p. 53.
56. Ibid., p. 54.
57. Ibid., p. 49.
58. On Gandhi's career see DNB 1941-50, pp. 282-6 and on Das, Dictionary of National Biography (Indian), vol. 1, pp. 339-43.
59. For example Joseph A. Schlesinger, 'Lawyers and American Politics: A Clarified View', Midwest Journal of Political Science, 1 (1957), pp. 26-39; Eulau and Sprague, Lawyers in Politics, passim; Mogens W. Pedersen, 'Lawyers in Politics: The Danish Folketing and United States Legislatures' in Samuel G. Patterson and John C. Wahlke (eds.), Comparative Legislative Behavior: Frontiers of Research (New York, 1972), pp. 25-63; P.L. Hain and James E. Piereson, 'Lawyers and Politics Revisited: Structural Advantages of Lawyer-Politicians', American Journal of Political Science, 19 (1975), pp. 41-51.
60. On Namier's categories see Structure of Politics, chapter I.
61. Guttsman, British Political Elite, pp. 145-50.
62. Ibid., pp. 186-94.
63. Ibid., pp. 173-80.
64. DNB 1922-30, p. 715.
65. Heuston, 'Lord Halsbury's Judicial Appointments', pp. 524-5.
66. Prest, The Inns of Court, p. 20.
67. Anthony Giddens, 'Elites in the British Class Structure', in Anthony Giddens and Peter Stanworth (eds.), Elites and Power in British Society (Cambridge, 1974), pp. 14-15. See also R.W. Johnson, 'The British Political Elite, 1955-72', European Journal of Sociology, 14 (1973), pp. 38-9.
68. For example, in the index of Guttsman's British Political Elite there are twelve references to the public schools and five to the universities while the inns of court are unlisted.

Chapter Seven

THE BAR AND BENCH IN SOCIAL AND HISTORICAL PERSPECTIVE

Recently Professor Eliot Freidson urged his fellow sociologists to treat the professions 'as an empirical entity about which there is little ground for generalizing as a homogeneous class ...'. 'The task of the theory of the professions', he wrote, 'is to document the untidiness and inconsistency of the empirical phenomenon....'(1) In this final chapter I will follow Freidson's advice by using the data I have collected on the bar and bench in the eighteenth and nineteenth centuries to test the validity of commonplace assumptions about the chronology and progress of professionalisation in England.(2)

I must begin with a brief account of the orthodox interpretation of the rise of professionalism, but before doing so I want to enter one caveat. The tendency in summarizing the views of a number of scholars on a given issue is to simplify in the interests of clarity and brevity, consequently any exercise of this sort runs the risk of misinterpretation. I hope that I have avoided this pitfall and have correctly represented the opinions of those authors whose works I am discussing here. The most important of these are Philip Elliott, <u>The Sociology of the Professions</u>; Terence Johnson, <u>Professions and Power</u>; M.S. Larson, <u>The Rise of Professionalism</u>; Harold Perkin, <u>The Origins of Modern English Society</u>; and W.J. Reader, <u>Professional Men</u>.

The traditional view of the professionalisation process is as follows: In the early modern period, lasting until the end of the eighteenth century, the gentlemanly professions - divinity, the bar and physic - were dependent upon the patronage and social ideals of the aristocratic ruling class while at the same time the large majority of new recruits to these high-status occupations were the sons of landed gentlemen and peers. The social base from which professional men would hope to attract business was very narrow, since the middle classes had not yet begun to make widespread use of their services. As a consequence, elite consumers were in a position - through their monopoly over demand and their control of clerical livings, hospital appointments and government sinecures - to act

the role of patron to clergymen, doctors and lawyers. In
these circumstances the professional could not assert his expert, independent and disinterested opinion as we would expect
from him today. On the contrary, his primary function was to
please his patrons. His success in this arena was measured by
his social graces, gentlemanly virtues, classical education
and his willingness to provide services that conformed to his
patrons' expectations.(3) Since in such an atmosphere characteristics like initiative, innovation, professional skills and
knowledge were not emphasized but rather discouraged, it is
not surprising that little progress was made in extending the
frontiers of professional knowledge and its systematisation.(4)
T.H. Marshall has neatly summarized the traditional view of
the pre-modern professions as follows:

> The professions were, in English parlance, the occupations
> suitable for a gentleman. This idea naturally flourished
> in societies which distinguished sharply between life lived as an end in itself, and life passed in providing the
> means which enabled others to live as free civilized men
> should. The professions in such a society were those
> means to living which were most innocuous, in that they
> did not dull the brain, like manual labour, nor corrupt
> the soul, like commerce.(5)

All of this changed in the wake of the industrial revolution and its social and economic aftermath. While there is
not complete consensus on when the transformation occurred,
the traditional view sees the years between the end of the Napoleonic Wars and the passage of the Reform Bill of 1832 as a
watershed in the history of the professions in England. We
are told that while the term 'profession' is used to describe
occupations on both sides of this chronological and qualitative divide, the pre- and post-industrial versions have little
more than their names in common.(6) The new model of professionalism that was emerging at this time was the result of the
collapse of the old patronage system and the advance of scientific knowledge. Professional men were no longer dependent
upon a relatively small group of wealthy patrons. The increasing wealth of the middle classes opened up new, more diversified sources of business to the members of the professions.
Consequently, individuals who now made use of professional
services were no longer upper-class patrons whose money and
social standing meant that they could call the tune, but rather clients who were dependent upon the learned opinions of
the doctor, lawyer or clergyman. These new clients were not
the social superiors of the professional men but their equals
or even their inferiors.(7)

At the same time a dramatic change occurred in the recruitment patterns of the professions. Just as the monetary
and ideological connections that had previously bound

professionals to the landed classes loosened, so the percentage of the sons of landed gentlemen and aristocrats who entered the professions declined and their places were filled by members of the middle class.(8) The emphasis on the traditional classical attainments declined in favour of a system of professional education suited to the needs of the expert and bolstered by examinations designed to test competence. Concurrently with this development, the state of professional knowledge improved as a result of scientific discoveries and the advance of 'cognitive rationality'.(9) Spheres of practice became more clearly defined with the increasing division of labour.(10) In turn these improvements increased the status of the professions and created conditions conducive to the formation of monopolies over specific types of services. Furthermore, by stigmatising or legally prohibiting practice by individuals who had not acquired official qualifications and by limiting the number of recognised practitioners, the professions endeavoured to guarantee a secure living to their members.(11)

Finally the establishment of formal training and the creation of societies and associations gave the professions a greater sense of corporate unity and esprit de corps. Members were socialised to accept a common view of their relationship with the lay public and of the character of their work, while at the same time codes of ethics and etiquette were introduced that on the one hand regulated the relations between client and professional and on the other reduced competition and conflict between the professional men themselves.(12)

We can now examine critically the traditional view of professional evolution that I have just sketched, beginning with the contention that the pre-industrial professions were dependent upon aristocratic patronage. According to Blackstone this was not an accurate description of the mid-eighteenth-century bar. He claimed that litigants were not the patrons of the barristers but their clients, and as such dependent upon the lawyers' expert knowledge and skills. Of course it is conceivable that Blackstone was describing an ideal relationship rather than the historical reality of his day. In order to make a conclusive determination in this case, we would want to know the social class of litigants; unfortunately data on this subject are not available at present for the eighteenth century. Thus we are forced to fall back on evidence that has been collected for the period 1560 to 1640. According to Christopher Brooks, of the individuals who appeared in causes in the Courts of King's Bench and Common Pleas in those years, only 20 to 30 per cent belonged to the aristocracy or landed gentry. The remaining 70 to 80 per cent included yeoman farmers, merchants, artisans, labourers, professional men and their widows.(13) While these statistics do not necessarily indicate the social class of eighteenth-century litigants, it would be surprising indeed if the middle and lower classes had ceased to appear in these courts or if they had been unrepresented by counsel there.

There were two other factors that probably reduced the dependence of barristers on upper class patrons. The first was the professional division of labour between the barristers and the attorneys. Specialisation of function in the legal profession pre-dated the industrial revolution and it was considered contrary to professional etiquette for barristers to consult directly with lay clients without the intervention of an attorney by the late eighteenth century. Consequently the lower branch, acting as an intermediary, shielded the barristers from domination by upper-class litigants. A second factor was the decline in the percentage of members of the bar from the landed classes, that we will discuss in more detail below. This phenomenon meant that few eighteenth-century landed gentlemen had the requisite knowledge of the law to interfere in counsel's conduct of a case. Finally barristers were remunerated separately for each brief they accepted; according to J.H. Baker, the formal permanent retainer largely disappeared during the early modern period.(14) Taken together these factors demonstrate in the clearest possible terms that barristers received their fees from a socially diversified clientele long before the coming of industrialisation. Furthermore, by the eighteenth century the ability of upper-class litigants to dictate the conditions of work to members of the bar and to retain control over the conduct of cases was extremely limited.

There was one type of patronage that did play an important role in promoting careers of barristers, namely connections based on contact networks. As we saw earlier this type of sponsorship, usually undertaken by family or friends, was most important in the early years at the bar. These connections gave a fledgling practitioner the chance of trying his luck in court, but they could only be exploited to their full potential when combined with professional ability. Patronage alone could not guarantee success in the law. The principal reason for this limitation was competition. There were always more barristers than briefs, and while a solicitor might be willing to favour a recently called counsel with some business, he would certainly not have been willing to risk his clients' interests on a long-term basis if the man proved himself incapable of winning in court fairly regularly. Gentlemanly manners, sociability and good connections could not overcome a lack of ability, at least not at the bar.

According to the orthodox view, the two principal characteristics of modern professionalism - autonomy and an absolute monopoly over practice - were products of the post-industrial era. This interpretation does not fit the case of the bar. The upper branch achieved a national monopoly over advocacy in the superior courts of law and equity in the late sixteenth century as the call to the bar at one of the four inns of court became recognised as the sole qualification for practice. Autonomy came much later, but still long before the industrial revolution. During the Tudor and early Stuart periods the judges of the Royal Courts and the Privy Council regularly interfered in professional affairs. Yet soon after the Restoration, in 1664 to be more precise, the last order by either body was issued. From that time forth the only appeal from the decisions of the inns was to the judges not in their official capacity, but rather as senior members of the profession. Lord Mansfield formally recognised the autonomy of the bar in 1780 at a time when industrialisation was still in its infancy.(15)

In two recent studies of the professions we find the following descriptions of the social class of professional men:

> In mid-[nineteenth] century English society...occupations and their honorific titles reflected class origins. Barristers, physicians, and clergymen belonged to the gentry; while solicitors, surgeons, apothecaries, engineers and most civil servants came from artisan and commercial backgrounds.(16)

> In fact, [in the late eighteenth century] the elite professionals of the traditional corporations tended to reserve entry into their ranks to those who they considered their social peers.
> Thus despite the existence of a minority of very successful middle class practitioners, the "first-class" marks of professional distinction were practically monopolized by aristocratic or quasi-aristocratic elites.(17)

With regard to the bar these generalisations are incorrect. Even in the early seventeenth century only half of the barristers were the sons of aristocratic or gentry families.(18) In the first half of the eighteenth century the landed representation had declined to less than 40 per cent, and then to less than 30 per cent by the outbreak of the American Revolution. This distribution did not apply only to the rank and file of the bar but also to the elite. Of the central superior court judges appointed between 1727 and 1760 - men who were called to the bar between 1700 and 1730 - just under half were from landed origins. Among the generation appointed between 1760 and 1790 this declined to just under 30 per cent and for those who were raised to the bench between 1790 and 1820 it was less than 20 per cent.(19) Thus it is clear that the middle classes, especially the professions, were the major source of recruitment to the bar and bench before the coming of the industrial age, while in the eighteenth century landed members constituted no more than a decreasing minority.

This brings us to the issue of the social attitudes of the professional men. In this instance the traditional view is somewhat closer to the mark than it has been on the other topics discussed here. The evidence, primarily the occupational choices of the sons of the high court judges, the frequency of purchase of large landed estates by members of the judiciary, and their adoption or rejection of primogeniture in the disposal of their wealth and property, suggests that already among the judges appointed between 1790 and 1820 there was a decline in the percentage who adopted aristocratic values and perceptions. But the real change occurred in the following generation - 1820 to 1850 - when the judges and their families abandoned the view that the law was a stepping stone to the gentry; instead they were content with their status as the leading and wealthiest professional men of their day.(20)

In most theories of professionalisation, the development of esoteric knowledge and its diffusion among practitioners by means of formal and systematic education constitutes a crucial stage. Professional men are distinguished by their possession of specialised knowledge and skills that make their services essential for society and profitable to themselves, at the same time justifying their demands for total autonomy from lay supervision. In most instances the creation and systematisation of professional knowledge is associated with the industrial revolution and the advances in science, technology and organisation that came in its wake. In fact the history of the bar tells a very different story. Legal knowledge is not scientific but normative, resting as it does on precedents that have been fixed over the generations.(21) Its use is limited to those who have been trained in the mysteries of the law, and in fact for centuries legal and social reformers have complained that professional jargon and forms render the law incomprehensible even to the best educated of laymen. Not only was legal knowledge both esoteric and specialised prior to the industrial era, but efforts had also been made to rationalise it. One of the most famous and influential attempts to systematise the law was Sir William Blackstone's Commentaries, which were the fruit of his labours as Oxford University's first Vinerian Professor of English law. These volumes were published between 1765 and 1769. Yet if the nature and organisation of legal knowledge were modern prior to the era of industrialisation, the form in which it was taught unquestionably belonged to the ancien regime, until the second half of the nineteenth century when compulsory lectures and examinations were introduced at the inns of court. On balance however, there can be little doubt that by the second half of the eighteenth century, at the latest, the bar had achieved that 'cognitive commonality' that Professor Larson sees as an essential component of modern professionalism.(22)

According to the traditional interpretation, improvements in professional education and consequent increases in status, cohesion and independence depended on the establishment in the nineteenth century of the modern qualifying association.

Without doubt the inns of court were the oldest professional societies in the realm, yet they failed to approach the nineteenth-century ideal. However, despite their abdication of responsibility for the education of law students, their completely undemocratic constitutions and their apparent lack of concern with the interests of their junior members, the inns, along with the circuit messes, were able to generate a strong sense of corporate unity among the members of the bar. In fact it may not be too much to claim that the <u>esprit de corps</u> that existed among the barristers was the immediate precursor of the colleague-orientation that characterises the modern professional man.

The clearest expression of this phenomenon was the existence of a recognised code of professional etiquette, albeit an unwritten one, in the second half of the eighteenth and the first half of the nineteenth centuries. The earliest circuit mess records that have as yet been found, dating from the years immediately after the end of the Napoleonic Wars, contain restrictive practices that define acceptable professional behaviour. While we do not know the full history of the customs of the bar, some rules, for example the prohibition against direct access to lay clients, have their origins in the eighteenth century and even earlier.(23) Furthermore the bar was not the only profession to develop a system of etiquette by the beginning of the nineteenth century. In 1803 Dr Thomas Percival, a Manchester physician, published his <u>Medical Ethics</u>, that dealt principally with defining the proper relationship between medical men.(24) This was only three years after the founding of the Royal College of Surgeons, and it preceded the passage of the Apothecaries Act by 12 years, the invention of the stethoscope by 16 years, the establishment of the nucleus of the British Medical Association by 29 years and of the General Medical Council by 55 years. The existence of codes of behaviour in both the legal and medical professions in the early decades of the nineteenth century casts severe doubt on the accuracy of a recent generalisation by Professor Larson about the timing and evolution of professional etiquette. According to her, the 'regulation of intraprofessional competition' by means of recognised rules of conduct was only achieved in the last stages of the professionalisation process.(25)

My aim in the preceding pages has not been to prove conclusively that fully-fledged professionalism existed at the bar in the eighteenth century, although I do believe that it had become a prototype of the modern profession by the time that the first Reform Bill was given the royal assent. What I hope to have demonstrated here is that any attempt to establish a natural history of the professions or an ideal chronology of professionalisation is doomed to failure. Our real task, as Professor Freidson has proposed, is to document and analyse the peculiarities of each profession and not impose artificial models upon them for the sake of simplicity.(26) Moreover, while there can be little doubt that the social transformation of nineteenth-century England helped to speed up the evolution of the professions, the case of the bar suggests that it is incorrect to see the industrial revolution as a watershed in their history.

By the time that this study opens in 1835, the bar had achieved most of the essential features of professionalism: autonomy from lay control; a well-defined field of competence and an absolute monopoly over practice; a systematised body of knowledge even if it was not particularly rational, according to its many critics; a socially diversified clientele that was dependent upon the opinions and advice of the barristers; corporate unity and at least the beginnings of a system of professional etiquette; and developing social attitudes and behaviour that reflected middle-class, rather than aristocratic, ideals. In this light we are compelled to ask the question: if the Victorian era was not an age of professionalisation for the bar, then what role did it play in the evolution of the profession?

A critic of my interpretation would point out that the professionalisation of the bar continued well into the reform era. The years from 1834 to 1895 witnessed three parliamentary investigations of the legal profession, the introduction of a formal educational system as a means of ensuring competence if not excellence, and the creation of a professional association - the Bar Council. But when we take a closer look at these reforms, we find that they did not change the basic fabric of the profession. There was no diminution of the absolute autonomy of the bar, as Parliament persistently refused to impose controls from the outside. The final bar examinations were not particularly rigorous and their role in quality control was negligible. Pupilage, not lectures, remained the principal means by which barristers acquired the tools of their trade. Finally the Bar Council had only advisory powers and it totally failed to democratise the inns of court, much less to replace them as the governing body of the profession. In fact, taken as a whole, changes in the organisation of the bar and in its educational system after 1830 were not directed towards the collective upward mobility of the profession - a goal usually viewed as synonymous with the professionalisation process - but rather towards preserving the independence, power and status that had already been achieved, albeit by some fine tuning and minor concessions where necessary.(27)

On the more personal level, the Victorian era witnessed members of the bar grappling with problems that are of central concern in today's overcrowded professions, most importantly the search for alternative careers. Although the number of qualified barristers trebled between 1835 and 1885, practitioners in England increased by only 50 per cent. The threat of professional unemployment was a very real possibility, as the journals never failed to point out. Yet fortunately for the barristers, severe overcrowding at the English bar coincided with the emergence of new employment opportunities in the public service and in the law itself. The home civil service was expanding as the state took an ever-increasing role in directing the economy and society. Barristers seemed to be ideally suited to fill positions as inspectors, commissioners and secretaries in various government departments. They also had a virtual monopoly over positions as full-time legal advisers particularly to the Home Office, the Foreign Office and the Treasury. Of even greater importance in this regard were the colonies. The colonial bars absorbed more than ten per cent of the men called at the inns of court in the later decades of the nineteenth century. In addition, there were numerous legal offices to be filled throughout the length and breadth of the empire, while in India there was a large civil service establishment that was in need of men with legal qualifications. Finally the world of business served as an important field of enterprise for members of the late Victorian bar, both as a principal occupation and as a means of supplementing incomes from other sources.

These employment opportunities prevented the emergence of a militant and powerful group of briefless barristers who could have posed a major problem for Britain and may even have become a focus for social and political discontent, as had other lawyers in the not-so-distant past.(28) In fact their role was just the opposite; the barristers were pillars of nineteenth-century stability. Rarely if ever had the gentlemen of the long robe figured as prominently in the political affairs of Britain as they did during the reign of Queen Victoria, and this despite the impact of social change. In 1835 Alexis de Tocqueville had dubbed the members of the bar 'the younger branch of the English aristocracy'.(29) Fifty years later the old ruling class was in decline but the barristers did not go the way of their 'elder brothers'.(30) On the contrary, they had adapted to circumstances and in the process had become fully integrated members of the new governing elite.

NOTES

1. Eliot Freidson, 'The Theory of Professions: State of the Art', in R. Dingwall and P. Lewis (eds.), Sociology of the Professions (London, forthcoming). I would like to thank Professor Freidson for permitting me to see a typescript of this article prior to publication. The quotation is found on p. 23 in this version and other pertinent comments in this regard on pp. 3 and 25.

2. The evidence that is summarised here is by and large found in the present work; Duman, The Judicial Bench; and Duman, 'Bar in the Georgian Era'. References have been given

in instances where no previous mention has been made of particular arguments or data in this study. I am grateful to Dr Wilfrid Prest of the University of Adelaide for suggesting to me the need to re-examine the orthodox interpretation of professionalisation.

3. Johnson, Professions and Power, pp. 65-7; Larson, Rise of Professionalism, pp. 12, 57, 88; Bledstein, Culture of Professionalism, p. 20; Elliott, Sociology of the Professions, p. 27.

4. Larson, Rise of Professionalism, p. 90; Johnson, Professions and Power, p. 72.

5. T.H. Marshall, 'The Recent History of Professionalism in Relation to Social Structure and Social Policy', Canadian Journal of Economics and Political Science, V (1939), p. 325.

6. For example, Philip Elliott distinguished the eighteenth-century 'status professionalism' from the nineteenth-century 'occupational professionalism'. Elliott, Sociology of the Professions, pp. 14, 32. See also Larson, Rise of Professionalism, pp. xvi, 2-3, 51; Reader, Professional Men, p. 2; Johnson, Professions and Power, p. 52; Perkin, Origins of Modern English Society, p. 254.

7. Larson, Rise of Professionalism, p. 57; Perkin, Origins of Modern English Society, p. 254; Johnson, Professions and Power, p. 52.

8. Larson, Rise of Professionalism, pp. 12, 90, 98; Bledstein, Culture of Professionalism, p. 20.

9. Larson, Rise of Professionalism, p. 44.

10. Ibid., pp. 31-52; Reader, Professional Men, p. 11.

11. Larson, Rise of Professionalism, pp. xvii, 54.

12. Ibid., pp. 41-2, 46.

13. Brooks, 'Litigants and Attorneys', pp. 46-8.

14. Baker, 'Counsellors and Barristers', p. 210.

15. Duman, 'Bar in the Georgian Era', p. 86 and notes 1-3 in that paper.

16. Bledstein, Culture of Professionalism, p. 20.

17. Larson, Rise of Professionalism, p. 12.

18. Prest, 'The English Bar, 1550-1700', p. 70.

19. Duman, 'Bar in the Georgian Era', pp. 90-5. In fact among the more senior judges there was a higher percentage of landowners' sons but they were largely the sons of farmers and minor gentry.

20. Duman, The Judicial Bench, chapters 5-7.

21. Duman, 'Pathway to Professionalism', pp. 617-18.

22. Larson, Rise of Professionalism, p. 40.

23. Baker, Counsellors and Barristers, passim.

24. Waddington, 'Medical Ethics', p. 39. Waddington also notes that Percival's work developed out of a conflict in Manchester's medical community that occurred in 1789. The first privately printed version of the work was published in 1794.

25. Larson, Rise of Professionalism, p. 46.

26. Freidson, 'The Theory of Professions', p. 25.

27. On this point see the comments in Ibid., p. 26.
28. For example, in the English Civil War and the American and French Revolutions.
29. Tocqueville, Democracy in America, vol. 1, pp. 287-8. On Tocqueville's view of English lawyers and aristocracy see David Spring, 'An Outsider's View: Alexis de Tocqueville on Aristocracy, Society, and Politics in Nineteenth-Century England', Albion, 12 (1980), p. 125.
30. Tocqueville, Democracy in America, vol. 1, p. 288.

Appendix

RULES OF THE NORFOLK CIRCUIT CLUB

Extracted from the Circuit Books in the custody of the Recorder & codified pursuant to the resolution of July 18, 1856.

Constitution of the Club
All motions respecting the Constitution of the N.C.C. shall be preceded by motion at the Assize Town preceding that at which such motions are to be brought forward.

Election of Members
    1. First every candidate may be proposed & seconded after the Bar Dinner at either of the Assize Towns.
    2. That the election whether of ordinary or honorary members should be by ballot after the Bar Dinner.
    3. That candidates may be proposed at either of the Assize Towns - but the ballot shall be confined to Aylesbury, Cambridge, Bury, Ipswich & Norwich.
    4. That six members shall be necessary to form a ballot & that no gentleman shall be elected except by a majority of two thirds of the members present.
    5. That no gentleman shall be proposed until he shall have actually joined the circuit & shall have appeared at an Assize Town.
    6. That no gentleman shall be proposed who shall have been a member of any other circuit for 10 years.

Bar Dinners
    1. That any member who is presented at an Assize Town ought to attend the Bar Dinner.
    2. That no charge for luncheon provided for any member shall be included in the Bar Bill.

Practice
    1. That no member ought to send his clerk to an Assize Town unless he intends to attend that Town.
    2. That members be allowed to lodge at an hotel in Aylesbury, Bedford & Huntingdon.

3. That no member shall enter an Assize Town before the commission day. (Amended as to Cambridge.)

4. That no member who has ceased to attend his Sessions for three years & who after that interval appears thereat in a particular case for a stipulated fee shall be at liberty to take a common brief in any other case thereat even tho' no junior has joined during that interval.

5. If a special counsel attended at any Sessions & there be no junior disengaged can a senior to him accept a brief with him on the understanding that such special counsel shall lead or take the whole lead of the cause.

No decision was come to on this point - but on discussion the feeling of the members present was in the negative.

[Amendment] For Practice Rule 2 - That members be allowed to lodge at Hotels on all Towns on the circuit.

Source: Norfolk Circuit Book, 1864.

SELECTED BIBLIOGRAPHY

PRIMARY SOURCES

Manuscripts

Bryce MSS, Bodleian Library, Oxford
Cairns Papers, Public Record Office
Carnarvon Papers, Public Record Office
Coleridge MSS, Bodleian Library, Oxford
Joseph Foster, Entries at the Inns of Court to 1800, University Library Cambridge
_____, Register of all Barristers called down to 1887, University Library Cambridge
General Council of the Bar, Minute Books, Senate of the Inns of Court and the Bar
Giles Puller Collection, Hertfordshire Record Office
Halsbury Papers, British Library
Home Circuit Minutes, Wine Committee of the South-Eastern Circuit Mess
Lloyd, R.L., 'Inner Temple Admissions', 3 vols., 1960 typescript, Inner Temple Library
Martin Leake Papers, Hertfordshire Record Office
Monk Bretton Papers, Bodleian Library, Oxford
Norfolk Circuit Minutes, Mr John Blofeld QC
Selborne Papers, Lambeth Palace Library
South-Eastern Circuit Minutes, Wine Committee of the South-Eastern Circuit
James Fitzjames Stephen Papers, University Library Cambridge
Talfourd Diaries, Berkshire County Library
Western Circuit Minutes, Wine Treasurer of the Western Circuit
Wharncliffe Minuments, Sheffield Central Library
Wills and Registers, Principal Probate Registry, Somerset House

Parliamentary Papers

Inns of Court Commission, BPP XVIII (1854-5)
Judicature Commission, Second Report, BPP XX (1872)
Monopolies and Mergers Commission, Barristers Services (6th July, 1976)
Return of the Owners of Land (England, Wales and Scotland), BPP LXXII (1874), (Ireland), BPP LXXX (1876)
Royal Commission on Legal Services (October, 1979)
Select Committee on County Courts Jurisdiction, BPP XI (1878)
Select Committee on the Inns of Court, BPP XVIII (1834)
Select Committee on Legal Education, BPP X (1846)
Select Committee on Official Salaries, BPP XV (1850)

Parliamentary Debates

Hansard, 3rd series

Newspapers and Periodicals

Law Journal
Law Times
Pall Mall Gazette
The Times

Books and Articles

Alverstone, Rt. Hon. Viscount. Recollections of the Bar and Bench, 1914
Bar Committee and Bar Council Annual Statements
Blackstone, William. Commentaries on the Laws of England, 4 vols., Oxford, 1765-9
Baildon, W.P. Lincoln's Inn Admission Registers, 2 vols., 1896
———. Lincoln's Inn Black Books 1422-1845, 4 vols., 1897-1902
Boase, Frederick. Modern English Biography, 6 vols., 1965, reprint
Bryce, James. The American Commonwealth, 2nd edn., 2 vols., 1889
Burke's Landed Gentry, various editions
Burke's Peerage, Baronetage and Knightage, various editions
Campbell, Sir George. Memoirs of My Indian Career, 2 vols., 1893
Circuit Tramp. Pie Powder, 1911
Debrett's House of Commons and Judicial Bench, 1880
Dicey, A.V. 'Legal Etiquette', Fortnightly Review, n.s. 2 (1867), pp. 169-79

Directory of Directors, various editions
Escott, T.H.S. England Its People, Polity and Pursuits, 1891
Foster, Joseph. Alumni Oxonienses 1715-1886, 4 vols., Oxford, 1888
———. Men-at-the-Bar, 1885
———. Register of Admissions to Gray's Inn 1521-1889, 1889
Gathorne-Hardy, Hon. A.E. (ed.). Gathorne Hardy First Lord Cranbrook, A Memoir, 2 vols., 1910
Haldane, Richard Burdon. An Autobiography, 1929
Hardcastle, M.S. (ed.). The Life of John Lord Campbell, 2 vols., 1881
Harris, George. The Autobiography of George Harris, 1888
Hess, Henry. The Critic Black Book, 1902
Law List, various editions
Liddell, A.C.G. Notes from the Life of an Ordinary Mortal, 1911
Palmer, Roundell, Earl of Selborne. Memorials Family and Personal 1766-1865 and Memorials Personal and Political 1865-1895, 4 vols., 1896-8
Parmoor, Lord. A Retrospect, 1936
Plowden, Alfred Chichele. Grain or Chaff? The Autobiography of a Police Magistrate, 1903
Rentoul, Sir Gervais. This is My Case, 1944
Rolt, Sir John. The Memoirs of the Right Honourable Sir John Rolt 1804-1871, 1939
Roxburgh, Sir R.F. Lincoln's Inn Black Books 1845-1914, 1968
Ruggles, Thomas. The Barrister or Strictures on the Proper Education for the Bar, 2 vols., 1792
Simon, Rt. Hon. Viscount. Retrospect, 1952
Smith, Adam. An Inquiry into the Nature and Causes of the Wealth of Nations, New York, 1937
Snow, C.P. Time of Hope, Harmondsworth, 1962
Stenton, M. (ed.). Who's Who of British Members of Parliament 1832-1885 and 1886-1914, 2 vols., 1976-78
Sturgess, H.A.C. Register of Admissions to the Honourable Society of the Middle Temple, 3 vols., 1949
Thackeray, William. The History of Pendennis, Harmondsworth edn., 1972
Thomson, H. Byerley. The Choice of a Profession, 1857
Tocqueville, Alexis de. Democracy in America, 2 vols., New York, 1954
Trollope, Anthony. The Way We Live Now, 1969
Venn, J. and J.A. Alumni Cantabrigenses 1754-1900, 10 vols., Cambridge, 1940-54
Walton, Robert. Random Recollections of the Midland Circuit, 2nd series, 1873
Warren, Samuel. Introduction to Law Studies, 2nd edn., 2 vols., 1845
Whishaw, James. A Synopsis of the Members of the English Bar, 1835
Williams, F. Condé. From Journalism to Judge, Edinburgh, 1903

Witt, John George. *Life in the Law*, 1906
Who Was Who
Wynne, Edward. *Eunomus or Dialogues Concerning the Laws and Constitution of England*, 4 vols., 1785

SECONDARY SOURCES

Abel-Smith, Brian and Stevens, Robert. *Lawyers and the Courts: A Sociological Study of the English Legal System 1750-1965*, 1970
Adler, Dorothy R. *British Investment in American Railways 1834-1898*, Charlottesville, Va., 1970
Arnould, J. *A Memoir of Thomas, First Lord Denman*, 2 vols., 1873
Atlay, J.B. *The Victorian Chancellors*, 2 vols., 1906
Auerbach, Jerold S. *Unequal Justice: Lawyers and Social Change in Modern America*, New York, 1976
Aydelotte, W.O. 'The Business Interests of the Gentry in the Parliament of 1841-47' in G. Kitson Clark, *The Making of Victorian England*, 1962, pp. 290-305
Baker, J.H. 'Counsellors and Barristers', *Cambridge Law Journal*, 29 (1969)
_____. *An Introduction to English Legal History*, 2nd edn., 1979
_____. 'Solicitors and the Law of Maintenance 1590-1640', *Cambridge Law Journal*, 32 (1973), pp. 56-80
Banks, J.A. *Prosperity and Parenthood*, 1954
Bellot, H.H.L. 'The Exclusion of Attorneys from the Inns of Court', *Law Quarterly Review*, 26 (1910), pp. 137-45
Bennett, J.M. (ed.). *A History of the New South Wales Bar*, Sydney, 1969
Best, Geoffrey. *Mid-Victorian Britain 1851-75*, St. Albans, 1971
Bledstein, Burton J. *The Cultural Professionalism*, New York, 1976
Bolton, W.W. *Conduct and Etiquette at the Bar*, 5th edn., 1971
Braibanti, Ralph (ed.). *Asian Bureaucratic Systems Emergent from the British Imperial Tradition*, Durham, 1966
Brooks, C.W. 'Litigants and Attorneys in the King's Bench and Common Pleas, 1560-1640' in J.H. Baker, *Legal Records and the Historian*, 1978
Buckee, G.F.M. 'An Examination of the Development and Structure of the Legal Profession in Allahabad 1886-1935', unpublished Ph.D. thesis, University of London, 1972
Calhoun, Daniel H. *Professional Lives in America: Structure and Aspirations 1750-1850*, Cambridge, Mass., 1965
Carr-Saunders, A.M. and Wilson, P.A. *The Professions*, Oxford, 1933
Clark, George and Cooke, A.M. *A History of the Royal College of Physicians*, 3 vols., Oxford, 1964-72

Cock, Raymond. 'The Bar at the Assizes: Barristers on Three Nineteenth Century Circuits', Kingston Law Review, VI (1976), pp. 36-52

Cockerell, H.A.L. and Green, Edwin. The British Insurance Business 1547-1970, 1976

Cooke, Robin. Portrait of a Profession: The Centennial Book of the New Zealand Law Society, Wellington, 1969

Cornford, J.P. 'The Parliamentary Foundations of the Hotel Cecil' in Robert Robson (ed.), Ideas and Institutions of Victorian Britian, 1967

Cowan, C.D. Nineteenth Century Malaya, The Origins of British Political Control, 1961

Crewe, Ivor (ed.). British Political Sociology Yearbook, 1974

Day, Arthur. John C.F.S. Day: His Forebearers and Himself, 1916

Dean, Sir Arthur. A Multitude of Counsellors, A History of the Bar of Victoria, Melbourne, 1968

De Montmorency, J.E.C. John Gorell Barnes, First Lord Gorell, 1902

Dickson, P.G.M. The Sun Insurance Office 1710-1960, 1960

Dogan, Mattei. 'Political Ascent in Class Society: French Deputies 1870-1958' in Dwaine Marvick (ed.), Political Decision Makers, New York, 1961

Duman, Daniel. 'The Creation and Diffusion of a Professional Ideology in Nineteenth Century England', Sociological Review, n.s. 27 (1979), pp. 113-38

_____. 'The English Bar in the Georgian Era' in Wilfrid Prest (ed.), Lawyers in Early Modern Europe and America, 1981, pp. 86-107

_____. The Judicial Bench in England 1727-1875: The Reshaping of a Professional Elite, Royal Historical Society, forthcoming

_____. 'Pathway to Professionalism: The English Bar in the Eighteenth and Nineteenth Centuries', Journal of Social History, 13 (1980), pp. 615-628

Durkheim, Emile. Professional Ethics and Civic Morals, 1957

Edwards, J. Ll. J. The Law Officers of the Crown, 1964

Elliott, Philip. The Sociology of the Professions, 1972

Erickson, Charlotte. British Industrialists: Steel and Hosiery 1850-1950, Cambridge, 1959

Erlanger, Howard S. 'The Allocation of Status Within Occupations: The Case of the Legal Profession', Social Forces, 58 (1980), pp. 882-903

Eulau, Heinz and Spague, John D. Lawyers in Politics, A Study in Professional Convergence, Indianapolis, 1964

Ferns, H.S. Britain and Argentina in the Nineteenth Century, Oxford, 1960

Feuchtwanger, E.J. Disraeli, Democracy and the Tory Party, Oxford, 1968

Fisher, H.A.L. James Bryce, 2 vols., 1927

Freidson, Eliot. Profession of Medicine, A Study of the

Sociology of Applied Knowledge, New York, 1972
———. 'The Theory of Professions: State of the Art' in R. Dingwall and P. Lewis (eds.). Sociology of the Professions, Macmillan, forthcoming
Gann, L.H. and Duignan, Peter. The Rulers of British Africa 1870-1914, Stanford, 1978
Gardiner, A.G. The Life of Sir William Harcourt, 2 vols., 1923
Gerth, H.H. and Mills, C. Wright (eds.). From Max Weber, Essays in Sociology, 1970
Giddens, Anthony. 'Elites in British Class Structure' in Philip Stanworth and Anthony Giddens (eds.), Elites and Power in British Society, Cambridge, 1974
Goldthorpe, John H. Social Mobility and Class Structure in Modern Britain, Oxford, 1980
Graham, Richard. Britain and the Onset of Modernisation in Brazil 1850-1914, Cambridge, 1968
Greaves, H.R.G. 'Personal Origins and Interrelations of the Houses of Parliament', Economica, 9 (1929), pp. 173-84
Griffith, J.A.G. The Politics of the Judiciary, 1977
Guttsman, W.L. The British Political Elite, 1963
Hain, P.L. and Piereson, James E. 'Lawyers and Politics Revisited: Structural Advantages of Lawyer Politicians', American Journal of Political Science, 19 (1975), pp. 41-51
Halevy, Elie. England in 1815, 1961
Hall, A.R. The London Capital Market and Australia 1870-1914, Canberra, 1963
Hanham, H.J. Elections and Party Management: Politics in the Time of Disraeli and Gladstone, 1959
Harries-Jenkins, Gwyn. The Army in Victorian Society, 1977
———. 'Professionals in Organizations' in J.A. Jackson (ed.), Professions and Professionalization, Cambridge, 1970, pp. 53-107
Hazell, Robert (ed.). The Bar on Trial, 1978
Heeney, Brian. A Different Kind of Gentleman, Parish Clergy as Professional Men in Early and Mid-Victorian England, Hamden, Conn., 1976
Heuston, R.F.V. Lives of the Lord Chancellors 1885-1940, Oxford, 1964
———. 'Lord Halsbury's Judicial Appointments', Law Quarterly Review, 78 (1962), pp. 504-32
Hobhouse, L.T. and Hammond, J.L. Lord Hobhouse, A Memoir, 1905
Holdsworth, Sir William. A History of English Law, 17 vols., 1922-72
Honey, J.R. de S. Tom Brown's Universe, The Development of the Public School, 1977
Jackson, W. Turrentine. The Enterprising Scot: Investors in the American West After 1873, Edinburgh, 1968
Jenks, Leland H. 'Britain and American Railway Development', Journal of Economic History, XI (1951), pp. 375-88

Johnson, R.W. 'The British Political Elite, 1955-72', European Journal of Sociology, 14 (1973), pp. 35-77
Johnson, Terence. 'Imperialism and the Professions' in Paul Halmos (ed.), Professionalisation and Social Change, Keele, 1973, pp. 281-309
———. Professions and Power, 1972
Johnston, Alexander. 'The History of the Two Counsel Rule in the Nineteenth Century', Law Quarterly Review, 93 (1977), pp. 190-1
Katz, Fred E. 'Occupational Contact Networks' in Sigmund Nosrow and William E. Form (eds.), Man, Work and Society, New York, 1962, pp. 317-21
Kimble, David. A Political History of Ghana, The Rise of Gold Coast Nationalism 1850-1928, Oxford, 1963
Larson, M.S. The Rise of Professionalism, A Sociological Analysis, Berkeley, 1977
Laski, Harold. Studies in Law and Politics, New Haven, 1932
Laslett, Peter. 'The Wrong Way Through the Telescope: a note on literary evidence in sociology and historical sociology', British Journal of Sociology, XXVII (1976), pp. 319-42
Lucas, Paul. 'Blackstone and the Reform of the Legal Profession', English Historical Review, 77 (1962), pp. 456-87
———. 'A Collective Biography of the Students and Barristers of Lincoln's Inn 1680-1804: A Study in the "Aristocratic Resurgence" of the Eighteenth Century', Journal of Modern History, 46 (1974), pp. 227-61
MacLane, John R. Indian Nationalism and the Early Congress, Princeton, 1977
Marshall, T.H. 'The Recent History of Professionalism in Relation to Social Structure and Social Policy', Canadian Journal of Economics and Political Science, 5 (1939), pp. 325-40
Millerson, Geoffrey. The Qualifying Associations: A Study of Professionalisation, 1964
Misra, B.B. The Indian Middle Classes, Their Growth in Modern Times, 1961
Mitchell, B.R. and Deane, Phyllis. Abstract of British Historical Statistics, Cambridge, 1971
Morgan, Jennifer. 'The Judiciary of the Superior Courts 1820-1968', unpublished M. Phil. thesis, University of London, 1974
Morrison, Charles. 'Kinship in Professional Relations: A Study of North Indian District Lawyers', Comparative Studies in Society and History, 14 (1972), pp. 100-25
Mowat, R.B. The Life of Lord Pauncefote, 1929
Namier, Lewis. The Structure of Politics at the Accession of George III, 2nd edn., 1957
O'Boyle, Lenore. 'The Problem of an Excess of Educated Men in Western Europe 1800-1850', Journal of Modern History, 42 (1970), pp. 471-95
O'Brien, R. Barry. The Life of Lord Russell of Killowen, 1901

Osipow, Samuel. *Theories of Career Development*, New York, 1968
Parkinson, C. Northcote. *British Intervention in Malaya 1867-77*, Singapore, 1960
Paterson, A.A. 'Judges: A Political Elite?', *British Journal of Law and Society*, 1 (1974), pp. 118-35
Patterson, Samuel C. 'Comparative Legislative Behavior: A Review Essay', *Midwest Journal of Political Science*, 12 (1968), pp. 599-616
Pedersen, Mogens W. 'Lawyers in Politics: The Danish Folketing and United States Legislatures' in Samuel C. Patterson and John C. Wahlke (eds.), *Comparative Legislative Behavior: Frontiers of Research*, New York, 1972
Payne, P.L. 'The Emergence of the Large-Scale Company in Great Britain 1870-1914', *Economic History Review*, XX (1967), pp. 519-42
Perkin, Harold. *The Origins of Modern English Society 1780-1880*, 1969
Peterson, M. Jeanne. *The Medical Profession in Mid-Victorian London*, Berkeley, 1978
Podmore, David. 'Lawyers and Politics', *British Journal of Law and Society*, 4 (1977), pp. 155-85
Prest, Wilfrid, 'Counsellors' Fees and Earnings in the Age of Sir Edward Coke' in J.H. Baker (ed.), *Legal Records and the Historian*, 1978, pp. 165-84
———. 'The English Bar, 1550-1700' in Wilfrid Prest (ed.), *Lawyers in Early Modern Europe and America*, 1981, pp. 65-85
———. *The Inns of Court Under Elizabeth I and the Early Stuarts 1590-1640*, 1972
Reader, W.J. *Professional Men*, 1966
Richards, P.G. *Patronage in British Government*, 1963
Rippy, J. Fred. *British Investments in Latin America 1822-1949*, Minneapolis, 1959
Robinson, Ronald and Gallagher, John. *Africa and the Victorians*, New York, 1968
Rosencrantz, Armin David. 'The Role of Lawyers in the House of Commons', unpublished Ph.D. thesis, Stanford University, 1970
Ross, J.F.S. *Parliamentary Representation*, 2nd edn., 1948
Rostow, W.W. *British Economy of the Nineteenth Century*, Oxford, 1948
Routh, Guy. *Occupations and Pay in Britain, 1906-1960*, Cambridge, 1965
Rubinstein, W.D. *Men of Property, The Very Wealthy in Britain Since the Industrial Revolution*, 1981
———. 'Men of Property: some aspects of occupation, inheritance and power among top British wealthholders' in Philip Stanworth and Anthony Giddens (eds.), *Elites and Power in British Society*, Cambridge, 1974, pp. 144-69
———. 'New Men of Property and the Purchase of Land in Nineteenth-Century England', *Past and Present*, 92 (1981),

pp. 125-47
_____. 'The Victorian Middle Classes: Wealth, Occupation, and Geography', Economic History Review, XXX (1977), pp. 602-23
_____. 'Wealth, Elites and the Class Structure of Modern Britain', Past and Present, 76 (1977), pp. 99-126
Saul, S.B. The Myth of the Great Depression, 1969
Scarlett, Peter Campbell. A Memoir of the Right Honourable James, First Lord Abinger, 1877
Schlesinger, Joseph A. 'Lawyers and American Politics: A Clarified View', Midwest Journal of Political Science, 1 (1957), pp. 26-39
Schmitthener, Samuel. 'A Sketch of the Development of the Legal Profession in India', Law and Society Review, III (1968-9), pp. 337-82
Simpson, A.W.B. 'The Early Constitution of the Inns of Court', Cambridge Law Journal, 30 (1970), pp. 241-56
Singh, Amar Kumar. Indian Students in Britain, New York, 1963
Spangenberg, Bradford. 'The Problem of Recruitment for the Indian Civil Service During the Late Nineteenth Century', Journal of Asian Studies, 30 (1971), pp. 341-60
Spence, Clark C. British Investments and the American Mining Frontier 1860-1901, Ithaca, 1958
Spring, David. 'The English Landed Estate in the Age of Iron and Coal', Journal of Economic History, 11 (1951), pp. 3-24
_____. The English Landed Estate in the Nineteenth Century, Its Administration, Baltimore, 1963
Stephen, Caroline Emelia. The Right Honourable Sir James Stephen, Gloucester, 1906
Stephen, Sir James Fitzjames. A History of the Criminal Law of England, 3 vols., New York, 1973, reprint
Stephen, Leslie. The Life of Sir James Fitzjames Stephen Bart., 1895
Stevens, Robert. Law and Politics, The House of Lords as a Judicial Body 1800-1976, Chapel Hill, 1978
Stevenson, John. Popular Disturbances in England 1700-1870, 1979
Stone, Irving. 'British Direct and Portfolio Investment in Latin America Before 1914', Journal of Economic History, XXXVII (1977), pp. 690-722
Stone, Lawrence. The Crisis of the Aristocracy 1558-1641, Oxford, 1965
_____. 'Prosopography', Daedalus, 100 (1971), pp. 46-79
_____. The University in Society, 2 vols., Princeton, 1974
Tate, C. Neal. 'Paths to the Bench in Britain: A Quasi-Experimental Study of the Recruitment of a Judicial Elite', Western Political Quarterly, 28 (1975), pp. 108-29
Tawney, R.H. The Acquisitive Society, New York, 1967
Thomas, J.A. The House of Commons 1832-1901, Cardiff, 1939
Thompson, F.M.L. English Landed Society in the Nineteenth

  Century, 1963
Vincent, John. _The Formation of the British Liberal Party 1857-68_, Harmondsworth, 1972
Waddington, Ivan. 'The Development of Medical Ethics - A Sociological Analysis', _Medical History_, _19_ (1975), pp. 36-51
Walker-Smith, Derek. _The Life of Lord Darling_, 1938
  ———— and Clarke, Edward. _The Life of Sir Edward Clarke_, 1939
Ward, J.T. and Wilson, R.G. (eds.). _Land and Industry, The Landed Estate and the Industrial Revolution_, Newton Abbot, 1971
Wilson, F.M.G. 'The Routes of Entry of New Members of the British Cabinet 1868-1958', _Political Studies_, _VII_ (1959), pp. 222-32
Winder, W.H.D. 'Courts of Requests', _Law Quarterly Review_, _52_ (1936), pp. 369-94

INDEX

Note: Peers are indexed according to the way that they are referred to in the text, either by family name or by title. In those instances where both names are used individuals are indexed according to their family name and the peerage title is given in parentheses.

Abraham, Augustus B. 161-2
apprentices 120n120
Asquith, H.H. 174, 184
assize courts 38, 84-5, 90
Atherton, Sir William 57
Attorney-General 76n137, 103
   authority of 33, 66, 103
attorneys and solicitors 26
   as advocates 4
   as pupil masters 82
   relations with barristers 43-4, 49, 94-5, 146
   status of 85
   see also connections and patronage
Australia 10, 122, 127, 130, 147
Aydelotte, William 166n27

Baggallay, Sir Richard 59
Baker, J.H. 202
Banks, J.A. 148
bar xiii, 1
   overcrowding 2, 8-9
   recruitment 16-19
   size of 1, 5-9, 50-1
   structure 114
bar association 67, see also Bar Committee and Bar Council

Bar Committee 68-70
Bar Council 70-1, 125-6
bar reform, in Parliament 206
   failure of 62-6
   in 1860s 56-8
   in early 1870s 58-62
bar reform, internal 66-71
Barnes, John Gorrel 83-4, 86
barrister/MPs
   ages at election 175-6
   legal officeholding 183
   ministerial appointments 189-90
   motivations of 176-84, 186, 191-5
   numbers 169-71
   occupations 195n6
   peerages 189-90
   political affiliations 171-2
   practising 174
   social origins 172-3
barrister/ministers
   ages at appointment 197n49
   number of 185-6
   occupations 187-9
   portfolios 187
   social origins 187-8
barristers

as landowners 154-5, 163-4
briefless 2, 21, 84, 86
common law 7-8, 38
definition of xiv
education 22-4
effects of county courts on 4, 9
equity 8
geographical origins 9-15
juniors 31, 61, 144
non-practising 1-4, 45
occupations of 4-6, 22, 27, 29, 207
practising 4-9, 143-50, 154-5
provincial 86-7
self-image xiv
social and occupational origins 16-22, 107-8, 203
barristers, colonial 5-6, 9-10
colonial-born 123, 138
education 123-5
English-born 123
prospects for 122
qualifications 121-2
social origins 123-5, 132-3
barristers, Indian
non-European 131, 133
opportunities for 134
social origins 132-3
Beales, Edmond 102, 119n97
Benjamin, Judah P. 145, 162
Bethell, Richard 145
Bigham, Sir John (Lord Mersey) 93
Birmingham 87, 88, 116, 164n5
Blackburn, Colin, Lord 112, 156, 182
Blackstone, Sir William
Commentaries 204
on barristers and clients 42, 201
on legal education 20, 23, 78, 82
on social quality 19
Blennerhasset, Rowland 178
Bowen, Charles 182, 184
Bowyer, Sir George 56-8, 60
Bramwell, G.W.W., Lord 127
Brassey, Thomas, Lord 172, 192
Bristol 86, 88
British Guiana 147
Brougham, Henry, Lord 55
Bryce, James, Lord 1, 84, 91-2, 156
Buckmaster, Stanley 145
Burford-Hancock, Henry 126
business classes 19, 107, 172-3, 192

Cairns, Earl 59-60, 62-4, 101
Cambridge, University of 20, 23-4, see also Oxbridge
Campbell, Sir George 135
Campbell, John, Lord 9, 81 112
careers, legal 114-15
early stages 45
ideal 78, 106
failures 96
judicial offices 100-2, 103-5
non-judicial offices 96-100, 102-3
careers, political
compatibility with the bar 103, 173-5
in America 190
in India 190-1
professional advancement 106, 176-84, 186
Caribbean 10
Carnarvon, Earl of 125-6, 138
Cecil, Lord Robert 191
Chalmers, David Peter 125-6
chambers system 83-4
Charley, W.T. 58
Chelmsford, Lord 181
chief judge, Lower Burma 135-6
chief justices, colonial 128-30, 137-8, 142n75
appointment of 125-6, 138
geographical origins 128-9
legal education 129
pre-judicial careers 129
salaries 137
circuit messes 37-9, 52-5

223

66, see also individual circuits
Clarke, Sir Edward 92, 103, 119n100, 145, 179-81
clients 42-3, 49, 200-1, see also litigants
Coleridge, Henry 97
Coleridge, Sir John Taylor 83, 96, 98
Collier, Richard P. 56-7, 182
Colonial Secretary
  legal appointments 125-6
colonies, crown 121
  legal patronage in 125, 128-30
colonies, self-governing (responsible) 121, 139n2
  legal appointments in 127, 128-30
commissioners of bankruptcy 95-7
company directors 156-7, 164
  social origins 157-8
  wealth 150-2
  see also directorships
connections and patronage 46, 82, 93-4
  attorneys 22, 46, 82, 91-3
  barristers and judges 91, 117
  businessmen 90, 93
  contact networks 84, 94, 202
  Indian bar 132
  landed classes 90
  touting 46, 89
Conservative Party 106, 171-2
conveyancers and equity draftsmen 9n45, 79, 82-4
Cornford, J.P. 175
Cotton, Sir Henry 93
Council on Legal Education 24
county courts 4, 9, 65
Courtney, Sir John Irving 162
crammers 115n15
Crawfurd, Edmund 57
Creasy, Edward 20-1, 81
Crump, Frederick 69

Darley, Frederick 130

Darling, Charles, Lord 193
Das, C.R. 148
Day, Sir John 127
Denman, Lord 96-7
de Villiers, John, Lord 130
devils 83, 116
Dicey, A.V. 39, 48, 197n44
directorships, Britain
  banking 159-60
  industry 159-61
  insurance 158-9
  land 159
  mining 159
  rails 158-60
  utilities 159
directorships, Latin America 161
directorships, other 163
directorships, United States 161-2
discipline, see professional discipline
Dodson, John G. (Lord Monk Bretton) 156, 192-3
Durham University 20
Dyke, Sir William Hart 126
dynasties, judicial 91, 117-18n61

Edge, James Broughton 101-2
education, see public schools, universities
education, legal 22
  at inns of court 16, 24
  bar examinations 78-81
  reform of 59
  see also Blackstone, Sir William and pupilage
Elliott, Philip 199
Erickson, Charlotte, 160
Erlanger, Howard 105
Escott, T.H.S. 92
esprit de corps xiv, 71, 114, 205
  and professional etiquette 37, 49
etiquette, see professional etiquette

Flower, Cyril (Lord Battersea) 192

Freemantle, Thomas (2nd Lord Cottlesloe) 167n43
Freidson, Eliot 199, 205

General Medical Council 64
Giffard, Hardinge (Earl of Halsbury) 68, 179-80
    judicial appointments 181-2
Gifford, Robert, Lord 90
Gladstone, William E. 103
Gorst, Sir John Eldon 180
Gray's Inn 2-3, 25-7
Griffith, Downes 101
Griffith, J.A.G. 181
Griffiths, Samuel W. 130
Guttsman, W.L. 191

Harcourt, Sir William 82, 103, 186
Hardwicke, Earl of 150
Harris, George 96
Hatherley, Lord 102
Herschell, Farrer, Lord 95
Hess, Henry 162-3
Heuston, R.F.V. 181
Hobhouse, Arthur, Lord 112
Hogg, Douglas 148
Holland, Henry T. (Viscount Knutsford) 193
Home Circuit 51, 73
Home Secretary 187, 197n44
Hoskyns, Leigh 163
House of Commons
    barristers in 169-71, see also careers, political
Hutchinson, Joseph 128

incomes 143-8, 152-3, 165
    colonial barristers 147-8
    elite practitioners 148
    English barristers 143-7, 164
India 10, 130-7, 147-8, 190-1
Indian Civil Service 134-5, 141n67
Indian high courts 131
Indian National Congress 132, 190
industrial revolution 13, 16
    and professionalisation 200, 204
    as watershed 206
Inner Temple 2-3, 20-1, 25-7
inns of court
    admissions 2-4, 25-6
    as professional association 204-5
    authority of 33-5, 37, 66
    benchers 34-7, 63
    calls 26-8, 83
    democratisation 34, 58, 67, 69
    exclusion of attorneys 26
    foundation of 1
    professionalisation at 27
    requirements and rules 20-22
    see also bar reform and individual inns
Inverarity, John D. 156
investments
    real estate 154-5, 204
    securities 155-6

Jackson, Sir Henry M. 61, 173
Jamaica 127-8, 147
James, Edwin 52
James, Henry, Lord (of Hereford) 93, 103, 119n100
Jervis, Sir John 6, 55, 144-5
Jessel, Sir George 145
Jeune, Francis H. (Lord St Heliers) 162
Johnson, Terence 199
judges, county court 100-2, 119n93-4, 177
judges, Indian
    appointments 134-5
    origins 137
    recruitment 136-7
    salaries 136
judges, superior court 98, 164, 203
    appointments and politics 181-4
    numbers 104
    social origins 203
judicial dynasties 91, 117

Kelly, Sir Fitzroy 80

Kenealy, Dr Edward 39

landed classes
  barrister/MPs from 172-3
  exodus from bar 12-13, 16, 202
  recruitment of barristers from 17-18, 107
Laing, Samuel 160
Larson, M.S. 199, 205
Lascelles, Francis Henry 126
law officers 95, 102-3
  as politicians 179-81
  see also Attorney-General
Leeds 86, 88
Liberal Party 106, 171-2
Liberal-Unionist Party 106, 171-2
Liddell, A.G.C. 93-4
Lincoln's Inn 21, 25-7
litigants
  social class 30n5 201-2
Liverpool 86-7
Lockwood, Sir Frank 119n100
Lofthouse, Samuel 7
London 10-11, 86-7
London, University of 20, 23
Lord Chancellor 59, 179, 184
Lucas, Paul 20
Lyndhurst, Lord 87

Macrae, Charles 160
McLaren, Charles (Lord Aberconway) 192
Macnaghten, Edward, Lord 178, 186
Manchester 86-8
Mansfield, Earl of 34, 203
Marjoribanks, Dudley (1st Lord Tweedmouth) 173, 192
Marjoribanks, Edward (2nd Lord Tweedmouth) 192
Marshall, T.H. 200
Mathew, J.C. 83-4
medical profession 113-14, 205
Melbourne, Viscount 184
methodology xiv-xv

middle class 107-8
  dominant position 16, 203
Middle Temple 2-3, 20-1, 25-7
Midland Circuit 51
Morley, Arnold 192
Morley, Samuel

Namier, Sir Lewis 191
Napier, Joseph 6
Nelson, R.R. 82, 92
Newcastle 88
Newfoundland 122
New South Wales 121
New Zealand 127
Norfolk Circuit 40, 44, 73n36, 210-11
  circuit retainers 45
  conduct on circuit 46, 211
  membership rules 47, 210
  relations with solicitors 43-4
  size 51
  two counsel rule 44-5
North America 9
North-Eastern Circuit 47, 50-1
Northern Circuit 50-1, 86-7
North Wales and Chester Circuit 45, 47
Norton, Thomas 127
Norwood, Charles 60-2

officeholders, colonial 125-30, 134-8
Oxbridge 24, 110
Oxford Circuit 50-1, 53
Oxford, University of 13, 20, 23-4, 111

Palmer, Roundell (Earl of Selborne) 55, 57, 92
  as Lord Chancellor 59-60
  general school of law 58-9
  legal appointments 101, 136
  reform of the inns of court 60, 62
Parliament 184

226

barristers in 65
see also careers, political and House of Commons
Patteson, Sir John 97
Pearce-Edgcumbe, Edward 161
Pearson, Charles J. 156
Peel, Sir Robert 175
Perceval, Spencer 184
Percival, Dr Thomas 205
Perkin, Harold 199
Peterson, M. Jeanne 112-14
Petty-Fitzmaurice, Lord Edmond 191
Plunkett, William 78
Pope, Samuel 162
Prest, Wilfrid 16
professional associations 33
professional autonomy 49, 71
  challenge to 59-60
  in 1780s 34
  from clients 42, 62, 202
  from official intervention 63, 203, 206
  respect for 65
professional classes 19, 172-3, 192, 203
professional discipline 33, 39, 67
  and trade unionism 48
  benchers 35, 37
  circuit messes 37-9
  reform of 57, 62-4
professional etiquette 33, 37, 68-70
  and patronage 46
  and professional identity 9
  attacks on 67
  categories 41
  circuit messes 39
  definition 72n29
  direct access 43-4, 146
  formalisation 68
  honorarium 41-3, 146
  informality 40, 52
  special retainer 45, 54, 74n60
  two counsel rule 45
professional ideal 154-5, 163-4
professional imperialism 121, 137-8
professional knowledge 204
professional socialisation 78
  see also esprit de corps
professionalisation 27, 29
  orthodox interpretation 199-210
  revised interpretation 201-6
  see also inns of court
professionalism xiii, 206
provincial bars, 86-89, see also barristers, provincial
public schools 22-4, 110, 153
Puller, Sir Christopher 136
pupilage 79-82, see also education, professional

quarter sessions courts 84-5, 90
queen's counsel 98-100, 106
  and politics 177-9
  as benchers 35-6

Reader, W.J. 199
recorders 95, 97-8, 176-7
Reeves, William C. 140n36
Reid, Robert (Lord Loreburn) 193
Rentoul, Sir Gervais 92, 174
revising barristers 95, 97
Ridley, Edward 182
Robinson, Henry Crabb 92
Rolt, Sir John 136
Romilly, Sir Samuel 145
Rubinstein, William 152
Ruggles, Thomas 112
Russell, Charles, Lord (of Killowen) 90, 95, 145
Russell, Sir George 161
Ryder, Granville Richard 160

Salisbury, 3rd Marquess of
  legal appointments 179-82
  political appointments 186
Scarlett, James (Lord Abinger)

227

Scott, John (Earl of Eldon) 85, 136, 145, 150, 165n23
serjeants-at-law 35, 98-9, 120n120
Seymour, William Digby 52, 71-2n13
Sheffield 88
Sheriff, William 128
Simon, John, Viscount 169, 186-7
sinecures 150
Smith, Adam 9, 146
Smith, Sir Montague 57
Snagge, Thomas 161-2
social mobility 19, 192, 194-5
South Africa 122, 130
South-Eastern Circuit 73
   on barrister/JPs 46-7
   size and character 51, 53
special pleaders
   as pupil masters 79, 81-2
   practice under the bar 31n45, 83
   see also pupilage
Stephen, Sir James Fitzjames 85, 95, 103, 117n58
Steward, Mark John 156
Stone, Lawrence 13
success, determinants of
   ability 11-12
   connection 112
   education and knowledge 107, 109, 111-12
   health 112
   luck 112-13
   occupational origins 107-8
   politics 110, 176-84
   see also connection and patronage
Sugden, Edward (Lord St Leonards) 145

Tagore, G.M. 131, see also barristers, Indian
Talfourd, Sir Thomas N. 96
Tate, C. Neal 105-6
Thesiger, Alfred 182

Thompson, F.M.L. 30, 189
Thomson, H. Byerley 6, 144, 146
Tocqueville, Alexis de 207
translation, judicial 104-5
Trinity College, Dublin 20, 23
Trollope, Anthony 163
universities 23-4, see also individual universities

vakils 131, 134, see also barristers, Indian
Victoria, Australia 122
Victoria, Queen xiii-xiv
Vincent, John 172, 176

Warren, Samuel 20-1
Watson, George 156
wealth, landed
   barrister/MPs 172-3
   barristers 153-5
   barristers' fathers 16, 18
   see also investments, real estate
wealth, personal 148-53
   cabinet ministers 150-2
   company directors 150-2
   judges 150-2
   MPs 151-2
   physicians 150
   practising barristers, 148-50
   see also investments, securities
Webster, Richard (Viscount Alverstone) 82, 93, 193
   appointment as Attorney-General 179-80
   see also careers, political and Clarke, Sir Edward
Western Circuit 47, 69, 72n24
   conditions on 53
   size 53
Wood, Sir Charles 159
Woodfall, Robert 101-2
Woods, R.C. 139n21
working classes
   rarity at the bar 19, 21
Wortley, James Stuart 81, 147
Wrensfordsley, Henry T. 126

For Product Safety Concerns and Information please contact our EU
representative GPSR@taylorandfrancis.com
Taylor & Francis Verlag GmbH, Kaufingerstraße 24, 80331 München, Germany

www.ingramcontent.com/pod-product-compliance
Lightning Source LLC
Chambersburg PA
CBHW061440300426
44114CB00014B/1771